Bodycheck:

Relocating the Body in
Contemporary Performing Art

B.S.U.C. - LIBRARY

00254003

Critical Studies

Vol. 17

General Editor
Myriam Díaz-Diocaretz

Assistant Editor
Esther von der Osten-Sacken

Amsterdam - New York, NY 2002

Bodycheck:

Relocating the Body in Contemporary Performing Art

Edited by

Luk Van den Dries
Maaike Bleeker
Steven De Belder
Kaat Debo
Kurt Vanhoutte

BATH SPA UNIVERSITY
NEWTON PARK LIBRARY

Class No.

Dawson

DISCARD

The paper on which this book is printed meets the requirements of "ISO 9706:1994, Information and documentation - Paper for documents - Requirements for permanence".

ISBN: 90-420-1500-4 (bound)
©Editions Rodopi B.V., Amsterdam – New York, NY 2002
Printed in The Netherlands

Contents

III. INTERVIEWS

Preface

This volume is an initiative of *Aisthesis: Research Centre for the Study of Language and Body*. *Aisthesis* was established in 1997 at the Theatre Studies Section of the Department of Germanic Languages and Literatures at UIA (University of Antwerp, Belgium), on the initiative of theatre maker and visual artist Jan Fabre and Luk Van den Dries, head of the Theatre Studies Section at UIA.

Aisthesis refers etymologically to the Greek word for perception. *Aisthesis* comprises more than just visual perception; it stands for general perception with all the senses, as well as the impression that the perceived leaves on the body. In the original meaning of the concept, tactile and visual perception constitute a whole, and it was not until later (e.g. in the Kantian tradition) that this meaning was reduced to merely an eye that observes, without a body.

The purpose of *Aisthesis* is to provide a forum where the contemporary theoretical discourse on the status of the body in the arts can be further developed and studied in depth. The centre has set itself the task of examining the differentiated manifestations of the cultural corporeal image in an all-embracing perspective. By bringing together a number of scholars, the centre intends to provide new impetuses to research: through internal discussions, the means and the possibilities of theoretical reflection are explored and tested. Thus a kind of open space for reflection is created where participating scholars can search for the most appropriate tools for approaching recent developments in the arts. Though the main focus is on the performing arts, cross-fertilisation has certainly not been ruled out. In the long term, the centre intends to make a contribution to the scholarly discourse concerning the representation of the body in the arts. The surplus value offered by the research centre lies in the dialogue that is conducted with artists. The close collaboration with people working in the field creates a unique medium for cross-fertilisation between arts theory and artistic practice. The theoretical reflection on the representation of the body in the arts is constantly confronted with and inspired by conversations with artists who have succeeded in finding their own way in their particular field.

For more information: Vddries@uia.ua.ac.be

UIA – GER
Universiteitsplein 1
2610 Wilrijk – Antwerpen
Belgium

Acknowledgements

This volume could never have been written without the help of a great number of persons and institutions. We would like to thank the Province of Antwerp for providing us with a grant which helped to lay the scientific groundwork for the research centre Aisthesis and which made the publication of this book possible in the first place. Furthermore we wish to acknowledge the support of the Flemish Theatre Institute (VTI) which provided the resources and funds to render possible many of the translations ('The Sublime Body', 'Allegories of the Fall', 'Theatricality – Invisibility – Discipline', 'Images Preserved in Liquid: A Foreword', and the interviews with Romeo Castellucci, Jérôme Bel, Marc Vanrunxt and Thierry Smits). We are grateful to Hélène Frichot, Claire Tarring and Maggie Bowers for proofreading the translations. We thank Annemie Vanhoof who did a wonderful job in the early stages of this publication and who made possible a lot of the contacts with the artists. Finally, our thanks to Jan Fabre and the many artists who collaborated, for their ongoing inspiration and enthusiasm.

Notes on Contributors

Maaike Bleeker is associated with the Amsterdam School for Cultural Analysis, Theory and Interpretation (ASCA – University of Amsterdam) and is preparing a Ph.D. thesis on the impact of corporeality on the acquisition of experience during performances. The term 'experience' encompasses all the affective and cognitive processes by which the perceived is given meaning. The focus is on the role of corporeality within these processes. As such, her research into the meaning of the body not only studies the body, but also the concept of meaning itself. Furthermore, her research occasions reflection on 20th-century thought on the relation between body and soul. A central aspect of the experience of performances is corporeality as an interference; the disturbance of expectations requires a different, more active manner of watching.

Steven De Belder studied philosophy, history and theatre sciences at the universities of Antwerp and Ghent. He works at the University of Antwerp (UIA) as Research Assistant of the Fund for Scientific Research-Flanders, preparing a Ph.D. thesis on the figure of the everyday in theatre and the theatricality of the everyday.

Katrien Jacobs is assistant professor in New Media at Emerson College. She studied at University of Maryland, College Park, where she wrote a Ph.D. thesis on dismemberment myths in 1960s/1970s performance art. She has published several articles on feminism, pornography and new media art in journals such as *Wide Angle* and *Paralax*. She is a filmmaker and emerging new media artist who is devoted to visualizing theories on the body, sexuality, and performance art. A Ford Foundation Grant (-Ism, 1996) and Research and Learning Grant (Edith Cowan University, 1998) enabled her to conceptualize and carry out video/diversity teaching projects for undergraduate students. Her documentary *Joseph Beuys in America* won a Rosebud Award in 1996 and was screened for PBS television and the American Film Institute.

Dietmar Kamper is connected to the Institüt für Soziologie of the Berlin Freie Universität. He published, among others, *Die Wiederkehr des Körpers (1982)*, *Transfigurationen des Körpers: Spuren der Gewalt in der Geschichte (1989)*, *Abgang vom Kreuz (1996)*, *Im Souterrain der Bilder: die Schwarze Madonna (1997)*.

Peter Mason holds an M.A. in Literae Humaniores and a Ph.D. in Anthropology. His books on visual representations include *Deconstructing America: Representations of the Other (1990)* and *Infelicities: Representations of the Exotic (1998)*. He is currently associated with the experimental workshop and exhibition project Cuerpos Pintados in Santiago de Chile.

Eric Raeves is a Belgian choreographer, dancer and costume designer. He is an autodidact. Raeves has worked regularly with choreographer Marc Vanrunxt, both as a dancer and a designer, and he also danced for Jan Fabre. He has been developing an oeuvre of his own since 1988.

Frank Reijnders is connected to the Art Historical Institute of Amsterdam University. He published, among others, *Kunst, geschiedenis, verschijnen en verdwijnen (1984)*, and *Metamorfose van de barok (1991)*.

Luk Van den Dries is professor of Theatre Studies at the University of Antwerp (UIA). He is co-editor of *Kritisch Theaterlexicon* (VTI). He wrote on performance Analysis (*Omtrent de opvoering. Heiner Müller en drie decennia theater*, 2001) and on theatre in Belgium (*Luk Perceval*, Kritisch Theaterlexicon, 2001); he edited a volume on the representation of the body (*Geënsceneerde lichamen*, 2000) and coedited with Rose Werckx a book on René Moulaert (*René Moulaert en de Belgische avant-garde 1920–1930*, 1992). He coedited together with Dina Hellemans en Marianne Van Kerkhoven several volumes on political theatre in Flanders.

Kurt Vanhoutte studied germanic languages, theatre & drama and cultural studies at the universities of Brussels (VUB), Antwerp (UIA) and Berlin (Humboldt). He published several articles on the representation of the body in theatre. Vanhoutte was granted a fellowship by the Fund for Scientific Research – Flanders (F.W.O.-Vlaanderen) and conducted research at the University of Antwerp, where he wrote a Ph.D. thesis on the position of theatre in today's mediatized society: *Theatre through the looking-glass of the new media – an investigation into the allegory of corporeality in the technological era guided by Walter Benjamin*. Vanhoutte proposes Benjamin's conception of allegory as a method to think the paradox of the technological body within the theatre, free of excessive ontological anxieties and self-deluding transcendent remedies. Currently he is connected to the University of Antwerp as a Postdoctoral Fellow of F.W.O.-Vlaanderen. His main research focus is on the significance of technology and messianic patterns in contemporary theatre.

Myriam Van Imschoot is affiliated with the Institute of Cultural Studies, K.U.Leuven. Granted a fellowship by the Fund for Scientific Research-Flanders, she conducts research on improvisational dance in postwar avant-garde. She is a publicist on dance. She is the initiator and founding member of SARMA, an online discursive vehicle for dance and performance criticism.

Luk Van den Dries

Bodycheck: Introduction

In ice hockey, the term bodycheck refers to a specific move for gaining control of play. The opponent is tackled hard, his sturdiness tested, with the purpose of stealing the puck away from him. It is a blow from body to body, a dynamic clash of physical strength, which will determine the continuation of play. It is a fierce collision of players in armour, theatrically exaggerated for the arena of the lustful eye.

In this book, too, the body is checked and there is physical confrontation. Not in the hockey ring, but in places where the body is moulded into an artistic shape, where it is staged on the interface between showing and watching. In this book, we shall deal with the body in the (performing) arts. In the theatrical arena, too, the thin line between real and theatrical violence is an important line of approach to the work of many performing artists. The representation of the violence that is exerted in society against corporeal images is a constant source of inspiration. The artist tackles this hardening of corporeal images in order to counteract the coagulation of the body. H/She explores the body, searches for unexpected openings, causes surprise by suddenly moving in a different direction, and thus introduces liquidity to the corporeal image, renders it mercurial. The image of the 'bodycheck' is therefore also an apt metaphor for describing the researcher's work. H/She too searches for openings in existing schools of thought and prevailing concepts by trying out new lines of approach through unexpected collisions. The scientist's pen is like the hockey player's stick, constantly looking for new connections and surprising directions.

Of old, the theatre is a place where views of mankind and the world are traded. Theatre is the most anthropomorphic art form: in theatre, man, his thoughts and actions, and more importantly his failures and lack of action, are always central. In the classical historiography of theatre, attention is almost exclusively focused on the contents of these portrayals of man, on the conflicts between man and the world that are told and shown on stage. It is, however, also possible to write a history of theatre on the basis of its corporeal manifestations, on the basis of the way in which these portrayals of mankind have literally been given shape by the actors. This would result in an entirely different story. Such a history would be about shame and the oppression of the female body, which remained taboo on stage for many ages. Greek drama would, first and foremost, become a stage for the obscene body, with actors playing the parts of satyrs with the aid of sexually explicit props. One could demonstrate on the basis of commedia dell'arte the connection between the use of masks and physiognomic typologies, which would later become a trademark of racist ideologies. The Russian revolution brought forth a new body in theatre: the body as a machine part, acrobatically oiled and uniformly made. It was a collective body in which the individual was silenced. And a little later this century, the broken, aching and hypersensitive body of French essayist and theatre maker Antonin Artaud could be regarded as the harbinger of the ecstatic body: a mixture of exaltation and destruction of the body that is so typical of corporeality in contemporary art.

The body on stage tells its own history: an often secret, oppressed story which may nevertheless be a much more powerful tool for showing the scars of the world in which it lives than official historiography. Foucault demonstrates this quite magnificently in his analyses of power and sexual ethics.

This book shifts the focus of attention from the content of portrayals of man to their material inscription, to the way in which they are given shape by staged bodies. This is not new of course. For some time now, the social sciences have been showing a remarkable interest in the human body. Never before has the body been so emphatically present as today. The disciplining of the body, its cultural (trans)formation, its genetic codification and the opposition against these predetermined corporeal images through play with sexual identities are at the centre of current artistic and theoretical discourse. The title of Judith Butler's book *Bodies that Matter* has proven to be programmatic for cultural scientists' overwhelming interest in the manifestation of human bodies. Material corporeality is a hot item in current research. This book shares this wide interest in corporeality, while also adding some new insights.

This study stems from a shared interest on the part of cultural scientists and artists, compounded in the Aisthesis research group. The aim of this research group is to inquire into the representation of the body in contemporary (performing) arts. It is not so much the description of a certain artistic practice that takes our interest as the analysis of current manifestations of the body on stage. The focus is mainly on developing new concepts for approaching the body, and on exploring theoretical avenues that allow one to grasp corporeal images more accurately. This theoretical research is constantly fed and checked through co-operation with artists whose work deals explicitly with the body. We consider the research that artists and cultural scientists conduct in this field to be perfectly complementary, and have tried to compile this book on that very basis.

In more ways than one, the application of corporeality in the (performing) arts is, in other words, the actual starting point of this study. Contemporary research on the stage itself prompted its conceptualisation. The various theoretical articles that have been included in this book all stem from a fascination with what happens to the body on stage. The inability to grasp this kind of artistic research with the existing terminology and methodological tools was sufficient reason to follow new theoretical paths and try out other concepts. Even if the link with contemporary corporeal practice has not been made explicit in a number of these articles, it is always tributary to it. Thinking about the body is thus steered directly by the scenic representation of that body. It is a dialogue about and with bodies.

But that is not the only way that artistic research comes to the fore in this study. We were also interested in the corporeal concepts that artists themselves use when talking about their work. How do artists conceive the body itself? Which prefigurations are attached to the body? What are the starting points for corporeal research? This confrontation has resulted in a number of interviews with artists in which they discuss in greater detail their own practice. The interviews with seven artists, each of which conducts research in the field of corporeal (re)presentation in a totally different way, constitute an adequate range of views on the body.

The co-operation with artists becomes even more concrete in the portfolio by choreographer Eric Raeves. He was asked to grasp the essence of his own studies of the human body through the medium of photography. The result is a series of photographs in which the same theatrical principles are represented as Eric Raeves applies on stage – especially the denaturalisation of the body. As a pivot between the theoretical and the empirical part of the book, this portfolio offers a breathing space, a visual break.

We are convinced that the bringing together of these two voices – the theoretician's and the artist's – will result in a pleasant kind of friction when reading this book. Not in the sense that the voice from within 'checks' on that from without – certainly in the field of corporeal research this kind of opposition is entirely outmoded – but as complementary ways in which to carry out research into the body on stage today.

The artistic research that is dealt with in this study is rooted primarily in a European practice, which brings us to the second accent in this book: a choice was made for the Dutch-language area (Flanders and the Netherlands). Since the 1980s, this language area has been the scene of some genuinely interesting developments in the performing arts. Particularly

with regard to artistic research into corporeality on stage, some quite radical work has been produced which has since served as a model for many
other artists working in various areas of the performing arts. Jan Fabre's
eight-hour performance *Het is theater zoals te verwachten en te voorzien
was* (*This is theatre as could be expected and foreseen*) (1982) and Anne
Teresa De Keersmaeker's *Fase* (*Phase*) (1982) are two early examples
of the radicalisation of the body on stage. Throughout the 1980s and up
to the present day, the body has been the central junction in the artistic
research by a new generation of artists working from quite divergent
perspectives.

There are many reasons for the sudden and concentrated surge of
artistic renewal in this part of the world. First of all, there is the lack of any
great theatrical tradition, which in the major European countries is often
experienced as a burden of inheritance that continues to dominate the world
of theatre. As such there is more room in the Dutch-language region for wil-
fulness and for hyperindividual statements. Another factor is the extremely
open attitude that is adopted to what is going on elsewhere. Flanders and the
Netherlands have always taken care to programme whatever was regarded
as important in other places. This radically anti-chauvinistic attitude meant
that both countries soon became familiar with the work of very different
performing artists (Pina Bausch, Peter Brook, Tadeusz Kantor, The Wooster
Group, Bob Wilson etc. ...). A third and equally important factor is the
amount of support these artists have received, first from producers and subsequently – albeit rather hesitantly – from the government as well. As a
result, all these artists have been able to develop autonomously. They were
not absorbed by larger theatres, but were able to work individually. All this
has resulted in a truly fruitful theatre climate.

This localism is, paradoxically, also internationally oriented, as the
entrenchment in a local cultural environment is interwoven with and
dependent on international contexts. The locality is impure, in more ways
than one. Some artists, for example, felt an urge to come and work here,
enticed as they were by a stimulating artistic climate. This is how American
choreographer Meg Stuart ended up in Flanders, and today her work is an
integral part of the European context. Other artists featuring in this book
have strong personal ties with artists and producers in this small region. The
work of Parisian choreographer Jérôme Bel for instance has been included
in the programming of several Flemish theatres on a regular basis and he has
been given the opportunity to create several performances here. The same
holds for Italian director Romeo Castellucci and his company Societas
Raffaello Sanzio: his position at the top of the European avant-garde is

partly due to the co-productions he has been able to realise with the Holland Festival in Amsterdam and the KunstenFestivaldesArts in Brussels. On the other hand, many Flemish artists who have made it internationally are obviously dependent on different producers in other European cities such as Rotterdam, Hamburg and Frankfurt. The grants they receive from local authorities are inadequate to create fulfilling artistic work. Artistically they are tributary to the stimulating climate, while economically they are dependent on European partners. This does not mean that the artists who have been included in this study are operating in a sort of hybrid European context of avant-garde theatre, but that a network of locally anchored structures feels an affinity with the work of certain artists and takes responsibility for it. In other words, it concerns a subdivision of precisely located entities, not an open space of hybrid cultural forms.

This study by no means pretends to offer a comprehensive overview of the research into corporeality on the contemporary European stage. We thought it more interesting to opt for a rather limited range of artists whose work would enter into an interesting interaction with the search for new theoretical concepts in the study of corporeality. The confrontation between new theoretical insights and a self-willed artistic practice was an important criterion in selecting texts for this book. When necessary, the notion of 'European avant-garde' was actually abandoned in order to allow a relevant interaction between theory and practice. This holds especially for Katrien Jacobs's discussion of masochism in the film/performance work of Maria Beatty. Apart from that, our selection was inspired by the consideration that a lot of interesting work in the field of corporeal representation has drawn hardly any theoretical attention. This does not mean that we consciously opted for lesser-known names. We considered it a priority to venture into theoretically less explored territory, to deal with relevant contemporary work and artists who have singularly stood the test of theory. Hence the inclusion of relatively well-known names such as Wim Vandekeybus, Meg Stuart and Romeo Castellucci, all of whom are, however, usually dealt with in a journalistic context, and are hardly ever discussed in a more theoretical way. Beside these artists, there are less well-known names such as Eric Raeves, Marc Vanrunxt, Jérôme Bel, Thierry Smits, Gerardjan Rijnders and Krisztina de Chatel, whose research into corporeality tempts to new theoretical standpoints.

As we have already pointed out, frameworks have sometimes been flung open in order to clarify the interaction between theory and practice. This is particularly true of the framework that is the performing arts itself. A very broad definition of the performing arts has been applied, so that it would embrace many different forms of theatre, dance and dance theatre. Furthermore, the occasional switch is made to other forms of artistic expression such as painting, film, video and sculpture. After all, trends in the field of corporeal (re)presentation that are observed in other forms of art correspond to what is happening on stage. This way, we want to liberate the body on stage from its theatrical isolation, in order to make it a focal point in the debate on corporeality in our culture.

Beyond Oppositions

And so we arrive at the third accent in this study, namely the range of theoretical formulations of the representation of the body in the contemporary (performing) arts. With this book, we not only try to introduce relevant but lesser-known artistic research into a broader context, but we also wish to contribute to the theoretical developments in this field. The discourse on this theme often focuses on the axes of cultural determinacy of corporeality versus the authenticity of the body as a counterforce. As a matter of course, we arrive at the building site of corporeal identity where very different forces (disciplining versus hyperbolic reflection) are at work.

The body as a construction site of very diverse cultural codes has been studied for several decades from a feminist point of view. According to feminist research, the gender construction is the most regulating of all cultural determinations. In her essay 'Masochism, or the Cruel Mother in Maria Beatty's Pornography', Katrien Jacobs ties in with the gender body in order to further develop it in a context which feminism itself finds hard to come to terms with: pornography. This field has always been treated by feminism as the pre-eminent terrain of phallocratic oppression. But where does that leave lesbian porno? Or sadism and masochism, where sexuality and violence explicitly provoke each other? With Deleuze and others, Katrien Jacobs argues that the erotogenic body is not a nostalgic reminiscence of a pre-Oedipal phase, a construction by means of which psychoanalytical theory has colonised sexuality. On the contrary: the body is a 'desiring machine'. In all its unpredictable appearances, the erotogenic desire fragmentises the body, breaks it up and rephrases it 'as an open-ended and performative category'. This infinite multitude of possible shapes of desire is exemplified by means of S&M scenes from Maria Beatty's film and video work. From this, we learn that the body as a 'desiring machine' cannot be reduced to an image or an essence, but always fluctuates between concreteness and virtuality. This flux oscillates between several extremes and haunts every attempt to pin the body down.

On a theoretical level, this flux is mirrored in the refusal to bury one-self in an opposition of corporeal views. Quite a few articles in this book try to avoid the sort of oppositions which the discourse on the human body is instilled with. Not in order to leave the truth (if there is such a thing as the truth when talking about the body!) aside (the body is both culturally determined and potentially authentic), but to boost the discourse on this topic itself. In his article 'Theatricality–Invisibility–Discipline', Steven De Belder expounds on Peggy Phelan's concept of 'invisibility'. Phelan literally tries to avoid the cultural inscription of the body by making it invisible. According to Phelan, visibility is a condition for an immediate recuperation in saleability and productivity. The only way out is to actively disappear. Through this disappearing act, Phelan avoids 'the subject's involuntary absorption into the definition by the other'. As opposed to the visibility of cultural subjectivism, she puts forward an active invisibility. Steven De Belder tries to avoid Phelan's antithetical attitude by introducing the concept of repetition. In repeating the visibility and its obvious theatricalisation, he wants to emphasise its recuperation so strongly that the body becomes both visible and invisible at the same time. Jérôme Bel's *Shirtologie* (*Shirtology*), a performance realised with a group of youngsters, demonstrates the effects of this (in)visibility.

In the article 'The Sublime Body', Luk Van den Dries builds on Kant's definition of the sublime as aesthetic experience. Kant uses the category of the sublime to secure the primacy of reason. Postmodern philosophers such as Lyotard reacted strongly against Kant's idealism and redefined the sublime as a regression in pure sensuality. The confrontation with the sublime results in the terror of the unknown and creates an intense shiver. For Lyotard, the rupture with the familiar, with each form of representation, is a precondition for arriving at the energy of the lustful. This treatment of the sublime, however, stays within the boundaries of the conflict between reason and libido. Again the antithesis which is so typical of contemporary thought on corporeality is avoided by opting unequivocally for the paradox. The sublime body is then no longer a body representing a subject, but is founded on the impossibility of filling up the void with pure presence. Fragments from the living exhibition of bodies by Eric Raeves and images from Romeo Castellucci's work clarify the 'filled void' of corporeal representation.

Kurt Vanhoutte has a similar point to make, albeit from a totally different perspective. He again observes an opposition in reflection on the body. The embrace of technology by theatre, which goes back to the futuristic symbiosis of man and machine in the early 20th century, goes hand in hand with a diabolic denunciation of that same technology. This allows Vanhoutte to introduce the theme of the fall of man. In today's era of the new media, technology still carries with it the fear for a mechanisation of man. According to this belief, technology will cause the fall of man's natural aura. On rereading Benjamin's theory on aura and his concept of allegory, this opposition is resolved, which enables us to bring body and machine together in a more complex relationship. The possibilities of this largely unexplored theoretical field are illustrated in the performance *CyberChrist* by Belgian choreographer Thierry Smits.

Another opposition which continues to dominate the study of theatre as a spectre is that between showing and watching, between actors and audience. In his article, Steven De Belder observes how difficult it is to find a perspective which at once encompasses production and reception. This is certainly true in relation to corporeal representation. Research is mostly limited to the analysis of staged corporeal images and to the way in which the body has been given shape scenically. The fact that perception is also connected with corporeality is usually ignored. This perception incarnate is the topic of Maaike Bleeker's article 'Disorders that Consciousness can Produce: Bodies Seeing Bodies on Stage'. The two points of view in theatrical communication, watching and playing, are conceived as a relationship between bodies. This relationship is constructed on the basis of psychoanalytical concepts – which, for that matter, also run as a thread through this collection of articles. Lacan's 'mirror-stage' in particular serves as a paradigm in this bodily way of watching. The single direction that is implied in this action is complemented with 'inner mimicry', a concept which Bleeker borrows from John Martin. This concept refers to a manner of looking that is reflected in other bodies, but does so from its own kinaesthetic consciousness and is therefore searching for 'responsiveness'. It is like a dialogue between bodies, as it were. The performance that is used as a test for this theoretical apparatus of concepts is *De Zieleweg van de Danser* (*The Path of the Dancer's Soul*) by directors de Chatel and Rijnders. It quotes a text by Kleist about the representation of bodies, reaffirming the integration of theory and practice, one of the starting points for this book.

Paint Screen

Apart from the invigoration of the debate on certain oppositions in the field of corporeal representation, this book is dominated by another important theoretical accent. For bodily representation is anchored in the skin, perhaps even tattooed onto it. The skin is not only a transparent screen on which all kinds of culturally determined corporeal images are projected; it is, first and foremost, matter which transforms itself. The skin itself, its material structure, its openings, its complexion draw attention. The skin is comparable to the paint screen Frank Reijnders writes about in his article 'The Hide of Marsyas: Some Notes on the Screen of Painting'. The comparison to the status of paint structure in the history of painting, from Titian to Pollock, clearly shows how the materiality itself of all those layers of paint, scattered and splashed by fingers and brushes or buckets and sticks, applies a very literal layer in the image. The paint screen itself brings about the metamorphosis between matter and image. In exactly the same way, the many examples in this book of corporeal practice on the contemporary stage point to the skin as the place of transformation. The performer's skin is the carrier of an inscription process, just like paint on canvas. This is not to be confused with the prima causa, a kind of essential bottom layer. The materiality of the skin constantly interferes with the cultural images it incorporates. By analogy with the 'paint screen' in painting, we could therefore speak of the 'skin screen'.

If one skins the body, the bones are exposed. This bone structure is the topic of Peter Mason's article, occasioned by the installations of John Blake. The bones which John Blake exhibits have been taken out of their structure, have literally been torn from their context, in order to acquire new functions in a context that is quite different from supporting the body. Positioned in a gallery or in the architecture of a bunker, the bones start to transform. They transmute from anthropomorphic matter into an architectural principle, from human blueprint into ruined remains, from invisible interior into exterior extension of the body. The truly exciting thing about Blake's bone structures, however, is that they always belong to the border area between life and death, between presentation and representation, as a result of which they evoke a constant ambiguity. They are dead remains which remind us of bodies, traces of immobilised movement. Because of their position in space, however, they are also building blocks of life. The inside of movement is thus made tangible. The extremely fragile row of horizontally suspended vertebrae clearly reflects the dubious status of the body in Blake's work: powerful yet fragile, familiar and yet totally alien.

What then is the body on stage? Or, in more general terms, what is it we talk about when we talk about the body? This most essential and unanswered of questions is posed by Dietmar Kamper. In Western culture, the body is the most detrained principle. Detrained in an ascetic sense, i.e. stripped of its own material well-being, disciplined to obedience and constricted by knowledge. Even when the body is no longer oppressed by reason, and almost declared invisible, it is organised as an imaginary construction. The body answers to images of bodies, it becomes an imaginary double of the spirit, and therefore appears as an abstraction yet again. This desire for a duplication of the familiar is applied quite literally in the practice of cloning. All that could possibly be different is tamed in the clone, and reduced to Similarity. As such, cloning represents an attempt to restrain the primary fear of decay and death. All these attempts to incorporate the body have not resulted in our coming to grips with it. The body falls apart in different fragments. But as the body, in its capacity as the Other, eludes any meaningful grip, it creates opportunities for coming to terms with mortality.

What then is the body? The many answers that are put forward in this book are in no way conclusive. Each in their own way, though, they try to take the debate a little further, by building on hypotheses and propositions that one encounters in the recent literature. In the same way as the navel makes a knot in the skin so that the body would not be forgotten, this book wants to tie together very diverse disciplines, points of view and lines of approach in order to prevent the body from grinding to a standstill. In that sense, it applies to the body one of the body's most essential characteristics: change.

Translated by ICTS

I. Essays

Maria Beatty, Still image from *The Elegant Spanking*
(Courtesy of Maria Beatty)

Maria Beatty, Still image from *The Black Glove*
(Courtesy of Maria Beatty)

Katrien Jacobs

Masochism, or The Cruel Mother in Maria Beatty's Pornography

'You are dreaming,' she cried. 'Wake Up!' She grasped my arm with
her marble hand. 'Wake up' she repeated, this time, in a low, gruff
voice.

Von Sacher-Masoch

Introduction: Performing Masochism

This essay proposes a theory of women's sexuality and eroticism as conceived in masochistic screen performances. The essay will center around
the work of Maria Beatty, an internationally renowned masochist performer and independent filmmaker who works at the edges of the New York
porn industry, having been nurtured by an older generation of performance artists such as Carolee Schneemann and Annie Sprinkle, and as a
professional submissive by the dominant school of New York dominatrixes.[1]
In this essay, the theory of masochism applies to performance and film
aesthetics, and is primarily derived from recent analyses of Gilles Deleuze's
Masochism: Coldness and Cruelty, an introduction to Von Sacher-Masoch's
diaries which was originally published in 1967. Although Deleuze's study
has been developed into a comprehensive film theory for classical narrative film by Gaylyn Studlar in *In The Realm of Pleasure: Von Sternberg,
Dietrich and the Masochistic Aesthetic* (1988), the aim of this essay is to
examine such theory in light of a new generation of filmmakers and theorists, and the culture of lesbian pornographic short films and videos.

A central figure in Deleuze's study is the 'cruel mother' as a larger
than life archetype and proponent of anti-reason who participates in sexual
politics by obsessively carving out new zones of the sexual body and bodily
awareness. The essay will explain 'masochism' as a gradual surrender to
such 'feminine' body sculpting, resulting in desire which isolates fragments
of the body and networks fragments between shifting erotogenic zones.
The slow and ritualized process of networking zones (through pain and
pleasure rituals) is the subject of Beatty's porn repertoire as she represents
masochism through stylized, fetishistic film aesthetics. The mother-figure
also becomes a central trope in critiques of psycho-analytical theory such
as Teresa de Lauretis' study *The Practice of Love* (1994). De Lauretis shows
that lesbianism is a sculpting of the body that does not rely on phallic

imaginaries. 'Mother' functions as an absent figure who does not consolidate the young woman's existing body but creates experimental deviations and alternate zones. This process of disassembling and reassembling the female body is shown in Beatty's lesbian s/m film *The Black Glove* (1996) as a peculiarly dark and primeval impulse. Both Deleuze and de Lauretis believe that such forces may lead to new types of bodily imaging, perception or even sexual politics. De Lauretis posits that a renewal of the female body occurs through 'lesbian desire', a doubling of the lost maternal body in other female bodies. (De Lauretis 1994: 25) Female bodies do not awaken this loss as negativity, but as limitless desire or searching for zones of the body which seem lost, are conjured up temporalily, then lost again to fantasy. The essay will show that the body-visions of feminist and queer scholars such as Teresa de Lauretis, Luce Irigaray, Elizabeth Grosz and Judith Butler are cinematically evoked in aspects of Maria Beatty's pornography. As theorists have come up with structuralist definitions of the body which replace female gender and genitals with bodies as perverse textualities and sites of construction, Beatty's movies show the ecstasies of pain and pleasure involved in exhibiting processes of construction – the raw somatic fragments and uncanny debris produced in private acts of erotic cruelty or societal dismemberment.

Current proponents of Deleuze's study insist on his presentation of sadism and masochism as distinctive psychic modes of perversion and cultural practices. Masochism is no longer seen as a sexual strategy which leads to sadism, but as one which channels desire into consensual and formalized modes of performance. Deleuze brought a radical shift to Freudian psycho-analytic theory as he viewed masochism as a sexual game and an erotic meditation on the flawed nature of gender inscription and authoritarian law and order. Deleuze challenged Freud's essay '*Beyond the Pleasure Principle*', in which he claimed that sadism and masochism were complementary perversions operating in one psyche, whereby masochism's tendency to self-destruction develops a tendency to enact sadistic brutalities against others. Freud also equated sadism with the emergence of a gendered masculine subject, which would be a more natural development in the male. Deleuze critiqued Freud's affirmation of a genital sexuality inherited from the father, and instead celebrated the masochist as a gender-fluid subject who desires an identification with the mother. Moreover, rather than enacting cruel compulsions onto others, the masochist develops introspective performance strategies for the renewal of his/her own sexual identity. Renewal occurs through an intense process of disorientation and bodily discomfort which Deleuze calls the 'art of destruction'. This art of destruction requires the subject to imagine an altered image of the autonomous body through formalized rituals of cruelty in which s/he expresses a wish for reconstruction through identification with the mother. (Deleuze 1991: 57–69)

In her essay 'The Birth of Sadomasochism', Catherine Dale summarizes the general historical and political significance of Deleuze's 'masochizing' of sado-masochism:

> The principles of contemporary practices of eroticised pain make sadism morally unlivable and as politically dubious as it was in the eighteenth century but with the cruelty exercised in two world wars the term sadist has been reserved for an intonation peculiar to the evil afoot exclusively in the twentieth century. Conversely, masochism has become increasingly for the twentieth-century, both formally, with regards to identification, and ethically, in its relations of power. The nominal arrival sadomasochism then coincides more accurately with its becoming ethically, politically, aesthetically and sexually masochism which 'borrows' the name sadism as an authentic addition to its fantastic cruelty. (Dale s.d.: 6)

Dale then explains that masochism is generally presented as the 'most attractive, palatable and livable of the two perversions'. (Dale s.d.: 6) According to Deleuze, sadist performers act out the death instinct in demonstrative forms, by multiplying and condensing cruelty; whereas masochists use contemplative modes of perception and performance which enact and subvert law and authority. He describes the subversive nature of masochistic fantasies as follows:

> We all know ways of twisting the law by excess of zeal. By scrupulously applying the law we are able to demonstrate its absurdity and provoke the very disorder that it is intended to prevent or conjure … A close investigation of masochism reveals that while they bring into play the very strictest application of the law, the result in every case is the opposite of what might be accepted (thus whipping, far from punishing or preventing an erection, provokes and ensures it. It is a demonstration of the law's absurdity). (Deleuze 1991: 88)

Deleuze's distinction between sadism and masochism has implications for sketching performative modes of power exchange in s/m practice, for film and performance aesthetics, and for a feminist theory of sexuality.

Such areas of investigation are explored, for instance, in Leoni Knight's video *The Father is Nothing*, which is an audio-visual experiment around Deleuze's theory. The masochist's longing for the mother in this video is shown and celebrated through water imagery and an encounter between a woman and a male-to-female transsexual. The father's libidinal economy surfaces in blunt references to fascism; sounds of sirens, masses calling Sieg Heil, a cadence of goose-steps and leather boots. The polarized gender vision in this video is Deleuzian, but can also be explained in reference to Klaus Theweleit's study *Male Fantasies*, which depicts the event of fascism as a historical consciousness which misrecognizes 'feminine' forces – the body, bodily waste and fluids, representing them as dangerously erupting masses. (Theweleit 1986)[2] In *The Father is Nothing*, the reference to a history of fascism and patriarchal excess recedes in the background and becomes a faint memory-image which flashes by and sporadically interrupts the s/m encounter. This is a love story narrated from a masochistic perspective in that it reveals a theatricalized eroticism clearly distinct from the 'sadist' ego-libido.

Gaylyn Studlar explains the masochist's longing for the mother as the desire to approach a dominant figure who is not a substitute for a hidden father, but a controlling agent and as such the perpetual object of the child's curiosity.[3] A romanticized depiction of such desire in a more recent lesbian video, would be Maria Beatty's *Let the Punishment Fit The Crime* (1996), where Beatty appears as a naughty little girl in love with her mother. The girl steals her mother's make-up kit and applies it to a hidden collection of dolls; painting the eyes and genitals with nail-polish, sticking hairpin needles into the bodies in preparation of a sacred offering. As the girl's gaze turns to the mother in anticipation of punishment, the camera transforms the mother into a suave *femme fatale* and a desirable and voluptuous sexual partner. After a long series of repetitive spanking shots – the core of the pornographic content – we can see the mother caress her girl's behind with a soft powder puff, and calmly smoke a cigarette. The mother becomes a good mother as she permeates the girl with love and desire, and carries her through the last stages of sexual climax.

In the s/m contract between the lesbian performers, it is stipulated that the submissive partner surrenders to the dominant female, who performs the role of a stern but attractive mother. Studlar believes that the mother/ dominatrix directs the subject towards a pre-oedipal life, and 'masochistic desire merges the plenitude of the mother with the subject's need for suffering'. (Studlar 1988: 15) In a search for a dual feminine role, the masochist fantasizes a good mother who assumes and appropriates bad mother traits. Studlar adds that the masochist's gender is less important to the perversion's basic dynamics, as performance revisits areas of sexual development which are reminiscent of an infantile bodily awareness and less dependent on gender identification. (Studlar 1988: 16) Through the subject's identification with the mother and a disavowal of the father's patriarchal role, gender identity becomes transmutative. Studlar explains: 'As Deleuze remarks, the masochist believes it possible to become both sexes. Polymorphous, non-procreative, nongenital sexuality undermines the fixed polarities of male and female as defined by the patriarchy's obsession with presence/lack, active/passive, and phallic genitality'.[4] Deleuze's treatise argues that cruelty is fantasized and sought in the construction of various mother/dominatrix archetypes, such as the hermaphrodite: '... who creates havoc in the patriarchal family, inspires the women of the household with the desire to dominate, subjugates the father, cuts the hair of the son in a curious ritual of baptism and causes everyone to dress in clothes of the opposite sex'. (Deleuze 1991: 47–48)

As this essay will show, masochistic performativity is largely conceived of as a set of fantasy scenes which the subject holds in suspense and carefully merges with the actuality of private/public performances, art works and filmic reproduction. It is important to note that 'the mother' is not a rigid entity within the performance dynamic. The mother is rather viewed as an enabling and open-ended sign, an adaptable character within s/m practices, and a debatable role-model within feminist theory. The mother-figure grew out of a 1960s oppositional consciousness which questioned psycho-analytic theory and patriarchal sex education models, and which entered film theory to revise theories of eroticism and gendered agency within the film text and spectatorship. By investigating the work of recent lesbian pornographers, the essay hopes to modify and rethink Deleuze's formulation of the masochist aesthetic, as it enters a world of new technologies, pornography debates, and feminist thinking.

The Stage Setup of Masochism: Dungeon/Dreamscreen

In masochistic performance, performers are engaged in the exchange of sexuality and eroticism. Sado-masochism's aesthetic impulse, however, always works as a kind of anti-art. As Dale observes: 'Leather, chains, masks and handcuffs, common equipment during war, political oppression and torture, become stylized and fetishized as does the choreographed performance of many s/m scenes'. (Dale s.d.: 16–17) The dungeon is full of kitsch yet distinguishes itself precisely from a regular prostitution house in its simulation of stage environments (rather than bedrooms). The New York s/m house Pandora's Box, for example, consists of a Medical Room, a Classroom, a Times Square room, a Dungeon, a Virtual Reality room, and a Versailles room. Inside Pandora's Box, blue velvet-covered walls open and close like sliding doors and regulate an ongoing traffic of clients who decide to act out masochistic fantasies inside the different rooms. Visitors in the Versailles room can get sexual release in ostentatious aristocratic environments, furnished with fireplaces, marble statues, gilt frames, and brocaded thrones. To the uninformed outsider, Pandora's box aspires to accommodate the codes of conduct of the upper-class. However, the dungeon also contains a protocol of subterfuge and enables clients to act out and reconstruct socially ingrained roles and responsibilities.

A famous literary example of masochistic subterfuge would be Jean Genet's play *The Balcony* (1958), which anticipated the s/m subculture's growing desire to shatter myths of paternal authority. The satirical patriarchal stock characters such as the Judge, the Bishop, the General, and the Police, are juxtaposed with the more complex egalitarian character, the political revolutionary Roger. Roger's masculinity exemplifies tension between a world of political activism and a sheltered world of erotic cruelty. In the final scene of the play, at the height of a Paris revolution, Roger undergoes an identity crisis and escapes from the streets of Paris into the s/m house to act out a Chief of Police in the vicinity of an obeying slave. After his clumsy performance, Roger castrates himself in a paradoxical attempt to impersonate and annihilate his desire for power. Roger is thrown out of the s/m house by the proprietress, Madame Irma, who disdains his lack of performative rigor and his lunatic gesture of self-mutilation which also stains her new carpets with blood. Roger's tragedy is presented as the dramatic epiphany of a wavering masculine psyche in the modern era. A new dimensionality in his queer identity emerges through his simultaneous impersonation and castration of authority. However, even though his castration entails a rejection of an oppressive, genital-oriented culture, he fails to fully impersonate the masochistic 'art of destruction' and becomes a tragic character.[5]

Masochism is similarly attained by male and female subjects, who develop performance strategies in a search for the mother. Not only does the masochist's disavowal of phallic power calls for the suspension of orgasmic gratification and symbolic likeness to the father and his law, but such fantasy also enables a gender-fluid position of voyeurism and spectatorship in cinema. (Studlar 1988: 16) Studlar's theory of subjectivity is ultimately a film theory which envisages a gender-fluid identity for the film spectator, and she questions feminist theory and queer theory which assumes a more rigid gender position for the viewer and the pleasures of film spectatorship. Studlar is thus one of the first feminist film theorists to have challenged the theoretical view which excludes the female from the structures of cinematic pleasure and libidinalized looking. (1988: 45)[6] Studlar believes that the spectator is inventive and insurrectionary as s/he enters cinematic viewing strategies to question gender roles and patriarchal eroticism. Moreover, as Mary Conway shows in the recent essay 'Spectatorship in Lesbian Porn', lesbian-produced porn more than any other type of porn imagines female viewers in ways of constructing cinematic pleasure. (1997: 91–114)

Masochistic perception of sexuality is closely aligned with cinematic spectatorship in that the masochist constructs a virtual world through which s/he lives out fantasies which neutralize the real in the imaginative ideal. Studlar uses the concept of the 'dream-screen': 'Through the dream screen – the formation of the cinematic apparatus as environment – the spectator is encouraged to play out the ambivalent oral stage conflict of union/differentiation with the fetishistic substitute for the mother'. (1988: 25, 190) Studlar thus presents the masochistic stage as an environment which mediates between virtual 'cinematic' screens and material spaces. As will be shown in the last section of this essay, the masochistic stage as dream-screen is currently being reconstructed through new virtual technologies such as home video and Internet.

The Cruel Mother in Maria Beatty's Pornography

In her study *The Invention of Pornography*, Lynn Hunt claims that pornography has since its emergence had a paradoxical relationship to democracy. It was invented in the period of modernity (1500–1800) in response to the perceived menace of the democratization of culture through forms of mass communication. Pornography emerged as a legal term denoting selected and censored publications '… in the context of the careful regulation of the consumption of the obscene so as to exclude the lower classes and women.' (1993: 9–45) To the present day, it has been a challenge for women to have access to pornography and the masochistic stages.

Sexual flagellation as a masochistic practice, for instance, has for centuries been recognized by the industries of sex and medicine as a healthy instrument of erotic stimulation for male recipients. In the 17th century, German doctor Johan Heinrich Meibaum (1590–1655) wrote the first in a series of influential treatises about the medical benefits of sexual flagellation, indicating that it cured the adult male subject of madness, melancholy caused by unhappy love, erotic mania, skinniness, bodily weakness, but above all impotence. This idea became institutionalized in the flagellation house, where male patients would be sent out to be spanked or 'cured' by female dominants. Ian Gibson's study *The English Vice: Beating, Sex, Shame in Victorian England and After* further documents spanking stories which featured regularly in the British newspapers as a form of hidden pornography. Needless to say that women, mostly portrayed as dominant characters within the fantasies, were actually discouraged from acting out erotic fantasies in newspapers or public s/m houses. Masochism was still mostly a male invention, although some authors indicated its potential to arouse female subjects. Take for instance John Cleland's porn classic *Memoirs of Fanny Hill* (1749) which narrates an intense encounter between Fanny and the young, impotent Mr Barville. Cleland details the whipping session and conveys how Fanny herself gets pleasantly aroused during the session. After a mutual spanking and a nice dinner with Mr Barville, Fanny is suddenly overcome by 'itching ardors' and 'a prickly heat' which makes her shift and wriggle in her seat. Finally, Mr Barville helps her get full satisfaction by means of spanking and full intercourse.

Published in the 1920s in Victorian England, Havelock Ellis's case-study *Florrie*, narrates the life of a suffragette who pursued feminism in public life and begged for chastisement and confinement in private life. Ellis as an early emancipated psycho-analyst taught Florrie how to accept her fantasies and gradually encouraged her to have her first orgasm through flaggellation. A fully self-authored and persistent spanking fanatic was Edith Cadivec who wrote her memoirs in *Confessions and Experiences* and *Eros: the Meaning of My Life* (1920–1924). Cadivec gave an explicit account of her masochism and explained it as a cry for the intense physical touch and affection of her mother who passed away when she was nine years old.

A recent wave of s/m videos such as Maria Beatty's cast a new light on the sexual nature of female masochism. In a stage setup which resembles a bourgeois parlor, Beatty and her partner Rosemary Delain conceived of their debut film, *The Elegant Spanking* (1995). Like most of her other short films, *The Elegant Spanking* portrays a childhood memory and longing for mother–daughter gratification. The film is shot in black and white, uses a classical spanking setting, and builds towards the gradual display of naked buttocks, meticulous and repetitive spankings carried out by the stern mistress's hand, and the submissive's sexual climax. Beatty is dressed up like a servant girl 'Kitty', who is naughty as she fantasizes contact with the mistress's bodily fluids. In a dissolving dream sequence scene, we can see how Kitty steals the mistress's pearls which the mistress used for masturbation purposes. The stark black and white contrast in the opening shots of the video brings to mind a film aesthetic prevalent in silent, expressionist movies. The repetition of nicely framed eye-shots indicates that Kitty is a voyeur, who carefully watches her mistress's body and begs for her attention.

Although Kitty is submissive in the s/m scenario, her point of view shot represents the unseen director of the masochistic performance and film text.[7] In a daringly explored tension between nostalgic film composition reminiscent of the silent film, and an assertive lesbian bodily display, *The Elegant Spanking* subverts the point of view shot of commercial s/m pornography. The stylized mise-en-scène makes reference to older experiments in photography and film art. Beatty's well crafted 'buttocks' compositions in particular, harken back to underground pornography and the birth of audio-visual technology in the 19th century. A catalogue of Nazarieff's collection *Jeux de Dames Cruelles Photographies 1850–1960* (1992) shows lesbian spanking scenes which have been integral to the institution of photography since the mid-19th century. Most pictures zoom in on the submissive's naked and girlish butt cheeks as fetishized body parts. The two glaring cheeks surrounded by black stockings and white lace petticoats are an expressionistic black and white contrast which features strongly in *The Elegant Spanking*. The oldest classroom punishment scenes mostly depict the dominatrix participant as an older, uptight woman, while the submissive is a younger woman. The staging of age difference between the dominant and submissive partners accentuates the *trompe l'oeil* character of the flaggellation scenes and hides their sexual intent. Browsing through Nazarieff's collection, one can see a break-down of illusionism and the emergence of desire and pleasure in the more recent photographs. Beatty's nostalgic films revisit the old-day punishment scenes, yet also admit to masochism's subversive function and show how partners have intimate physical contact, and reach mutual satisfaction and orgasm.

Beatty's masochism constructs an actual/virtual stage for enacting scenarios of dominance and submission. Studlar shows that a formalized masquerade aims to control and delay the moment of consummation:

> Providing characters with a transformational visual mode of self-definition, masquerade functions as a performance that controls the enticement of desire. Through the temporality of masquerade, gratification is delayed and masochistic suspense is formalized. (1988: 70)[8]

Joseph Von Sternberg's films for instance, who are the main focus of Studlar's analysis, often portray female characters engaged in role-switching. Studlar's main thesis is that the multiple female roles, stereotypes, and mothering images allure to the (female and male) spectator's masochistic imagination.

Maria Beatty shows a range of female voyeurs and divas in her short films. In the film *The Black Glove* (1996), she moves her voyeuristic submissive persona inside a secluded space and writes a solipsistic narrative which leads to the dominatrix's torture of her breasts and vagina. The film opens with a stylized slow motion sequence showing lady-like stiletto heels tapping into a polished floor. Beatty, tied up from head to heel, is then delivered to the dominatrix's room inside a soft velvet wrapping. The dreamscreen of *The Black Glove* still resembles *The Elegant Spanking*, as the infantile longing for maternal touch is translated and aestheticized into consensual lesbian role-play. However, *The Black Glove* shows more clearly how the voyeur brackets the other into the realm of the private consciousness.

The bodily worship of *The Elegant Spanking* has been replaced by a stainless steel fetish, a shining pinwheel and surgeon's hemostats which are slowly applied to Beatty's submissive body. Before she deprives herself of all sensory perception by donning a black mask, black lace panties (her own) are stuffed into her mouth. The camera then zooms into her vagina, and her white labia are slowly pulled apart by means of other shining instruments, then to be covered with black candlewax. Towards the very end of the film, a woman's hand with black velvet glove enters the picture and tempers the cruelty. This absent third player appears as a shadow on the submissive's body, and her voice fills the soundtrack with siren-like humming and orgasmic sounds. The contrast between soothing nature sounds and imagery, and candid portrayals of bodily torture, is crucial to Beatty's works. It is explained by the artist as an attempt to show a painful state of bliss, or the bodily ecstasy following sexual climax (little death).

With *The Black Glove*, Beatty sinks deeper into the masochistic model of filmmaking, because desire is also portrayed as a state of mind rather than a physical condition. The submissive's 'other' is no longer a living partner but an abstract formal entity. While Beatty still entertains the mysterious countenance of the mistresses, the film no longer presents the living women's aura and relationship pangs, as did *The Elegant Spanking*. In order to trace Beatty's development from spanking fanaticism in *The Elegant Spanking* to internalized masochism in *The Black Glove*, it is helpful to recall Deleuze's ideas on coldness and cruelty. Following Freud in *Beyond the Pleasure Principle*, Deleuze explains that masochism, death or destructive instincts are exhibited in the unconscious in conjunction with life instincts. Destruction, and the negative at work in destruction, always manifests itself as the other face of construction and unification as governed by the pleasure-principle. (Deleuze: 30) Deleuze believes that the 'negative' impulse in masochism strives towards a 'positive' outlet or a redeeming cycle. Redemption is established through an intense physical ordeal which intensifies sense-perceptions and transforms them into distorted formal entities – the art of destruction. In this respect, the masochistic voyeur envisions a de-humanized sexual experience, or at least explores the tension between bodily sensations and the body as representation. Deleuze concludes that there is a fundamentally cruel aesthetic perception process in masochism in its disavowal and freeze-framing of aspects of reality.

Reading the diaries of Von Sacher-Masoch, Deleuze takes notice of the baron's austere sense-perceptions, and how they infringe law and order upon the living environment:

> It has been said that the senses become 'theoreticians' and that the eye, for example, becomes a human eye when its object itself has been transformed into a human or cultural object, fashioned by and intended solely for man. Animal nature is profoundly hurt when this transformation of its organs from the animal to the human takes place, and it is this painful process that the art of Masoch came to represent. (1991: 69)

Before Masoch pledges to surrender his life and luxury to the whims of a Russian mistress, he reclines in a comfortable chair and exposes the senses as 'cruel theoreticians' to objects of the decadent environment. Masoch dissects the environment and tries to give up the distinction between his bodily sensations and the body as representation. He calls this cultural state of transmuted sensualism, 'super-sensualism,' and he finds in inanimate works of art the reflection of his love for women who resemble cold, marble statues or paintings in darkened rooms. Although Masoch falls in love eventually and expects to be utterly emotionally hurt by his mistress Wanda, he makes a first *cruel* leap between physical s/m personas and their disembodied reflections. Materially speaking, Masoch gives up his estate to become a servant, laborer, and slave to Wanda's court; only to be further mistreated, humiliated and finally dumped by the Russian empress.

Through a process of disavowal of living, organic aspects of sexuality, masochists aestheticize physicality and create two-dimensional images as fetishes. As Deleuze writes:

> The fetish is therefore not a symbol at all, but as it were a frozen, arrested, two-dimensional image, a photograph to which one returns repeatedly to exorcise the dangerous consequences of movement, the harmful discoveries that result from exploration. (1991: 52)

Here the most obvious connection between Masoch and Beatty can be seen – the construction of a fetish which initiates the process of desire and becomes the ultimate incarnation of a formal aesthetic experience.

The luring voice and soft fabric (black glove) of the absent woman play an important role in *The Black Glove*, as mistresses Morgana and TV

Sabrina apply inanimate and cold instruments to Beatty's body – hemostats, and the rubber mask. According to Deleuze, the coldness of masochistic art is not the negation of feeling altogether, but the disavowal of sensuality. Through disavowal, the sexual experience is turned into a state of waiting and suspense, representing a dormant fusion of the ideal and real in the masochist's fantasy. Waiting divides into two currents: '… the first represents what is awaited, always late and always postponed, the second something that is expected and on which depends the speeding up of the awaited object'. (1991: 71) In *The Black Glove*, Beatty waits for the absent woman to torture the vagina. There is a tension delicately maintained between the cold, impersonal application of instruments by Sabrina and Morgana, and the hot, searing pain of candlewax, the substitute for sensuality, the reward following suspense.

Masochism is read by Deleuze as the desire to formally repeat and reconstruct a regeneration rite. The deeper the process of desexualization, the more powerful and extensive could be the process of resexualization. As we have seen before, the latter upward movement is suggested in *The Black Glove* by means of the sounds and the absent third player, whose voice and softness recall an earth goddess or maternal type. She typifies Beatty's lost childhood and is idealized in the process of waiting, as the other mistresses prepare her for her candlewax ritual. If a fetish can be defined as the last object that a child sees before the awareness of the castrated mother, *The Black Glove* portrays the maternal glove as fetish. The black candle, which is shaped like a phallus, is the symbol of the process of castration (this is an ironic joke of course). (1991: 31)

Whereas Deleuze views the death drive as an inherently aesthetic and tragic faculty of erotic sense-perception, Jacques Lacan presents it as a formation of the ego which is not unique to masochism itself. New Lacanian theorists have focused on the symbolic nature of the death drive and contradicted clinical psychologists who consider s/m as a painful repetition of a traumatic experience.[9] Lacan views the subconscious as a form of reason, logic, and pleasure, governed by signification rather than natural instincts. According to Richard Boothby in *Death and Desire: Psychoanalytic Theory in Lacan's Return to Freud* (1991), Lacan theorizes the death drive as a primordial force of exclusion, a process of alienation which splits the subject from itself and from the external world through language and symbols. In the transition from libido to ego, imaginary *Gestalts* (shapes) act as a buffer or filter which refuses the transmission of energy.

Following Lacan, we can approach Beatty's cinematography as the fragmented language which documents the gap between the unconscious and signification. Her masochistic and solipsistic dream imagery thus becomes symbolic of the act of communication itself, narrating a process of separation between parent and child and asserting the primacy of language in the development of life/art. One could say that Beatty reaches conscious expression only by means of disguise, distortion and displacement and she replaces the original lost object of desire with a substitute – the fetish. (Boothby 1991: 202, 80) The next section of the essay will investigate how masochism's tendency towards fetishism can be understood within a feminist framework.

Feminism and Masochism

About 7 years ago, in her article 'Daughter of the Movements: The Psychodynamics of Lesbian s/m Fantasy', Julia Creet asked herself to what degree feminism as an intellectual and activist movement had lost its credibility with a younger generation of women in search of new definitions of sexuality. Due to feminism's lack of recognition of masochism as a sexual identity, Creet pronounced a rebellion against feminist modes of public culture: 'The symbolic Mother has come to be the repository of the prohibitions of feminism … feminism itself has become a source of approval or disapproval'. (1991: 144) As a supervizing symbolic mother, American anti-pornography feminism in particular, has often denounced womens' public sex work and/or pornographic artwork, thus supporting an alliance with right-wing censoring organs.

In *Bad Girls and Sick Boys*, Linda Kauffman demonstrates how the 1986 Meese Commission on Pornography appropriated the extremist anti-porn arguments of feminists Catherine MacKinnon and Andrea Dworkin to issue extremist measures against pornographic film and photography. MacKinnon and Dworkin had negatively defined pornography as 'the sexually explicit subordination of women, graphically or in words'. (Kauffman s.d.: 233–243) In the early 1990s, the Christian fundamentalist Jesse Helm's infamous amendment to the American Senate proposed to censor 'indecent' art depicting 'sadomasochism, homoeroticism, the exploitation of children and individuals engaged in sex acts'. Helm's amendment reflected a moral panic in religious and in feminist circles around pornography, a political development which has had a disastrous effect on public exhibitions of queer and s/m sexuality. Gayle Rubin predicted this development in the mid-1980s in her seminal essay 'Thinking Sex: Notes for a Radical Theory of the Politics of Sexuality'. Rubin wrote:

> It is always risky to prophesy. But it does not take much prescience to detect potential moral panics in two current developments: the attacks on sadomasochists by a segment of the feminist movement, and the Right's increasing use of AIDS to incite virulent homophobia. (Rubin in Kauffman 1993: 33)

Rubin then suggested that sexually radical communities and their pornographic works be discussed outside the institutions and discourses of feminism in order to prevent the construction of a class of women 'perverts'. Nearly a decade later, in *Presence and Desire: Essays on Gender, Sexuality and Performance*, Jill Dolan reiterates that a prevailing feminist anti-pornography rhetoric ultimately censors deeply layered erotic lesbian imagery. Dolan wrote: 'The Jesse Helmses of the United States aren't the only ones legislating representation from ideologically, morally, and ethically righteous positions'. (1993: 179) A contemporary writer, sex educator, and porn star, Carol Queen summarizes 'feminism's false analysis' of pornography in the British magazine *Skin Two*:

> [Feminism] has made the mistake of overestimating its area of expertise, assuming that because it does a good job in cultural and political analysis of gender, economics, and power, it can proceed to analyse everything, including sex ... Some women are deeply damaged by this absence of support. Others are simply turned off by feminism. For of course most of us do not eroticise spanking and other pervy joys out of any lack of self-worth ... How on earth can feminist (and others) imply our desire for pleasure is a source of weakness or worse? (1996: 87)

Masochism's positive aura within contemporary women's movements and film cultures is shown in Sasha Water's *Whipped* (1997), a documentary which features three 'life-style' dominatrixes and owners of major New York dungeons: Carrie Coakley, Ava Taurel, and Sonya Blaze. *Whipped* focuses on the relationship between the dominatrixes and their male slaves and highlights their everyday politics and feminist activism. In one of the most endearing scenes of this documentary, Ava Taurel introduces a class of women apprentices to the principles of female domination, a set of coded performance practices which can be applied to private sex practices or public sex work. The film shows the entire class break out in laughter when one apprentice hesitantly whips a male submissive in front of the camera. Taurel's workshop teaches women to gradually accept and embody the role of the mother/dominatrix, to interpret and act out the role in front of diverse clients, to acquire the technical skills of bondage and the discourse of humiliation, and to endorse the fantasy as a material practice in the dungeon and/or in the private imagination.

More provocative scenes in *Whipped* highlight the intricate relationship between Ava Taurel and her black slave Girard. Whereas Taurel explains Girard's submission as an extravagant craving for affection resulting from early childhood trauma and brain damage Girard himself shows his discomfort and dissatisfaction being cast in this role. The film shows that Taurel and Girard respect and love each other, but are also caught up in a very rigid masochistic scenario. *Whipped* then follows the younger dominatrix Carrie Coakley during her pregnancy and marriage, and points to her necessity to embody fluctuating feminine roles and responsibilities. Carrie is shown as a strong woman torn between her radical sex activism such as leadership in New York City's organization 'lesbian s/m mafia', and a more traditional engagement with her family. *Whipped* poses ethical and feminist questions around the practices of dominatrixes by showing their complex search for a sexual identity within supportive activist women's networks.

In order to locate a theoretical framework which can locate the feminist impulse in s/m sexuality, I will start with the ideas of the French feminist philosopher Luce Irigaray. Irigaray argues that assertive female sexuality has been erased or misrepresented in the western philosophical tradition due to its being rooted in a Platonic illusionistic 'stage setup'. Irigaray imagines the prisoners in Plato's cave as physically *and* mentally immobile and unable to envision the bodily, dark space, the womb from which they came: 'Heads forward, eyes front, genitals aligned, fixed in a straight direction and always straining forwards, in a straight line'. (1985: 245) The cave as metaphor has emptied itself from any relation to the body, as she writes:

> … man's attributes figure only insofar as they have been made into statues, immortalized in deathly copies. Any reference that might have been made to it – if one could only turn around – is from the outset a *formal* one. The potency of the enchanter has always already been captured, *made into a corpse by morphology.* (1985: 355, italics in original)

Gillian Rose explains in 'Masculinist Theory and Feminist Masquerade', that Irigaray juxtaposes the masculine morphology as 'corpse' with a feminine morphology as 'masquerade'. Femininity does not reverse masculinity, but functions as a series of refusals of and deviations from masculinity.[10] *Speculum of Another Woman* investigates the feminine masquerade as a new bodily discourse. Metaphorically speaking, the subject has to pass through a looking-glass (speculum) into a new territory of her own self-representation. The speculum differs from the Platonic mirror in that the subject is able to 'self-touch' and to mime modes of femininity.[11] Irigaray imagines a mother-child environment which gets displaced at the moment of birth, when the child takes exile from the womb, and the mother is symbolically reconstructed as a space of absence and transformation. This space becomes an immense space, and keeps challenging traditional perceptions of gender and the body.[12]

In the postmodern arts scene, feminist performance artists have responded to such ideas when they started to appropriate and parade the mythic functions *and* living properties of the body and sexuality in experimental performance works. For instance, Carolee Schneemann in *Interior Scroll* (1975) pulled a scroll out of her vagina and read aloud a text attacking a structuralist thinker who misread her body works. In 1991, Annie Sprinkle douched on stage in preparation of her 'public cervix announcement' in which, aided by speculum and flashlight, she allowed audience members to look at her cervix.[13] Feminist theory and performance art has been crucial to the development of s/m masquerades in lesbian s/m videos.[14]

In recent years, Elizabeth Grosz has reinvestigated Irigaray's theory to formulate a new phenomenological view on the body. Grosz rejects the Platonic idea that the body is a brute, or passive entity, but sees the body itself as constitutive of systems of meaning.[15] In *Volatile Bodies*, she redefines the body using Deleuze's post-oedipal framework of the 'Desiring Machine.'[16] The body becomes a desiring machine when it de-humanizes the object of desire and dissolves into surrounding environments. The subject becomes one with the machine-like apparatus and senses its merging components as changing, segmented and discontinuous waves, flows, and intensities. Instead of aligning desire with the realm of fantasy and opposing it to the real, the machine stands for positive actualizations of the body within new technological environments.

Grosz refines her theory of the body in the essay 'Animal Sex: Libido as Desire and Death'. She argues that desire exhibits a logic of its own and always insists on a certain formlessness and indeterminacy. Grosz refers to the work of Alfonso Lingis and points to a merging of corporeal and erotic desire within the body as desiring machine. Lingis distinguishes between corporeal need and erotic desire, and explains that the latter craves strategies of 'pleasurable torment' in order to prolong and extend beyond physiological needs. Desire fragments and dissolves the unity and utility of the organic body and breaks up the teleological plans and tasks to perform.

The body constantly interrupts the subject's goal-oriented sexuality, rewriting it as an open-ended and performative category. Following Lingis, Grosz explains that the 'other' as object of desire deranges the physical order, harmony and industry of the subject. The body gets thoroughly confused as it is approached through diverse organs, zones, surfaces which are jealous of one another and want to get aroused '... not simply by pleasure, through caresses, but also through the force and energy of pain. Pain is as capable, perhaps more so, of inscribing bodies as pleasure. We cannot readily differentiate the processes by which pleasurable intensities are engendered from those by which painful intensity is produced'. (1995: 289) For Grosz, erotogenic zones are not necessarily nostalgic reminiscences of a pre-oedipal, infantile bodily organization; but they are sites-in-construction '... in the process of being produced, renewed, transformed through experimentation, practices, innovations, the accidents or contingencies of life itself, the coming together of surfaces, incisive practices, inscriptions'. (1995: 289) Grosz argues that in order to accept the machinic body as a powerful category of inscription and intensification, the Freudian 'hydraulic' model of sexual release, and the internally interlinked faculties of pleasure and death, need to be revised. The needs and functions of machinic body merge actuality/corporeality with virtuality/signification and are thus different from the Freudian and Lacanian model.

Electronic s/m

Merging the body with machinic environments, filmmakers and spectators are rewriting masochism inside the culture of lesbian s/m porn, which is accessed by a growing community of home video and Internet spectators, sex workers, artists and critics. Writers such as Pat Califia, for instance, successfully promote the masochistic body as a new setting for auto-ethnography and female pleasure. In *Public Sex: The Culture of Radical Sex* (1995) Pat Califia comments on new technological constructions of sex and fetishism in our culture: 'The latex fetish is an excellent example of the way human culture (especially technology) alters human sexuality'. (1994: 195)

Masochism as a psychic mode and cinematic viewing pleasure implies that the original fantasy of mother–child union remains unconscious and unremembered, and that gratification is forever postponed, even if reconstructed in the moment of spectatorship. (Studlar 1988: 21–25) Do lesbian porn films and Internet sites offer less sublimated narratives for the spectator? They encourage the spectator to produce and receive pleasure in the making of masochistic portraits – a new type of cinema and literature which is constructed in the process of exchanging and discussing private and public desires. In the introduction to *Bodies that Matter*, Butler defines the body as a '*process of materialisation that stabilises over time to produce the effect of boundary, fixity, and surface we call matter*'. (Italics in original) (1993: 9) The masochist body can be seen as an artificial boundary which is produced in an open-ended type of communication, a process of materialization which renders new meanings in different user contexts, such as e.g. the cacophony of Internet chatting.

Artists such as Maria Beatty and Pat Califia have modified the masochist aesthetic through subcultural production and Internet exchange of porn videos, by encouraging performance participation in live and Internet communities. Deleuze's theory of masochism precedes his formulation of the desiring machine and presupposes a separation between the spectator and his/her projected plane of illusions. This aspect of Deleuze's theory of masochism was explored by Gaylyn Studlar in her theory of classical narrative cinema, which envisioned an intensity of experience and imagined role-reversal in the act of constructing eroticism in dark movie theatres. In this precise moment when conservative censorship is struggling to extend its surveillance mechanisms from arthouse cinemas to Internet sites, the sexuality and theory of the masochist body is rewritten by artists and theorists and rescued from the dark within the less sublimated feminist and queer screen cultures.

Word of Thanks

I would like to thank Michelle Siciliano and Hélène Frichot for reading and editing the text. Joseph S. Schaub for ample feedback from the outset of the masochist project. Herbert Blau and Kathleen Woodward at the Center for Twentieth Century Studies for their enthusiasm and encouragement. Joseph Slade and Ruth Bradley for comments on an earlier version of the text, published in *Wide Angle*, July 1997.

Bibliography

Boothby, Richard. *Death and Desire: Psychoanalytic Theory in Lacan's Return to Freud*. New York: Routledge, 1991.
Butler, Judith. *Bodies that Matter: On the Discursive Limits of Sex*. New York and London: Routledge, 1993.
Califia, Pat. *Public Sex: The Culture of Radical Sex*. Pittsburg: Cleis Press, 1994.
Cetta, Lewis T. *Profane Play, Ritual and Jean Genet*. S.l.: The University of Alabama Press, 1974.

Conway, Mary T. 'Spectatorship in Lesbian Porn: The Woman's Film'. *Wide Angle*. Vol. 19, no. 3.

Creet, Julia. 'Daughter of the Movement: The Psycho-dynamics of s/m Fantasy'. *Differences*. Vol. 5, no. 2, 1991.

Dale, Catherine. *The Birth of Sadomasochism*. Unpublished manuscript.

Deleuze, Gilles. *Masochism: Coldness and Cruelty*. New York: Zone Books, 1991.

Dolan, Jill. *Presence and Desire: Essays on Gender, Sexuality, and Performance*. Ann Arbor, Michigan: University of Michigan Press, 1993.

Grosz, Elizabeth. *Jacques Lacan: A Feminist Introduction*. London: Routledge, 1990.

—. *Volatile Bodies: Toward a Corporeal Feminism*. Bloomington: Indiana University Press, 1994.

—. 'Animal Sex. Libido as Desire and Death'. *Sexy Bodies: The Strange Carnalities of Feminism*. Elizabeth Grosz and Eslpeth Probyn (eds). London and New York: Routledge, 1995.

Hunt, Lynn (ed.). *The Invention of Pornography: Obscenity and the Origins of Modernity, 1500–1800*. New York: Zone Books, 1993.

Irigaray, Luce. *Speculum of the Other Woman*. Ithaca: Cornell University Press, 1985.

Kaplan, Louise. *Female Perversions: The Temptations of Madame Bovary*. New York: Doubleday, 1991.

Kauffman, Linda S. *Bad Girls and Sick Boys: Fantasies in Contemporary Art and Culture*. Berkeley: University of California Press, 1998.

—. (ed.). *American Feminist Thought at Century's End: A Reader*. Cambridge: Blackwell, 1993.

Lauretis, Teresa de. *The Practice of Love: Lesbian Sexuality and Perverse Desire*. Bloomington: Indiana University Press, 1994.

Olson, Jenni (ed.). *The Ultimate Guide to Lesbian and Gay Video*. New York: Serpent's Tail, 1996. <http://www.planetout.popcornq>

Queen, Carol. 'The Bottom Line'. *Skin Two*. London, May 1996.

Rose, Gillian. 'Masculinist Theory and Feminist Masquerade'. *Body Space: Destabilizing Geographies of Gender and Sexuality*. Nancy Duncan (ed.). London and New York: Routledge, 1996.

Straayer, Chris. *Deviant Eyes: Deviant Bodies, Sexual Re-Orientation in Film and Video*. New York: Columbia University Press, 1996.

Studlar, Gaylyn. *In the Realm of Pleasure: Von Sternberg, Dietrich and the Masochistic Aesthetic*. New York: University of Illinois Press, 1988.

Theweleit, Klaus. *Male Fantasies* (Vols 1 and 2). Minneapolis: University of Minnesota Press, 1986.

Notes

[1] Among those dominatrixes are Ava Taurel and Carrie Coakley. Maria Beatty's reputation as film producer and director began with documentaries about performance art: the anthology *Sphinxes Without Secrets: Women Performance Artists Speak Out* (1991); *The Sluts and Goddesses Video Workshop or How to Be A Sex Goddess in 101 Easy Steps* (1992) in co-production with Annie Sprinkle; and *Imaging Her Erotics* (1994) in co-production with Carolee Schneemann. The performance art documentary *Sphinxes Without Secrets* was produced in response to the National Endowment of the Arts backlash against sexually explicit art. It brought together several performance

artists such as Lenora Champagne, Ellie Covan, Diamanda Galas, Holly Hughes, and Laurie Anderson and intended to narrate a women's history of performance art to counter-act restrictive legislation and censorship. Beatty was appointed director of this project, which was made possible with major grants from New York State Council on the Arts, Art Matters, Inc., and DCTV. Beatty's interest in *Sphinxes Without Secrets* was to produce (rather than debate) sexual politics and to participate in culture wars against the American conservative climate. Beatty later started to produce s/m videos which she decided to finance through her private sexwork rather than the more censored path of government funding.

[2] This study meticulously dissects pre-war German pop icons, propaganda, private documents in their repression of the 'red masses' who were associated with engulfing women, bodily forces, illnesses, and earth spiritualism. Theweleit explains fascist military rituals as the culmination of elite male fantasies erected in order to circumscribe a fear of social dissolution.

[3] In *Masochism: Coldness and Cruelty*, Deleuze distinguishes three 'mother' archetypes in Von Sacher-Masoch diaries; an Aphrodite who is dedicated to love and beauty. She generates disorder and stands up for the equality of women by attacking patriarchal institutions. The second is a sadistic type who enjoys hurting and torturing others but is liable to become a man's victim. The third woman represents an ideal mixture of both, and represents coldness as a disavowal or the intense and nurturing transformation of sensuality, 52.

[4] Studlar, *In the Realm of Pleasure*, 32. Studlar also mentions that Deleuze and Guattari further critique Freudian gender identification in the evocation of post-gender 'Desiring machines' in *Anti-Oedipus: Capitalism and Schizophrenia*.

[5] A. Norman O. Brown inspired reading of *The Balcony* is further outlined by Lewis T. Cetta in *Profane Play, Ritual and Jean Genet* (pp. 41–54). Cetta believes that the castration scene evokes the conflict of the desire of the immortal child for pure, polymorphous play; and the reality principle which imposes genital organization.

[6] Studlar refers to Laura Mulvey's seminal essay, 'Visual Pleasure and Narrative Cinema'.

[7] Although *The Elegant Spanking* grew out of a collaboration between Maria Beatty and Rosemary Delain, Beatty was in charge of most aesthetic aspects of the filmmaking process, imposing composition and editing styles onto the spanking narrative. Once *The Elegant Spanking* was launched into the New York s/m scene and gay and lesbian film festival circuits, it caused exaltation, raving successes and emotional turbulence in the life of the producers.

[8] Studlar, *In the Realm of Pleasure*, 70.

[9] See for instance Louise Kaplan's *Female Perversions: The Temptations of Madame Bovary* for an example of humanist clinical psychology which denounces cold fetishistic tendencies in the masochist.

[10] Gillian Rose, 'Masculinist Theory and Feminist Masquerade', in Nancy Duncan ed., *Body Space: Destabilizing Geographies of Gender and Sexuality* (London and New York, Routledge, 1996) 56–75.

[11] See Elizabeth Grosz's on the ideas of Irigaray, in *Jacques Lacan: A Feminist Introduction*, and Judith Butler in *Bodies that Matter: On the Discursive Limits of Sex*, 37.

[12] See Gillian Rose, 'Masculinist Theory and Feminist Masquerade', in Nancy Duncan ed., *Body Space: Destabilizing Geographies of Gender and Sexuality*, 67–69.

[13] For a description of Sprinkle's performance, See Chris Straayer, *Deviant Eyes: Deviant Bodies, Sexual Re-Orientation in Film and Video*, 235.

[14] Reflecting on the role of the masochist aesthetic in postmodern arts and filmmaking, I also refer to Noel Burch's lecture 'The Sadeian Aesthetic', which he delivered at the Rotterdam Arts Festival of 1998. According to Burch, the cult of de Sade has made an alliance with high modernist abstract formalist art and avant-garde filmmaking as it encourages the spectator to enjoy the 'optical and formal aggressions which the medium makes possible, a disinterested, aestheticized approach to the representation of violence'. The cult of de Sade establishes a 'particular eroticisation of ethics and politics' in abstract art and writing which stems from the cult of a self-engendered genius artist who transformed the world and matter into the fetish artwork. In contradiction to sadism, masochism professes a different approach to the representation of erotic cruelty and enables the viewer to identify with the subject matter. Although Burch believes that such experience can be found in the more 'populist' experience of watching classical narrative cinema, one could also see applications of the masochist aesthetic in the sensual of femininity and the body in performance art and lesbian pornography.

[15] See *Volatile Bodies: Toward a Corporeal Feminism*, 17–18. Judith Butler similarly rejects the naive 'constructionist' corrections of 'essentialism' in the introduction to *Bodies that Matter: On The Discursive Limits of Sex*, 1–23.

[16] For a discussion of Deleuze and Guattari's desiring machines as a new feminist model, see Elizabeth Grosz, *Volatile Bodies: Towards a Corporeal Feminism*, 160–186.

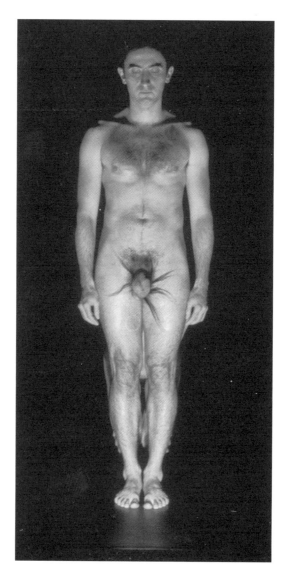

Jérôme Bel, *Jérôme Bel de Jérôme Bel*,
Photo: Lisa Rastl

Steven De Belder

Theatricality – Invisibility – Discipline

Introduction: Fields of Theatricality

'Theatricality' is a notion that, together with the concept of 'performance',[1] has become widespread in recent years. However as *theatrum mundi* it is an age-old metaphor, reinvented at the beginning of the 20th century as an analytical concept that developed later in two different directions. Firstly, it developed in scope, that is the number of areas where it has been used as a descriptive word (e.g. the best-known are Erving Goffman on everyday life and Norbert Elias on court life). Secondly, it developed in depth, within the framework of the research of the historical–anthropological origins of current theatre practices. The versatility the concept acquired was to the detriment of its clarity. At the same time, increased scope was created for a better understanding of the phenomenon of theatre. The explosion of the notion of 'theatricality' in the 20th century runs parallel to what Erika Fischer-Lichte calls the 'retheatralisation of the theatre' (Fischer-Lichte 1995a: 98), whereby theatre itself starts looking for its roots, its basic structures and for a changing relation to the 'outside' and toward other disciplines.

The theory of theatre hovers constantly on the dynamic border between offer and reception. However broad the sense we give to the term of 'theatricality', the articulation of a relation between offer and reception seems to be a *sine qua non*. This is true, as for more than a century theatre has been concerned with the removal or bridging of both dimensions. The 'cliché' conventions of bourgeois theatre, obsessed with actively producing a text before a passive audience, i.e. a mainly detached and intellectual relationship, was put under pressure by the appearance of the historical avant-garde. The audience got directly and, when possible, even physically involved; theatre makers refused to continue to produce a complete work and the theatre *process*, involving the two 'camps' in the production of the piece, was put first.[2] A significant part of contemporary research of 'theatricality' tries to identify the basis of these relatively recent developments and to connect them with historical apparitions and sources of the theatre, spanning the bourgeois capitalist division of labour and its idealistic philosophy of art.

However, a perspective that can encompass both production and reception appears difficult to attain. The scientist/critic/ ... is bound to take a position. Either they look at the audience from the point of view of what is being offered and at the ways the audience deals with it or, as a member of the audience, they pay attention to what the piece might mean or what they might experience and to what structure of meaning is being offered. Research is struggling with the relation between showing and looking, between *show* and *Schau*. Both are recognised as fundamental, but they often shape up to a *Gestalt* – you are aware of the presence of both of them without being able to see or comprehend them at the same time. On the one hand, we have Elizabeth Burns, for example, who places emphasis on the viewing:

> Behavior can only be described as theatrical by those who know what drama is, even if their knowledge is limited to the theatre in their own country and period. It is an audience term, just as the *theatron* was originally a place for viewing, an audience place. Behavior is not therefore theatrical because it is of a certain kind but because the observer recognizes certain patterns and sequences which are analogous to those with which he is familiar in the theatre.[3] (1972: 12)

On the other hand, we have the position that stresses the showing, the 'offering-of'. This view, starting with the theatre as an artistic phenomenon, implies the presence of an audience without treating it as such.

> Nothing other than the mere fact of exhibiting symbolisation (which brings forth symbolic violence) as an ersatz-satisfaction related to the level of deception at a certain moment in time, or in function of the disclosure or also total refusal of deception can justify the use [of the notion of theatricality – SDB]. (Münz 1998: 89)

This interpretation presupposes a symbolic audience at least with which one starts negotiating (hence the symbolic violence, the refusal of the status quo), but in a one-sided way.

It is Andreas Kotte who comes closest to an integrative wording, even when he opposes an independent use of the term of 'theatricality':

> The spectators scrutinise all circumstances and changes of the emphases and they react to them. They consider the ways of stressing (staging and playing) as the main function of the interactive happening (besides there are always other functions like conveying a message etc.) and from there they assess what happens as theatre. (...) In the so-called integrative definition of theatre, acting functions also as a necessary condition, but it is only experiencing (the perception) of the situation which is the sufficient condition. (Kotte 1998: 125)

In this description theatricality is an umbrella idea spanning both positions. Other attempts to occupy areas close to these positions, widening the scope for an independent concept of theatricality, are usually accompanied by many questions – when you move away from familiar territory, you may find yourself to be on shifting ground with a vague notion of something better somewhere else. 'Theatricality' is a very evident concept as long as it is used in an unreasoned or nominalist way. However, as soon as the term itself 'makes its appearance on the stage' and several semantic fields need to negotiate it and its interpretation for a sense of practicability, it turns into an enormous jumble of meanings. I mentioned 'to appear on stage' intentionally to show that even when analysing the term its metaphorical use remains very tempting.

'Theatricality' is a notion that always continues to function. It positions itself like a virus in the theory, questioning theory's idea of the relation between reality and fiction. It is a critical concept that takes up the illusionary and idealistic character of theatre to establish its relation towards reality, to criticise or even to replace it. 'Theatricality occupies the space between theory and practice, which both modes occupy.' (Brewer 1985: 14) To some people this impurity alone is reason enough to abandon the concept.

In this paper my intention is to connect the notion of 'theatricality' with two divergent fields: the Lacanian-psychoanalytical performance theory of Peggy Phelan's *Unmarked: The Politics of Performance* and the historic inquiry of Michel Foucault's *Discipline and Punish*. This may look a rather strange combination at first sight, bound to exacerbate further the nervousness around the notion. I intend neither to even them out, nor to attempt to comprehend theatre as such via some macro-cartel. All three of them as exclusive research instruments are too tautological to the concept of theatre and the appeal theatre theory makes to them may lead to a mutually circular justification. Thinking broadly may indeed conceal a lack of depth. Then their terms change into fetish concepts that, like viruses, can spread throughout all possible areas, not in the least into one another's. The fetish then takes advantage of the hesitation and the refusal to define the notion, according to Andreas Kotte. To him, 'theatricality' is a magic word that has now become so neutral that it does not add anything to the fields of research involved (Kotte 1998: 118–119). Kotte's criticism, however, is too much a defensive reflex by a discipline that notes how (a part of) its subject matter is seized upon and developed further by others. He himself reduces 'theatricality' to a subordinate derivative of the notion of 'theatre' that is to be well defined dynamically. But why should we not combine both of them? It is quite possible to approach concepts of theatricality in a critical way with a definition of theatre at the back of one's mind, not so much in order to promote them or to make them fall through, but to clarify and render more productive the ways they connect theatre and other areas. Equally, that hesitation coerces the critical user into looking consciously for their limits and keeping open the connection with other users and areas, which is an open and communicative operation that learns from use by others.

The advantage of starting from other theories is that they make people aware that theatre is a system that compromises a relatively autonomous functioning with influences by societal practices. This influence not only lies with a 'referential intention'[4] but with the total phenomenon/process of theatre. Besides, the danger of tautology is at least partly averted by the explicit commitment of the theories of Phelan and Foucault. Neither of them wants to accept the observing–analytical relation to their subject of research. Foucault qualifies objective analysis as extremely insipid (Foucault 1977b: 157), while Phelan considers her method an explicitly political instrument even though it is limited to the praxis in theatre.

In theatre, nothing is so unavoidably and conspicuously present as the human body. It is the meeting point of the communication between the artist and the audience. The 'retheatralisation of theatre' has put the body at the centre to the cost of the dramatic text. This was meant to oppose the intellectual structure of bourgeois theatre, the passivity of the spectator and the sublimation of bodily reality. However, in theatre the body presents itself to the *Schau*, the gaze of the spectator, who already holds a more dynamic and libidinal attitude. However, this *Schau* does not seem to be automatically capable of comprehending the many facets and dynamics of the body and threatens to turn it into a commodity, a consumable image. In this case the (male or female) spectator remains too passive and takes full advantage of the vulnerability the performer shows in his corporeality. The body continuously fails to respond to the energetic or critical ideal – it can only be comprehended or fixed in an image or in it being endlessly dissected into its tiniest particles.[5] Yet, the body remains the primary stake in the work of theatre makers. Art and its theory, busily concerned with saving the body from total encapsulation, may have made it into an even greater fetish than the commercial media industry could ever have imagined. Foucault's mechanism of disciplining the subject and his body haunts these attempts for desublimation. His theory itself draws on a theatrical terminology of rendering visible: the supervisor and the subject are aware of their own and each other's position, and the mechanism mostly occurs in a context of action with a clear-cut definition and effect (e.g. prison, classroom, hospital). The observation of this mechanism, and the effectiveness of blotting out and keeping some processes invisible, cries out for a radical reaction if we do not want to go on deceiving ourselves with our desperate attempts at rescue. Either we are silent about what we cannot say, or we start from this failure at a theatrical adventure with an unknown destiny.

This is why, according to Peggy Phelan, writing on theatre always becomes involved some complicity, becoming theatre itself. Even when this writing is to be repaid with finiteness and limitation of its sphere of action, even when the whole world is a theatre which involves everyone in maintaining the cheerful/terrible lie, the notion of theatre exists against the background of a tough, vague and always betrayed core of materiality: matter, actions and bodies. Nothing more than blood and bones. However passionately a theatre may embrace its opposite, or however proud it is about its hybrid and nomadic status, it always implicitly remains just theatre, i.e. 'consequence-lessening action' (A. Kotte). As a human action, limited in time and space, it is part of the world; it involves a communicative process that always makes it more than a sheer narcissistic game. This action may always question the difference between theatre and reality, like the historical avant-garde incessantly used to do, and this may still remain the motivation for the current use of the term. Nevertheless, it remains a sociological fact that that which calls itself 'theatre' must tolerate a limited societal functioning that should be exploited, without succumbing to obscurantism. This does not necessarily mean that conceptual analysis should be confined to formalistic semiotics of an art practice, because it is precisely there that thinking/writing lacks awareness of its own performative effect. But even when it is a consequence-*lowered* action, it is driven by a recurrent ethical desire.[6] The theatrical reality, i.e. the performance, refers to an active mediation between 'consumer' and 'product'. It is of minor importance whether this product is or is not capable of being reproduced. This ethical moment means that we do not remain silent; at least it becomes a game of staying silent, showing and concealing and perpetually starting over and over again.

This text is looking for possible attitudes towards the processes of disciplining, and the position of the body within them, as Michel Foucault has described them. What kind of answers can be given by theatre practice to the processes that have been outlined by Foucault and that we can still find at work more or less nowadays? What is the relation between the body and the disciplining process, of which it is simultaneously the subject and the object? Is it capable of and, if required so, willing to withdraw itself occasionally from the compulsion of conforming itself to the varying requirements of productivity? Is there really anything like a fully disciplined body, or do we encounter here rhetoric and a dramatic exaggeration of Foucault? If these questions only referred to possibly isolated, referential contents of theatre practice, the outcomes should be of little relevance for they would only disclose a naive political activism in the guise of art. The particular structure and context of theatre do not allow it to function as a detective of societal macro-structures. Neither do we aim at using the Foucauldian concepts within the artistic or social realm like some toolbox.[7] However, should these questions succeed in covering the whole practice, we would gain sight of some fundamental elements, for example, how is being dealt with discipline and freedom, with the body and the schemes it finds itself in? What is the real nature of the confrontation of theatre with its own presuppositions regarding the audience and picture quality? Moreover, the status of the discourse is also involved. The historiography and philosophy of Foucault can be conceived of as forms of performative writing, i.e. as theatre. Of course the danger exists of contamination and vagueness increasing once again, but this can, developing from Foucault, be used just as well as a tactic for influencing some practice in a careful and suggestive fashion.

This suggestiveness is a central quality of Peggy Phelan's work *Unmarked: The Politics of Performance*, where she looks for the theatrical opportunities for women and other groups to get up to speak and to make use of images, without immediately conforming themselves to those mechanisms that put them in a separate category in the first place. This bears upon those mechanisms whose efficiency and, most of all, the (unintentional?) involvement of both parties in it have been identified by Foucault. She proceeds by playing off their invisibility, pursuing the tactical possibilities of the observation that they do not have any power over their self-definition, rather than by trying to replace one dominant discourse with another, because of the great risk of recuperation. Her methodical suggestiveness consists in her attempt not to reveal too much the invisible in which she placed her trust whilst speaking about it herself. This is why she tries to write on the theatrical in a performative way. The term theatricality thus reappears at different levels: how is the invisible made theatrical in her opinion and what can the role be of her own writing here? The very emphasis on the invisible renders her theory quite versatile and inspirational even beyond the realm of feminism.

From the inspiration of Foucault, the question is raised of whether there exist opportunities for some resistance or distortion, more through the image of disciplining than through a direct denial, leaving room for something like an 'undisciplined body' or any 'remainder'. The ambivalence of the entanglement of discipline and 'rest' should prevent the urge of falling back on a false naturalism or primitivism, or on any other essentialist conception that replaces one straitjacket with another or that quickly allows itself to be incorporated powerlessly as something merely worth seeing. Seen from Phelan's standpoint, that 'other' is better kept hidden and not showing itself as overly powerful and vulnerable at the same time. We wonder whether it would be possible to fill the blind spot of invisibility with the image of its opposite and whether by showing the disciplining process the suggestion can also be made that this process cannot possibly be as complete as it presents itself. It is a possibility that Phelan herself has not actually taken into consideration, although in my opinion it would fit into her framework if it were extended somewhat and on condition that we remain aware of the necessary restrictions.

Visibility and Theatre: The Disciplining Process According to Michel Foucault

At the origin of each theory on what theatre is and should be lies the issue of the wording of what occurred in the visual field, of rendering communicative an event amidst its definitive absence. Martin Heidegger connects 'theory' and 'theatre' in one single root word, namely that of looking outward, an external aspect wherein something shows itself. The visible, as it presents itself, simultaneously offers itself up for questioning. It is incomplete without the idea it represents. Although Heidegger reserves this second movement to the theory (by relating the looking-at to the second part of theory),[8] it also strongly applies to theatre when we want to value both production and reception. Visibility is then the central term in all possible relations between the factors in the communication process that theatre is.

The basic structure of theatre, rediscovered in the twentieth century and the subject of historical theatre researches, is what can be seen, what is shown, show and *Schau*. Together with the whole visual image, other forms like auditory or linguistic communication are also intertwined. This is why a concert can be called theatrical, not because of the kind of music or the mere presence of an audience, but because of the extent to which music, or rather making music, can be presented and seen as meaningful in a visual way. Visibility, however, is neither a firm given nor a neutral medium. The dimension lingers in the frontline between production and reception. Within reception, the danger always exists of the visible being transformed into a consumer good that interrupts the communication process or that fully manipulates the spectator.

I will now go into the Foucauldian relation between visibility and theatricality in his history of the changing views of punishment and normal-ising practices. Foucault's notion of theatricality may be rather confused at first sight, all the more so since he does not define it anywhere. The meta-phor of theatre appears in both the 'theatre of corporal punishment' and panoptic thinking as well. On the other hand he distinguishes the panoptic as a *mechanism* from the 'theatre' of punishment and, by doing so, devaluates the metaphor of theatre in our time.[9] The main reason for that is that an audience as such would be non-existent in modern times as encapsulation has turned everyone into something viewed, an individual in front of a face-less government. However, in the evolution of the notion of punishment as well we can draw a parallel with the evolution of theatre itself. Central parameters to these evolutions are the relation between audience and executive power, position of the body in this process and the various ways of showing and viewing. An attempt at summarising the evolutions of these parameters follows.

The public ritual of punishment appears to be an excessive use of power against a criminal body. The body itself is more the leading actor of the event than it is the bearer of a criminal subject. It is a mediator for the projection of fear and fascination by the spectator, and the vehicle of power being exercised by the government as well. The direct usefulness of the body, which remains the object of torture beyond death, consists in the production of terror in the spectator, deterrence from committing crime and fear of the sovereign power and its laws. The body does not mean anything, but is subjugated to a meticulous procedure of interrogation and punishment. It is a bearer of the truth:

> [The body] constitutes the element which, through a whole set of rituals and trials, confesses that the crime took place, admits that the accused did indeed commit it, shows that he bore it inscribed in himself and on himself, supports the operation of punishment and manifests its effects in the most striking way. The body, several times tortured, provides the synthesis of the reality of the deeds and the truth of the investigation, of the documents of the case and the statements of the criminal, of the crime and the punishment. (Foucault 1977a: 47)

From the festive and religious character of the theatre originates a mode of negotiating between the authorities, that in the spectacle affirm themselves in an absolute manner, and the audience. Not only are the people present to undergo the terror passively, but on this occasion power demands that the people give their approval of its judgement and power. However, the event can turn out to be a violent reversal, offending and profoundly disarranging the ritual, when the terror of punishment suddenly turns into a fascination for the dying person who refuses to join in the game. Finally, visibility at this stage has an ambivalent character. On the one hand it is the manifestation of power, which deliberately seeks an audience, because it could also perform its repression of the illegal in a secret way.[10] On the other hand, it is a vulnerable operation, necessitated by the fact that sovereign power cannot yet continuously manifest itself and thus has to show off its supremacy every now and then. Richard van Duelmen, who investigated the same field, points out that this danger was to be averted or overcome via the festive nature of the event:

> Public executions gradually became *lavish* events that attracted many more spectators than any other conspicuous celebrations of the baroque era. (…) What the authorities intended by these punishments was undermined in the dramatisation they themselves encouraged of the execution rituals in order for the people to be able to celebrate them as an 'event' of their own. (Van Duelmen 1985: 180, italics in original)

The next discursive formation described by Foucault is characterised by the exhibiting of criminals. In his opinion, the change had been inspired by the awareness of the precarious economy of the public display of power. This exhibition, together with a clear calculation of the penalty and contextualisation, maintains its public nature, but instead of reckoning with the shock effect of corporal excess, a semiotic clearness simplifying the economy of punishment is being created. The body remains the core item, but it changes into a bearer of meaning. The punishment on the body refers to the criminal subject, calculates the penalty and the kind of punishment in relation to the nature of the crime, the motivation behind it and the biography of the subject. The body as a sign is no longer a medium of terror, but an obstacle that should prevent the audience from following its example.

Publicity too changes nature. Public punishment aims at being carried out much more frequently because it wants to intervene in the minds of the audience in a more specific way, leaving less room for any hero-worship of the criminal.

> This, then, is how one must imagine the punitive city. At the crossroads, in the gardens, at the side of the roads being repaired or bridges built, in workshops open to all, in the depths of the mines that may be visited, will be hundreds of tiny theatres of punishment. Each crime will have its law; each criminal his punishment. It will be a visible punishment, a punishment that tells all, that explains, justifies itself, convicts: placards, different-coloured caps bearing inscriptions, posters, symbols, texts read or printed, tirelessly repeat the code. Scenery, perspectives,

optical effects, *trompe l'oeil* sometimes magnify the scene, making it
more fearful than it is, but also clearer. (Foucault 1977a: 113)

For the audience the perspective is narrowed into a dominant and clear picture; the audience may not yet be addressed as individuals, in the linguistic communication it is at least subjectified. It is no longer a public body. The festive character too makes way for some kind of mourning ceremony.

The visibility of the marked body is deployed in an efficient way. The sovereign power partly withdraws from the scene. In its place come laws. Visibility turns into readability, the emanation of a regulatory system that is clear to all: the invisible law is laid bare. The body-as-an-obstacle temporarily continues to unite both poles: it is visible as a criminal body and as a corrected subject – the exhibition recuperates both aspects by function of the law. The public character of the performance, however, keeps provoking a threat of reversal and subversive fascination by the people. Therefore the framework will be totally changed at the next stage – i.e. the disciplining period.

When identifying the boundaries of disciplining, Foucault substantially extends the areas covered. What started as an evolution of opinions on punishing to end in the idea of the panoptic prison, now spreads like a virus throughout several areas of societal organisation. The application will be least successful in the site of origin – i.e. prison. I will not undertake a new summary of the whole process, but will confine myself rather to the three parameters.

To Foucault, the disciplinary movement first of all aims at enhancing the productivity of the body and its implication in the social-economic process. The body is treated *in a constructive fashion*. It is a machine and its training is conceived of as mechanics that precisely 'decompose' the body and its actions down to the smallest functional particles with their own function, located into the space, in a well thought out order. Military drilling exemplifies this best. After having been treated as a medium for fear and terror and a sign, the body here appears as mere force and energy. As an energetic volume, it is uniting the technological and organic realms. The technology of training aims solely at optimising those forces that are organically present. From this organic angle, the body is linked again to a subject, since an optimal disciplining occurs as individually as possible: purely mechanical physics too often raises the risk of revolt. (Cf. Foucault 1977a: 155)

As a principle, within the disciplining process, the audience ceases to exist as a whole. Each person is mobilised directly and is only active in discreet niches that are interconnected within a system which no longer comprises public spaces or displays. This is a consequence of the individu-alisation of the procedures: nothing holds as a general example, there are only relative orders. The sole spectator who remains is the supervisor, the power apparatus itself, which, to Foucault, is diffuse, non-localised, and certainly not to be conceived of as someone's property. The person who used to be a spectator is forced to become an actor himself in front of an anonymous audience. This relation becomes most explicit in the phantasm of the panoptic prison:

> They are like so many cages, so many small theatres, in which each actor is alone, perfectly individualised and constantly visible. (Foucault 1977a: 276)

Because he is imprisoned, but also by other techniques extending the surveillance, the actor is bound to join in the game.

> The penitentiary operation, if it is to be a genuine re-education, must become the sum total existence of the delinquent, making of the prison a sort of artificial and coercive theatre in which his life will be examined from top to bottom … (Foucault 1977a: 251–252)

Both quotations are the only places where we find the notion of theatre linked with disciplining. The theatrical component has obviously become quite weak. The panoptic universe may originate from the absolutist court/theatre,[11] but its main functions lie with the observation of conduct with a view to analytical knowledge and the adjustment of it to an optimal economic availability. As a result, the panopticon is more a laboratory than a theatre. This is why the recognition of this theatricality, the awareness that behaviour adapts itself to the (possible) presence of the watching eye, renders this mechanism vulnerable. For that reason, Foucault on the one hand considers the design of the panoptic prison the clearest example of the system ('a case of "it's easy once you've thought of it" in the political sphere') (Foucault 1977a: 206) whilst, on the other hand, it was immediately mistrusted, because:

> The power that operates and which it augments is a direct, physical power that men exercise upon one another. An inglorious culmination had an origin that could be only grudgingly acknowledged. (Foucault 1977a: 225)

The system of surveillance directly influences behaviour. It is exactly because of the permanently suggested gaze of others that people adapt their behaviour. In most cases, however, justification for it is wrapped up in a pedagogical, psychological or economic system; the prison is much more direct at this point. The dialectics of visibility and invisibility is thus the crucial factor in this system: as a principle, its proper functioning remains discreet and invisible and it reduces its objects into images and processes open for analysis.

> The Panopticon is a machine for dissociating the see/being seen dyad: in the peripheric ring, one is totally seen, without ever seeing; in the central tower, one sees everything without ever being seen. (Foucault 1977a: 201–202)

Visibility of the body loses the ambivalence it used to have in its former functioning: it no longer indicates any excess, nor can it, as a bearer of meaning, cause any friction with the inscription. Visibility equals a total readability and functionality. The visible body solely represents its own functioning, making use of an organic wording for a mechanical process. Visibility is a trap.

When speaking of theatre as a critical space, it may be useful to imply Foucault's view of the visible. In its very evolution both its force and instability have appeared and both the possibilities and dangers of a theatrical use of it can be suggested, for the disciplining process goes further than any criticism of representations can ever comprise. Even the natural body is already implicated in the productivity-centred thinking; it is a discursive construction. This is why a mere criticism of the subject notion as an original totality does not suffice when not implying the connection with bodily drilling and without avoiding being trapped in the presupposition of an original body preceding each exercise of power. According to Rudi Visker, Foucault simply wants too much when connecting power and knowledge; this original corporeality unintentionally keeps looming up on the horizon of his thought.[12] It is a tension which permeates his whole oeuvre. Foucault's inspiration, though, does not reside in the undercurrent of a 'return of the repressed', but in highlighting the functioning and limits of visibility, in advocating some invisibility and in disturbing what is self-evident. Moreover, this undercurrent is located at another level other than theory and methodology, i.e. the level of motivation that cannot possibly be realised. The contradiction Visker suggests is only partially valid; it is the paradox of disappearing, as expressed pointedly by Peggy Phelan when saying:

> We are, despite our best intentions, stuck with essences, and essentialisms. And perhaps never more fully than when the body of the beloved has vanished. For in that disappearance we are made to feel again that grief of our own essential absence from our deepest selves, our failure to answer our deepest questions. (Phelan 1997: 35)

The Active Invisibility: Peggy Phelan

If theatre wants to be an activity that takes a step out of everyday life, isolates a period of time and stages within that an action of its own, it encounters a problem with the definition of its relation toward reality. The operation of making visible risks being a vain attempt if it does not take into account the relative autonomy and the cognitive structure related to visibility. This is Peggy Phelan's starting point. To her, the theatrical is a possible and protected place where images and definitions of the self can breed, but also where the danger of commercial, sexist or racial recuperation is always a threat. In her opinion this is even implied in the endeavour to have these marginalised definitions represented.

Following Lacan, Phelan introduces the notion of the subject, which is on the borderline between the versatility of the semiotic framework and the leap into an energetic flux.[13] It originates from the urgency of constituting and giving voice to a definite authentic experience, and at the same time she is aware that each speaking and construing is a cultural artefact, which is always partially heteronomous. Speaking like this, however, itself a social interaction, is a constituent of the desire for self-manifestation. As a result of the criticism of metaphysical thought, it can no longer be a stable subject. It is bound to be a vulnerable and incomplete construction of images and meanings, which is caught in a game of exchanged glances, desires and images, balancing on the borderline between fiction and reality and is therefore always conceived of in a strongly theatrical way. The subject is a stage, the negotiating space between a self and its surroundings. The contribution of the Lacanian view of theatricality consists in making an attempt at looking at the construction and the functioning of the subject simultaneously from the viewpoints of both the spectator and the producer. The difference with such semiotic construction like in Erika Fischer-Lichte[14] lies in the body being not only a screen or bearer of signs, which as a medium is presupposed to possess a certain degree of neutrality. To Phelan, who thinks out of a feminist history and from a strong empathy to minorities that are the passive subject of definition by others, the body cannot possibly be a neutral object. It is to be closely linked with the notion of subject and therefore to be understood as extremely vulnerable as an object of desires and projections. Sometimes the body even seems to become an obstacle a little bit, because it indicates the material limit of the tactics of the invisibility which want to prevent the unlimited use of the body as a screen. Conversely, the advantage of her view of the subject, compared with the energetic alternative of Lyotard, is that it does not get bogged down in an exchangeability of bodies that would be neutralised instantly into an amorphous and essentialist volume. This would of necessity be a dead volume, because the reversibility of the economics of exchange is (or shall be) limited by the course of time and the finiteness of matter.

What does the role of the pair of visibility/invisibility in her view of the subject consist of exactly? Phelan starts from the famous mirror mechanism of Jacques Lacan: the subject constitutes in the other an image of himself/herself as he/she thinks/wishes to be in reality and like he/she supposes to be really seen by the other. The resulting representation is considered as a true reflection of a preceding reality. However, because the subject can never totally project himself in the look of the other, that unity remains a projected illusion, while in the resulting image the active contribution of the other is being denied. Concern, however, is not solely with the self-image. The subject anchors the image and meaning of the *other* within his own perspective, for from the above-mentioned illusion of the rightness of the self-image (through the other) he/she presupposes his own perspective to be an objective viewpoint. In Phelan's wording:

> One term of the binary is marked with value, the other is unmarked. Cultural reproduction takes she who is unmarked and re-marks her, rhetorically and imagistically, while he who is marked with value is left unremarked, in discursive paradigms and visual fields. He is the norm and therefore unremarkable; as the Other, it is she whom he marks. (Phelan 1993: 5)

The room and the perspective for the other subject have been delimited in advance in a pseudo-objective way. Analogous to Foucault, the 'un-marked' is the anonymous gaze which creates the space and the mode of action of the viewed; that regard does not even need to be present continuously. Therefore it is impossible to come to an autonomous or authentic (self-) definition by the Other within the existing economy of meaning. Visibility is a passive given, while the active pole remains concealed. If one tries to make another image of it directly, the result threatens to come back as a fetish in the economy of exclusion and to lose its effectiveness as an alternative. After all, a supplementary self-definition by the other is taken up within the originally circumscribed field. As a consequence, an augmented representational attention to subordinated definitions does not suffice to give them a place of their own within our pattern of thought. As long as an 'autarchic' self-image continues to prevail as an ideal, the inequality between the dominant self-sufficient frameworks of thinking and minorities will persist. Visibility is a trap here as well: 'If representational visibility equals power, then almost-naked white young women should be running Western culture'. (Phelan 1993: 10) Visibility no longer guarantees heroism, but marketability and productivity.

The visual field may comprise the possibility for the projected image to return the gaze actively and to reveal the illusory character of the auto-nomous subject: the subject does not see that it tries to see itself – actually there is a blind spot in its image. The incompleteness of the image arouses the demand or desire of the completion of that vacuum.

> The not-all of visual representation creates in the looker a sense that there is something 'beyond' the picture (and the signifying system itself) that is not shown – that is, the subject her or himself. This belief maintains desire. But for Lacan, there is nothing there at all. It is that (internal/ized) absence that visual representation always tries to recover. (Phelan 1993: 25)

The vanishing point in the classical perspective is the ideal point where everything meets. The unity of the picture emerging from it should confirm the truth of the representation, but at the same time it is the point where that unity is definitively broken as well, where the picture is absorbed into an infinitesimal point that escapes from our representation/domination. The theatricality of the subject is inter-subjectively recognised by that.

This, however, in its turn leads to a rather pessimistic symmetry that seems to confirm the deterministic connotations of psychoanalysis. Either the unity of the picture is an illusion that denies the difference or it is a traumatic error that cannot be corrected, the awareness that the picture seems to be indeed complete, though not an accurate representation. The latter, for Phelan, comes down to the awareness that radically the world can exist without the subject.

> The viewpoint and the vanishing point are inseparable: there is no viewpoint without vanishing point, and no vanishing point without viewing point. The self-possession of the viewing subject has built into it, therefore, the principle of its own abolition: annihilation of the subject as centre is a condition of the very moment of the look. (Bryson in Phelan 1993: 25)

Phelan is looking for a way of touching up the colour of that picture of little hope that is struck within that paradoxical and contradictory idea of the subject, and she finds it by siding with the object/the other who is being seen. Instead of making a new subject position out of it, she takes advantage of the extent of and ways by which the object is a construction of the conceited desires of the looking subject – the object as a screen, as it has been developed in film theory. Any alternative essence to be forwarded in its turn is absolutely out of the question, but an important complement to the object character lies with the possibility of actively looking back. By this looking back the expectations are disillusioned and an asymmetrical mutual relation is being established. After all, the returned glance is neither coming from a subject-unity that is to be confirmed, nor is it willing to resign itself to its external and reductive construction by the other. This is not to say that the looking-back would pass over the implicit wish to be seen: the returned look has neither a neutral nor an holistic character, but it attempts to create, actively but carefully, a new discursive space.

The asymmetrical relation considers the failure of the self-image and continuously putting off the satisfaction of that longing as a constitutive and positive fact.

> Identity emerges in the failure of the body to express being fully and the failure of the signifier to convey meaning exactly. Identity is perceptible only through a relation to an other – which is to say, it is a form of both resisting and claiming the other, declaring the boundary where the self diverges from and merges with the other. In that declaration of identity and identification, there is always loss, the loss of not-being the other and yet remaining dependent on that other for self-seeing, self-being. (Phelan 1993: 13)

Consequently, asymmetry surely never refers to eliminating the reciprocity, it is no one-way communication, but an open recognition of the other being requested to work together at your own identity. The scope of the identity of the subject becomes a hollow or empty site that can be occupied by pictures of bodies and language games, but that can never be incorporated.

How can this reversal be transferred to the visual field of theatre? To look means to ask for your look to be confirmed and to accept that this reciprocity can never be symmetrical as it is always incomplete and disturbed by the media you involve in it (the representation, the other as a screen, the differing of the other). By this very failure the true nature of our question for a reliable image becomes clear, even when it can no longer ever be answered, merely because of that.

> Seeing the real is impossible: eyes fail. Yet it is through this very impossibility that the given to be seen holds onto the real. (Phelan 1993: 19)

In the vanishing or staying empty of what was hoped for, the bud of hope begins to flower. Reality can only exist as a question and in all other cases it is but a mere imaginary effect of a desire that is short-circuited too soon. The tactics of invisibility capitalise on the desire for a fullness of picture and meaning, and is therefore always a parasitic operation. What remains invisible without being sought for cannot have any effect, and that is why it has to do with an 'active vanishing', a disappearing that needs to be noticed. That vanishing then is a theatrical operation: as an autonomous void it cannot produce any effect. The use of it starts functioning at the level of the frame within which pictures are being presented. The frames that enclose a picture and conduct its reception are being made unsteady by the absence of a conclusive entity. Out of this comes a wandering game of delaying and dynamics of perspective. The identification, the recognising look that incorporates the components of the picture into an external order, has been put off and distorted.

According to Carol Maver, these frames of the invisible can also be extended to other media, which leads to a broader conception of their application in the theatre. She borrows the metaphor of the glove from Merleau-Ponty; it has both an inside and an outside that cannot be simultaneously displayed visually, but do suggest one another. The inside refers to the outside by feeling, the outside to the inside by not-seeing.

> The invisible can include the visible (as it does in the word 'invisible' itself), yet the invisible goes beyond the visible and is not limited to the visible. However, in a culture that privileges the seen over the unseen, invisible caresses, invisible sounds, and invisible smells are often elided (overlooked). (Maver 1998: 196)

Yet, this is not to say that visible and invisible are exchangeable or totally complementary to one another, but that they are indeed linked by the incompleteness that keeps the question open.

In search of some concrete use of the theatrical means for this active disappearing, we hit upon Emil Hrvatin's analysis of the cry. The cry is a phenomenon that originates from the boundary of speech and body: unarticulated, it conquers the space, directs itself so massively toward the other so as to make any answer impossible. Each articulated answer reduces the cry into a partial event, while the scream is just meant and seen as a trace of total presence of the body.

> We want to see what is missing – the body which produces the voice, we want to give voice symbolic form. The voice is a part of the body, but once it leaves it, it leaves behind only traces of that body. The voice is spatialized, the voice produces space and becomes voice as object, the element that escapes the order of symbolisation – it is the rest (that which remains unlocated). (Hrvatin 1997: 83)

The cry produces a phantasm of a pre-discursive totality, the simultaneous attraction and impossibility of an original theatre. Impossibility, because the threat of the pre-symbolic within the cry is incorporated time and again, aestheticised in a repetition. Hrvatin refers to the opera soprano, at the same time both 'black hole of female pleasure'[15] (here it may be striking that the male cry in the opera takes mostly place off-stage) and some fetish for the audience.

Hrvatin also examines the possibility for the cry not to take place. The cry that has been uttered but has not been heard disappears into an image of itself, and leaves behind incomplete the space it promised to create. The absence of completion, of the trace the cry would place on the body, presents us with a void. The cry is simultaneously a trace that refers to the body and something that is projected by the body, a lack and an excess that, in its disappearing, leaves a question behind. When the dancers, half-way through the performance of Marc Vanrunxt's *Antimaterie (Anti-Matter)*, suddenly step out of their rather autarchic mental cocoons and stand up in front of the audience, giving voiceless passionate screams, then the vacuum, after having been present between dancers and audience all the time, suddenly becomes prominent – not by the sudden difference of the single breaching of that separation, but by the very failure of the cry, this vacuum turns into a space over which both parties can negotiate. The display of the invisible and the mystical becomes human and acceptable in the very failure of it. Any misunderstanding about the inaccessibility of that quest for the mystical and unspeakable that might arise from the idea that it had to be fully shared with the spectator has been dissipated by the awareness that search itself, not possession nor any other 'higher' communication, is the main point. The object of desire, in the picture of the body or its mental condition, stops being the only perspective. Instead of a mere difference, the perspective is switched and the quest for difference has become more important than any rash result. In the performances of Vanrunxt, we often find this tiny speck of matter outlining geometry, as a geographic frontier for the area of play, or as an intermittent, stubborn and frail tangible frame (dance floor, cloth-ing, etc.). Then the quest, the performing of the projected connection of motions occurs in an ever-surprising imbalance that does not dominate the happening as a failure, but every now and then upsets the anticipation of the gaze.

When we go back to the notion of 'theatricality', the relation between producer and consumer often appears to be circumscribed in terms of 'perspective'. The bourgeois and absolutist conception of theatre has firmly fixed both positions antithetically within an architecture that imposes one single perspective[16] presupposing a determinate idealised picture to be shared by both parties.

> Theatre is perspective. Making theatre does not equal performing something, but is about the determination of the point from where something *ought to be seen* and about turning a spectacle into a theatre that can be looked at in a *perfect* fashion. The theatre transforms both seeing and the spectacle. (Verschaffel 1990: 36, italics in original)

From Foucault and Lacan we learned how this central perspective is linked to the claim of knowledge, and with the leap of faith[17] necessary to turn that unique perspective into a logical condition for that knowledge by making it absolute.

Phelan explicitly shifts the perspective position inwards into the picture. This is not in order to let it coincide with that picture, which is actually the case in the vanishing point of the classical perspective that is firmly organised from one single point, nor does this perspective position fully absorb the idea of reality in any relativist solipsism. On the contrary, the theatrical quality is a relation that invites the spectator towards the difference between what he/she sees, what is represented and what remains out of the picture and wishes to be involved in that relation. The confrontation with reality as a phantasm, which the performer ventures by partially identifying himself with it out of the negative impulse of being (or wanting to be) different (from the dominant), is deemed to remain endlessly incomplete. Consequently, Phelan does not make the mistake of recklessly leaving the theatrical approach when it becomes dynamic so as to leap into reality – it is and keeps being a mechanism of substitution. If you transform it into a theory of performance, you remain in the aesthetic field. An enthusiastic leap outwards from there can be very painful indeed.

> The only way we can see if performance is an adequate substitute for ontology is through the staging of performances. In that enactment, however, we make conscious again the difference between performance and ontology: precisely what motivates the performance is that which ontology – the question of being itself – will not and cannot answer. (Phelan 1993: 105)

Phelan, in her multifaceted highlighting of the pictures and their frames, passes consciously over the cognitive claim of the perspective. Barbara Freedman argues that the fragmentation of the unique perspective can be linked to the tradition of a 'learned ignorance', connecting Socrates via Nicholas of Cusa to the Shakespearean comedies, from where the line can be extended up to some post-modern and Lacanian subjectivity.

She completes the scepticism about a fixed ground underpinning knowledge with other different approaches, whereby procedures like dream, fantasy and theatre parry the undeniable desire for knowledge with contradictory and paradoxical routes that neither deny nor make absolute the blind spot, but continuously keep it going. She complements theatre as 'show', i.e. as the opening up of a picture for viewing, actively rebuffing the desire of the audience, aiming at blurring all distinction between object, show and reception.

> Theatricality can only display the problematic of display itself, can only rehearse the paradox implicit in a spectator consciousness; it is that which constantly proclaims that what is seen is never where it is. (Freedman 1991: 52)

But even Freedman's enlargement of the perspective, which is not limited to simply incorporating the 'returned gaze' but opposes a qualitative interaction with it, still remains an intellectual operation, worrying about its own cognitive status within a strategy of ignorance. Not even in her study of comedy can she elude that. An informed ignorance threatens to remain an unfair strategy when it continues embracing knowledge as its main goal.[18]

Phelan, by contrast, creates some scope for an affective dimension that transcends knowing/ignoring and guarantees the maintenance of the interaction as a positive attention to desire. In this view, the unmarked-concept as negative is not only motivated by a longing for positiveness, but also aims at being effective. 'Performance enacts the productive appeal of the non-reproductive.' (Phelan 1993: 27) This becomes most explicit in her review of the photographs of Robert Mapplethorpe which are a complicated game with desires, expectations and shifts of frames. Pictures that at first sight confirm stereotypical opinions on race and sexuality, but with further consideration distort expectations. Mapplethorpe's black models link up perfectly with the myth of virile black masculinity, but they are displaced into a homosexual context and, what is more, they occupy the iconography of Greek classic sculpture. Moreover, by the fact that the models actively assume cliché poses, a complex picture arises. At first sight, it promises to meet the objectifying expectations of the onlooker, but on closer consideration it cannot possibly be caught in one single view. The obtrusiveness of the objectifying picture of the Same (i.e. the correspondences in virility of photographer, model and picture) arouses a desire for difference. There is, however, nothing but a permanent delay because of the linkage between race, sexuality and iconography and between the picture and the clichés it refers to (whereby the photograph turns into a picture of a picture). The spectator is to adapt his own perspective to find out that his own looking fails at the identification of what he/she is looking for. In doing so, he/she can give back to the photograph and the models their dignity and mystery.

> His photography demonstrates that love and understanding of a body, while always involving objectification, precisely because it is made over in the mind and eye of another, do not have to violate or eliminate the private grace and power of the model. (Phelan 1993: 51)

In entering into the ambiguities of the representation, the dimension that must not be objectified appears as an after-image of the visual brilliance of the photographs and the dizziness of the search for perspective. The unmarked is an 'unreality-effect' of that distortion. The visibility that remains embedded in the visible is separated from the object, from knowing, as Gilles Deleuze puts it:

> The visibilities are neither object forms, nor even forms that would reveal themselves in the contact with some light and thing, but forms of luminosity created by the very light and do not allow the things or objects to be replaced but like lightning, mere twinkling and glittering. (Deleuze 1986: 60)

In the spark itself, viewer and performer become connected, approaching one another without being assimilated or occupying one another for that matter. The theatrical space is always a fictional one, but it is inter-subjective in its fictional existence; it only exists with the agreement of both parties: concerted play and double play as well.

The Hole Within the Invisible, and How to Fill it With Slogans

In the previous sections, the notion of invisibility gradually underwent a shift. First of all, the active disappearance is expressed by opposing frames, but when we want to place more emphasis on the affective character we need to avoid leaving behind just a threatening void. Phelan herself feels the danger, but does not succeed in managing it. Let us go back to the example of Mapplethorpe: invisibility has to pass through the area of danger where the cliché has to be confronted head on. In the case of Mapplethorpe it is the nearness of the racist mythology of the virile black masculinity that is meant, in Cindy Sherman the recurrent image of the attractive woman that only disappears when there is physically nobody left. In respect of the painful performance-work of Angelika Festa, Phelan herself points out that this disappearance and decay threaten to be quite realistic up to the point where we leave the space of theatre to directly embrace that very reality. This is a small productive mistake that makes her ask whether the emotional and physical exhaustion of both the spectator and the performer is really the only access to the affective presence/absence she is emulating. On the other hand, however, this is also the logical consequence of her notion of invisibility in combination with her ontological opinion of the performance. Not until the end of her book does Phelan mention theatre as an art form. Moreover, even then her insistence on the ontology of the once-only presence-in-disappearance appears to be on the verge of an idealistic purism that annihilates the subversive possibilities of her theory. Although she starts from a notion of the subject which surely includes corporeality – already socially constructed as always, but for which she claims the right to determine her own definition – the body itself seems to change into an obstacle overnight. This is because in theatre it is always already present as a meeting-point for several cultural constructs. These constructions ultimately refer to an (imaginary) steady connection between body and subjectivity. It is this very stability that Phelan wants to undermine by putting first the failure and disappearance of the identification of construction and body.

> Performance approaches the Real through resisting the metaphorical reduction of the two into one. But in moving the aims of the metaphor, reproduction and pleasure to those of metonymy, displacement, and pain, performance marks the body itself as loss. (Phelan 1993: 152)

The issue, though, is too important to disappear totally for that matter – or rather, once vanished, never to reappear again. Therefore this disappearing needs to be specified further.

In the current theory of performance a lot of attention is drawn upon the single, fleeting character of the theatrical event, which is considered the best weapon against reproduction and commercialisation. Phelan here takes an outspoken stance. To her, it is a locus of absolute, single and live presence, in which copy or repetition can never be the same. Therefore, the performance as appearance of Reality can never be comprehended, unless approximately and incompletely in the mind's eye.

> Performance resists the balanced circulations of finance. It saves nothing, it only spends. While photography is vulnerable to charges of counterfeiting and copying, performance is vulnerable to charges of valuelessness and emptiness. Performance indicates the possibility of revaluing that emptiness; this potential revaluation gives performance its distinctive oppositional edge. (Phelan 1993: 148)

According to Philip Auslander, although this view may be attractive in its heroism, the ontological discussion is of little relevance, because theatre is always embedded in the prevailing cultural economy and therefore contingent. To him, the category of 'live performance' is an effect of authenticity originating from the fear of simulations and reproduction.

> On this basis, the historical relationship of liveness and mediatization must be seen as a relation of dependence and imbrication rather than opposition. (Auslander 1997: 55)

Because of this embedding into the cultural economy, a simple step beside is a delusion that only reaffirms this economy. The story of the live nature of events used as a selling point for the reproductions (e.g. pop musicians' tours increasingly serve as a means of promoting their records, cf. Auslander 1995: 204) is in line with the Foucauldian position on power that includes its own resistance in itself as the limit against which it defines itself. This is why the choice for uniqueness as the simple opposition to reproduction cannot be the best strategy.[19]

In this light, a simple and single departure from the stage would bring about nothing more than mere silence, which would soon be colonised by noise – instead of being a deafening silence. Nevertheless, my concern here is neither with a final rejection of the notion of invisibility nor with a capitulation before the idea that everything has to be reproduction for that reason – *end of story*. The question is how we can combine both insights into an effective and affective tactic. The impulses for it can be found throughout Phelan's text, but she does not know how to group them together.

In theatre the passing of time is constitutive. Therefore there is always a vanishing presence apart from the economic reproducibility of it. In this vanishing process, the term 'repetition' yields an important place. Referring especially to dance, André Lepecki writes that the paradox of the vanishing

> is that the repetition that informs it constitutes the same act which guarantees that the vanishing dance be always available for re-presentation and its reproduction. But isn't this paradox precisely the bulk of the hard work of being a dancer, of being a choreographer? Constant repetition, that is to say, in French, *répétition*, a continuous rehearsing? (Lepecki 1996: 73)

Repetition, as a conscious procedure, not only appeals to the memory of the spectator, but is to Lepecki a sign of the difference. In repetition the linear course of time is interrupted, the invisible, the Other, makes its appearance without taking it away or annexing it.

In order to track down what invades the unstable, vagrant, nomadic space of choreography (…) one must pay careful notice to those suspended moments, where gestures, sounds, landscapes are not (yet) visible as dance but point to the choreographic tension between physicality and imagination. (Lepecki 1997: 76)

The relation between physicality (body) and imagination (cultural inscription) can be seen in two different ways: physicality as an authentic experience or as a reified object; imagination as an externally imposed or internally negotiated social construction. The presence of both terms then always implies a risk. But we have learned how to look positively at such failure. Repetition is a sign of difference – the same performance will never be identical twice. The linkage between repetition and difference can be interpreted in several manners. Firstly, it can be interpreted as pure difference (Phelan – where we can question the necessity of repetition); secondly, this is not the point as one would strive for a qualitative ideal or commercial model over and over again (Auslander); thirdly, it can be interpreted as oscillating rhythm as well, where the interruption of time creates a new space where the visible can be looked at as vanishing, as a unity impossible to complete.

The tactic of the invisibility, of vanishing, opposes the involuntary vanishing of the subject in the definition by the other. The attempt to comprehend, understand and tell further each vanishing – vanishing as passing of time, and vanishing as dissolving into a picture – is an attempt at repetition. This repetition is doomed to fail, but is, exactly because of this, reusable as a tactic, according to Heidi Gilpin. She names this, using Freud, a mechanism of survival: repetition reveals a craving for control, but precisely in the theatrical moment this control is always evasive because of its impossibility. Together with Freud, Gilpin discerns two ways of relating to the vanishing: recollection reproduces the vanished as vanished, is oriented towards the past and causes the emotional state of grief, while repetition is an active attempt to get hold of things, generates joy, and – in Freud's view – is forward-looking as well.[20] Concerned with theatre, Gilpin tries to join both aspects.

Loss of presence is particularly apparent in a theatre of movement performance, where most often the presence (and not the verbal language, for example) of bodies on stage is apparent one moment, vanished the next. This loss must be recuperated through the act of recollecting, which according to Freud, is a substitute for repetition. Either we repeat the performance of absence, of abandonment, or we recollect the disappearance of this performance. (Gilpin 1996: 114)[21]

Repetition and recollection refer all the more strongly to the impossibility of their taking place, 'a critical acknowledgement of the impossibility of under-standing, of capturing somehow, that which cannot be recollected'. (Gilpin 1996: 114) Both the spectator and the actor are involved here. The spectator seeks in his recollection a re-presentation of the happening, wherein repeti-tion already has been used. The performer practices active repetition, but by its impossibility has to rely on his recollection. Hence, joy and grief are not divided in a neatly separated fashion between performer and onlooker respectively, but are essential to the process in their mutual implication.

For that very reason there is room for affect and respect within repetition, i.e. the active occupying a trauma-locus, and Phelan's active vanishing is given a richer content. Not only dissimulation and vanishing, but also *playing* is given back its position within the theatrical discourse. So we end up in the discourse on 'critical mime', where Elin Diamond quotes Mikkel Borch-Jakobson in an assenting tone:

> Who says that the stakes for the actor are knowledge, self-knowledge via
> (the gaze of) the other that freezes him into a statue, an idol? Isn't his
> joy (or his anguish) above all to *play* his role, to move *inside* the pathetic
> scene that he incarnates? And why, after all, should true life always be
> elsewhere, in front of me, in that double that augurs my death?[22]

To Diamond, concern is always with partial, played identifications that link up the subject and its surroundings, more in the manner of a bridge than as an accomplished consumption.

Diamond returns to Freud by mentioning affective mimesis which goes beyond an ironic identification that starts from the idea of superiority and remains fixed to the domain of cognition. What should we think then of Phelan's Lacanian framework? Have we not gone back to the starting-point she wanted to fight, i.e. the lack of autonomous self-definition and the rate of recuperation of the existing frames? According to Slavoj Zizek, such pseudo-identification defines only the totally immanent possibility of resistance within a power structure:

> The feature that actually maintains the identification, the famous
> Freudian-Lacanian '*einziger Zug*', the single stroke, [is] not the evident
> great official distinction, but a slight feature, even the one which marks
> the distance to the official hyphen. (Zizek 1997: 91)[23]

Phelan's starting-point was precisely the in-built difference within the phallocentric system that marks the female as other and keeps itself, as a defining agency, out of the picture. It seems to me that the affective aspect as a material effect is excess in relation to that recuperation. Let us also remember here the orientation toward the future that Gilpin sees in embracing repetition.

Nevertheless, we can also retain active vanishing within repetition as it can create a framework like an abyss surrounding the picture of the identification and repetition and, in doing so, always means these pictures are kept incomplete. The repetition is haunted by a question mark, a spot within the perspective behind which the rest is concealing itself so as not to be incorporated. Gilpin succeeds in prolonging this trace, taking as an example the works of the Polish director Tadeusz Kantor, where the object of repetition and vanishing is the very dying itself. There, death is present in a most obvious way: actors are strolling like zombies, purposeless. Puppets and mechanical tools still seem to be the most lively and coloured beings present. Dying is rehearsed/repeated, the vanishing and reappearing of the figures for Gilpin reveal the continuous investment of life and death in the theatre itself. The concern here is not with the simple replacement of living actors with puppets (or putting puppet behaviour first as an aim in itself) but with the contamination of both. Kantor was convinced that expression of life was not possible but could only be through the absence of life, through appealing to death.

> Presence can only be conveyed by absence (even the repetition of absence), that lack of message is precisely what signifies, and that the performance of emptiness makes a perception of existence possible. (Gilpin 1996: 120)

In Kantor's theatre identification and vanishing, affection and horror are merging into an abysmal repetition of the scandal of dying that suggests life just by not showing it.[24]

Let us finally bring together the three concepts this essay has been concerned with: theatricality – disciplining – invisibility. Can we fill the empty spot of invisibility with the picture of disciplining? Two frames would then be put in contact with each other. From the unmarked-construct a question is directed to the spectator, who marks the picture shown as uncompleted. This frame sets off a communication that allows a glimpse to be caught, beyond what is shown, of the desire for authenticity and solidarity, without highlighting it far too dominantly or vulnerably. The picture of disciplining taken in actively fuels, as it were, this desire, but does so in a negative way. The shown disciplining then appears to be deficient, a rash and painful interpretation of what plausible desire could be. Is it possible to suggest that, through the frame of invisibility and by the repetition/rehearsal of the vanishing of man in the invention of the externally defined subjectivity and a restricted corporeality, hope for a veracious and honest self-definition, for a relative, modest and open body-subject-relation can exist?

In the view of the 'unmarked' this veracity remains a spectre that loiters around the repetition of the same. It is not just a non-committal item for that matter, but the emanation of a desire for a fairer relation between subjects, between oneself, each other and each other's bodies. In the mysteriousness prudence becomes manifest, in seeking it appears the motive which is not an eschatological waiting for Good Times, but a repetition of failure, of dying and of life. It cannot be worded other than by suggesting, phenomenology or anecdotally. It is performative writing, betraying its object and at the same time driving it forth so as to prevent it from being caught by what is behind us. In doing so, disciplining is placed in a context that seeks the vacuum. It is not only the emptiness at the core of the disciplining process itself – this would only mean the uncovering of a structure, i.e. the trap of the demystification which in theatre is itself an empty gesture – but the emptiness around, the incompleteness of the picture and the awareness of the short-circuited longing for controllable bodies and subjects. It is here that pain and loving respect come together. The awareness of the seemingly insurmountable perversion and the powerlessness in the experience of the self is connected with the respect of the seeking and a recognition of human failure. The combination of both these frames, that as such may appear somewhat dry, detached and negative, breaks through towards a positive experience.

This gesture is a theatrical one. It re-theatralises disciplining, not by exposing the system out of the emptiness, but by looking back. It does so by presupposing the imaginary emptiness, by reusing the theatrical presuppositions of the process that the process itself does not want to know[25] and by appropriating them.[26] The idea of invisibility creates a framework in which the effectiveness of the disciplining can be reduced by making both parties involved, i.e. the onlooker and the viewed, the producer and the consumer, more interdependent. Aware that the analytical anonymous gaze does influence the behaviour of the viewed, the actor in question can actively join in the game and so cause some overproduction, an excess that also indicates a fundamental deficit. The spectator who notices that a trick is being played on his basic principles can start dealing more actively with his position – he/she knows that he/she is implied within the total frame of the theatrical moment. Furthermore, this gesture is theatrical because it is likely only to be possible in front of an audience, within the relatively autonomous and commonly shared zone of the performance. It has to make use of the particular status of reality of theatre, keep within it to hope for this step to be inspirational for the external field, maybe through its theatrical qualities. However, even in this shared and secured space it will remain a risk.

Shirtologie (*Shirtology*), the performance created by the Parisian choreographer Jérôme Bel with the youth-company 'De Victors' from Ghent, is an exquisite example of the appropriation of the disciplining theory, offering room for the unspeakable hope for humanity. The choreographer's still relatively recent oeuvre deals with body, identity and appearance in very varying ways. He is always looking for the conditions of the cultural construction and is seeking openly an answer to the question whether there is a zero-degree of cultural construction, with varying success. He sought this zero-degree in the immediate presence and nudity of the human body, stripped to the maximum from all interpretable signs. After the second piece, *Jérôme Bel par Jérôme Bel* (*Jérôme Bel by Jérôme Bel*), by his own account he came to the conclusion that this zero-degree did not exist. His following piece, *Shirtologie*, starts from the reverse viewpoint. Instead of looking for an origin, he fully challenges the process itself of the cultural construction of body and identity. By entering into this process himself and by totally reversing it, he succeeds in adding a refreshing and hopeful touch to the performance.

The procedure is quite simple: fifteen youngsters between fifteen and twenty years of age and an actor stay motionless on stage, all of them wearing several layers of T-shirts. Every minute (a time interval where literally nothing occurs) one of them takes off the top shirt. The T-shirts are printed with very divergent inscriptions: those of a commercial mass culture, signs by which people differentiate themselves from the one group and identify themselves with another. Sport clubs, pop idols, clothes trademarks, cartoons, environmental movements and events are reviewed. The removal of the T-shirts reveals some logic that both contains an internal order and is imposed from outside in a totally contingent way as well. Whenever a new T-shirt appears bearing a term or a picture referring to an order that can be carried out or making some link with previous pictures, some of them or the whole group carries it out until the next T-shirt continues the discourse. What seems to be a mere sign in which some identification takes place in a rather passive way now turns out to be a performative signal for immediate action. Furthermore, no words are spoken, no looks exchanged – the theatrical action consists solely of the orders, the inscriptions and the removal of T-shirts. Theatre is reduced to T-shirts.

T-shirts like that are immediately thought of as an external means in which one might project a part of one's identity. The shirt marks your personality as an adherent of some ideas, as a consumer of some product, as a supporter. The person who consciously stops wearing it may think back with pity on the time when he/she was still desperately seeking to be part of the game and completely in need of being identified with something. What occurs in this performance is different: it recognises the functioning but without any trace of nostalgia or regret. On the contrary, it starts from the total identification. In the time-spatial whole of this work of theatre, all actions have been determined by the T-shirts. Following their logic to the extreme, two movements arise. On the one hand, the logic of commerce and identification is given a hard edge as a pure example of social disciplining. The shirtology is analysed down to the last detail as an internalised obedience, while being looked at by others: you are wearing a shirt in order to be seen with it, with the consequence of making others identify with you. When this seduction of the other is no longer concealed under a mask, it becomes an obscene feature. On the other hand, the way the shirt is worn shows some creative trait, and the logic of commerce turns out to not be the only shirtology: new logics are invented on the spot, reasoned to the end and finally removed again. From this the performance yields some playfulness that breaks out of the monotony of the action. In this logic a game is played with identity, while this identity itself remains in the background: there is absolutely no direct communication either with each other, but via the T-shirts, or with the audience since the performers are gazing at them with as little expression as possible. The players don't try to prove their true personality at the backside of the absurd obedience to the codes. The neutrality of their posture suggests rather their full identification with it. Anyway, this neutrality can never be perfect for they are not trained actors, but precisely through this elaborate but restricted neutrality the personality comes forth. This is because it is not explicitly emphasised anywhere and because the shirtology at first sight even makes the person completely redundant. This is also clear from the likeness to the solo version of the piece, borne by the professional actor. This seems to be less interesting; there neutrality is not the point, non-communication is much less conspicuous. The performance seems then to be confined more to a linguistic and intellectual trick with '*mots et images trouvés*' (found words and images).

By the end of the performance, however, everyone is wearing monochromatic T-shirts with nothing written on them. For a moment it seems to be a moralistic final chord: will we not now hear the message that after all the games and displacements there is a basic, honest and authentic founding layer that unmasks the fuss with T-shirts as a superfluous game? It is significant that the first reaction is one of disappointment: this would be too easy, too idealistic and would reduce all the rest to a superfluous filling-in of time, to a stage of youth to be simply gone through. But the ultimate picture of the piece proves, in one single stroke, that it is exactly this direct use of authenticity that is easiest to recuperate: 'United Colors Of Benetton'. It is a counterpoint of this penultimate idealistic outpouring, a reinstallation of ambiguity[27] that appropriates the productivity of the prevailing economy in its own manner. This concluding picture is not a cynical embrace of the unavoidable commercialisation of honest feelings because it is linked back to the whole of the performance.

The theatrical aim of *Shirtologie* turns the performance into a particular testimony of cultural disciplining and the way we deal with it. Performances, aiming at showing something about present-day cultural life (and most of all of youth, which has become the paramount point of reference for cultural identity), often want to overwhelm too literally (by 'showing it as it is') with the overloaded diversities characteristic of this culture. *Shirtologie*, conversely, is a gigantic reduction of this experience, but in doing so catches the eye itself, looks back and opens up scope for understanding. In the reduction, the need for authenticity emerges, while in the abundance of other performances that quest is thrust in your face and loses its credibility. In the open space, the apparent neutrality of those young bodies, there is the tension between performer and audience: although they are all attractive boys and girls, they cannot be seized upon as an attractive picture. The grabbing excess of the cultural logic of identification, and the reduction of the piece into it, reflect the onlooker's gaze. It is concerned, however, not only with the spectator recognising in himself the conditions of his own looking or his own involvement in or distance to the mechanism. *Shirtologie* is not a didactical presentation forcing the spectator to revise the way he/she looks. But, in the reduction of the given, throughout the whole exhibition of simulacra, the possibility of some partial understanding is created as well. This strengthens the shared value of the theatrical communication and the feeling of mutual complicity to, and burgeoning resistance to, the heteronomous logic of the T-shirts. Whatever the identity of the youngsters on stage may be, they make you believe that this identity, beyond the reified images, remains truly possible.[28]

Translated by Jean Robesyn

Bibliography

Auslander, Philip. 'Liveness: Performance and the Anxiety of Simulation', in: Elin Diamond (ed.). *Performance and Cultural Politics*. London: Routledge, 1996.

Auslander, Philip. 'Against Ontology: Making Distinctions between the Live and the Mediatized', in: *Performance Research* 2(3), pp. 50–55, 1997.

Baumbach, Gerda. 'Immer noch Theatralität. Historisch-kritische Erwagungen in Anbetracht der russischen Theaterhistoriographie des frühen 20. Jahrhunderts', in: Rudolf Münz. *Theatralität und Theater* (hrsg. Von Gisbert Amm). Berlin: Schwarzkopf & Schwarzkopf Verlag, 1998.

Bleeker, Maaike. 'The Visible Human Project als het Schouwtoneel van de 21^e Eeuw', in: *Etcetera* XVI, 64, 19–23, 1999.

Brewer, Maria Minich. 'Performing Theory', in: *Theatre Journal* 37, 1, 13–30, 1985.

Bryson, Norman. 'The Gaze in the Expanded Field', in: H. Foster (ed.). *Vision and Visuality*. Seattle: Bay Press, 1988.

Burns, Elizabeth. *Theatricality: A Study of Convention in the Theatre and Social Life*. London: Longman, 1972.

Deleuze, Gilles. *Foucault*. Paris: Minuit, 1986.

Derrida, Jacques. 'The Theatre of Cruelty and the Closure of Representation', in: Jacques Derrida. *Writing and Difference* (translated by Alan Bass). Chicago: University of Chicago Press, 1978.

Diamond, Elin. *Unmaking Mimesis*. London: Routledge, 1997.

Duelmen Van, Richard. *Theater des Schreckens: Gerichtspraxis und Strafrituale in der frühen Neuzeit*. München: Beck, 1985.

Fischer-Lichte, Erika. 'New Concepts of Spectatorship: Toward a New Postmodern Theory of Theatricality', in: *Semiotica* 101, 9, 113–123, 1994.

Fischer-Lichte, Erika. 'From Theatre to Theatricality – How to Construct Reality', in: *Theatre Research International* 20, 2, 97–105, 1995a.

Fischer-Lichte, Erika. 'Theatricality: A Key Concept in Theatre and Cultural Studies', in: *Theatre Research International* 20, 2, pp. 85–89, 1995b.

Foucault, Michel. *The Order of Things: An Archeology of the Human Sciences*. London: Tavistock, 1974.

Foucault, Michel. *Discipline and Punish: The Birth of the Prison* (translated by Alan Sheridan). London: Penguin Books, 1977a.

Foucault, Michel. 'Nietzsche, Genealogy, History', in: *Language, Counter-memory, Practice: Selected Essays and Interviews*. Oxford: Basil Blackwell, 1977b.

Franko, Mark. 'Five Theses on "Laughter after all"', in: Gay Morris (ed.). *Moving Words: Re-writing Dance*. Routledge, 1996.

Freedman, Barbara. *Staging the Gaze: Postmodernism, Psychoanalysis and Shakespearean Comedy*. Ithaca: Cornell University Press, 1991.

Frijhoff, Willem. 'Foucault Reformed by Certeau: Historical Strategies of Discipline and Everyday Tactics of Appropriation', in: *Arcadia: Zeitschrift für Allgemeine und Vergleichende Literaturwissenschaft* 33, 1, 92–108, 1998.

Gilpin, Heidi. 'Lifelessness in Movement, or How Do the Dead Move? Tracing Displacement and Disappearance for Movement Performance', in: Susan L. Foster (ed.). *Corporealities: Dancing Knowledge, Culture and Power*. London: Routledge, 1996.

Hrvatin, Emil. 'The Scream', in: *Performance Research* 2, 1, 82–91, 1997.

Karskens, Machiel. 'De Lege Gereedschapsdoos van Michel Foucault', in: Machiel Karskens & Jozef Keulartz (eds). *Foucault Herdenken*. Best: Damon, 51–63, 1995.

Kotte, Andreas. 'Theatralität: Ein Begriff sucht seinen Gegenstand', in: *Forum Modernes Theater* 13/2, 117–133, 1998.

Laermans, Rudi. 'Theater/Politiek: Enkele Observaties', in: Yolande Melsert & Dennis Meyer. *Bewakers van Betekenis: Beschouwingen over Theater en Maatschappij*. Amsterdam: Theater Instituut Nederland, 1996.

Lepecki, André. 'As if Dance was Visible', in: *Performance Research* 1, 3, 71–76, 1996.

Maver, Caroline. 'Touching Netherplaces: Invisibility in the Photography of Hannah Cullwick', in: Della Pollock (ed.). *Exceptional Spaces: Essays in Performance and History*. Chapell Hill: University of North Carolina Press, 1998.

Münz, Rudolf. *Theatralität und Theater: Zur Historiographie von Theatralitätsgefügen* (hrsg. von Gisbert Amm). Berlin: Schwarzkopf & Schwarzkopf Verlag, 1998.

Murray, David (ed.). *Mimesis, Masochism and Mime: The Concept of Theatricality in Contemporary French Thought*. Ann Arbor: Michigan University Press, 1997.

Phelan, Peggy. *Unmarked: The Politics of Performance*. London: Routledge, 1993.

Phelan, Peggy. *Mourning Sex: Performing Public Memories*. London: Routledge, 1997.

Ransom, John S. *Foucaults Discipline: The Politics of Subjectivity*. Durham: Duke University Press, 1997.

Schramm, Helmar. 'Die Vermessung der Hölle: Über den Zusammenhang von Theatralität und Denkstil', in: *Forum Modernes Theater* 10, 2, 119–125, 1995.

Verschaffel, Bart. *Rome/Over Theatraliteit*. Damme: Vlees en Beton, 1990.

Visker, Rudi. *Genealogie als Kritik: Michel Foucault en de Menswetenschappen*. Nijmegen: SUN, 1995.

Zizek, Slavoi. *Het Subject en zijn Onbehagen*. Amsterdam: Boom, 1997.

Notes

[1] In this text 'theatricality' and 'performance' are used together and exchanged from time to time, although an analysis of 'performance' would reveal a great deal of differing connotations. 'Performance' here is meant as a term derived from 'theatricality', with more stress being placed on the active aspect of it.

[2] 'Erasing the border between art and life' is the characteristic of the historic avant-garde in Peter Bürger's influential but debatable *Theorie der Avantgarde* (Frankfurt: Suhrkamp, 1974). For an historic survey of the relation to the audience in the theories of the Avant-Garde itself, see San Sik Nam's *Der Faktor 'Publikum' in den Theatertheorien der Europäischen Avantgarde zwischen 1890 und 1930*. Frankfurt: Peter Lang, 1997.

[3] Burns is explicitly critical towards the attempts of theatre in the sixties at making the actor play himself rather than a part.

[4] By 'referential intention', I do not mean a referential content opposed to a theatrically autonomous form, but the total choice of a theatre maker, his total relation towards reality, which is the main concern of theatre theory.

[5] The most perfect version of breaking down, the Visible Human Project, i.e. two people cut up into millimetre-sized slices, reconstructed virtually and made visible via the internet, is itself a digital reflection of the *theatrum anatomicum*, and open for reduction into an image. Cf. Bleeker (1999).

[6] By 'ethical desire' I refer to the original drive for alterity; each naming or wording of it may be subsumed under the notion of 'ideology'. 'Ethical longing' is a kind of logical precondition for ideology, not a substance of its own. Ideology is too often presented as an arbitrary but unavoidably floating construction.

[7] According to Machiel Karskens, the famous metaphor of the toolbox, which Foucault loved because he did not like any worship of authors, is only useful for a purely political use and not for a historiography (Karskens 1995: 60). I, for my part, do not want to use Foucauldian analyses for the mere sake of historiography either. The theatricality of his method partly places it out of the reach of historiography (this is why historians do have a good deal of trouble with Foucault) as a meaningful picture with a limited, but active scope of action. Still, immanent analysis like this could also be a relevant area of research. Especially in dance studies it raises pertinent questions, under the condition that the conceptual apparatus is used in a balanced way; the latter implies, among other things, that Foucault is never concerned with macro-structures, but always with micro-political dimensions (e.g. see the works of Susan Foster).

[8] The quoted fragment to the full: 'The word "theory" stems from the Greek verb *theorein*. The noun belonging to it is *theoria*. Peculiar to these words is a lofty and mysterious meaning. The verb *theorein* grew out of the coalescing of two root words, *thea* and *horao*. *Thea* (cf. theatre) is the outward look, the aspect in which something shown is itself, the outward appearance in which it offers itself. Plato marks this aspect in which what presences shows what it is, *eidos*. To have seen this aspect, *eidenai,* is to know. The second root in *theorein*, *horao*, means: to look attentively at the outward appearance wherein what presences becomes visible and, through such sight – seeing – to linger with it.' Martin Heidegger. *Science and Technology* (in Freedman 1991: 48).

[9] 'We are much less Greeks than we believe. We are neither in the amphitheatre, nor on the stage, but in the panoptic machine, invested by its effects of power, which we bring to ourselves since we are part of the mechanism.' (Foucault 1977a: 217)

[10] Visibility in Foucault still remains a privilege of power. However, he notes that the privileged classes were granted a secret punishment or could have their faces covered. This may be understandable taking into account that sovereign power also had its reasons for not proceeding too harshly against its privileged citizens, i.e. for reasons of societal productivity, that would later lead to an increasing respect towards the body of ordinary people as well.

[11] Foucault suggests that Bentham, for the design of the panoptic prison, may have been inspired by the zoo of the Versailles Palace, where the king from the centre could observe animals' conduct in separate cages. Via the idea of the zoo we come to the absolutist court/theatre, where the king is the spectator of court life around him.

[12] See Visker 1995: 56–84.

[13] The distinction between the semiotic and the energetic is mentioned in the essay 'The Tooth, the Palm' by Jean-François Lyotard. In his opinion, semiotics is a negative nihilism, which under the guise of the representation keeps pushed aside and annihilates the original referent. The theatre reinforces this negativity by openly repeating the operation of giving meaning. Moreover, the semiotic distinction between signifier and referent is irrelevant to him in an exchange-value capitalism, which made total exchange-ability its hallmark. Consequently, he proposes an energetic libidinal theatre, where all relations are contingent and exchangeable.

[14] Erika Fischer-Lichte defines theatricality as a doubling of the sign-systems, always a sign of a sign, but with a greater versatility: 'Mobility is the prevailing feature in the case of the human body and the objects of its surroundings when they are used as theatrical signs. Here, a human body can be replaced by another body or even an object, and an object can be replaced by another random object or a human body because in their capacity as theatrical signs, they can signify one another.' (Fischer-Lichte 1995a: 88)

[15] Michel Chion, *La Voix au Cinéma*, Paris, 1982, quoted in Hrvatin 1997: 86.

[16] This seems to be a bit more complicated in the absolutist court theatre: it includes a doubling of the court's theatricality, because of 'the actors' both partly becoming audience to a performance and remaining under the look of the king, who preferably took his position in the middle gallery. On the other hand it seems to be a fractal operation, like when one single object between two mirrors gets multiplied into an infinite (pseudo-) complexity. Cf. Verschaffel 1990: 49.

[17] The term 'leap into faith' does not imply that we have to do with a fully unconscious process. In his analysis of Velazquez' painting 'Las Meninas' in *The Order of Things* (Foucault 1974: 3–16), Foucault just points out how this unique position – heralding the classical epistèmè – is deliberately taken by the king, but also upholds the tight connection between representation and the represented.

[18] 'Honest is he who speaks without knowing why, for hope to find this out. Honest is the one who says what he thinks he must say, for hope that this opinion will ever be shared by unknown, anonymous others. Honest is the one, who, without many illusions, uses powerlessness as a weapon against power because something like humanity cannot be expected but only hoped for. Nowadays, honesty is the only alternative to both cynicism and scepticism, even and most of all when the relation between theatre and politics is at stake.' (Laermans 1996: 83)

[19] 'The presence, in order to be presence and self-presence, has always already begun to repeat itself, has always already been penetrated. Affirmation itself must be penetrated in repeating itself. (…) It begins by penetrating its own commentary and is accompanied by its own representation, in which it erases itself and confirms the transgressed law.' (Derrida, 249)

[20] Repetition and recollection are the same movement, except in opposite directions, for what is recollected has been, is repeated backward, whereas genuine repetition is recollected forward. Repetition therefore, if it is possible, makes a person happy, whereas recollection makes him unhappy.' Søren Kierkegaard, Fear and Trembling/ Repetition, in Kierkegaard's writings, VI, p. 170, in Gilpin (1996: 112).

[21] Gilpin refers to European dance and physical theatre, but it also applies to other genres. This is because for some time in contemporary text theatre, the emphasis shifted away from active reproduction of a drama text towards the total process, where the body is present/absent next to the text.

[22] Mikkel Borch-Jakobson, *Lacan: The Absolute Master*, Stanford University Press, 1991, pp. 70–71, in Diamond (1997), p. 115.

[23] In doing so, Zizek radicalises the Foucauldian notion of the immanence of power and resistance: the definition of the power comprises the obscene core which is projected outward upon the peripheral cases. 'The obsessive focus on the naked body of women that fuels both high art and pornography is itself a stand-in, a substitute for the perhaps-more-fervently-desired image of a penetrable male body. (…) High art's and pornography's continual exposition of the possibility of men's penetration of women's bodies via the 'male gaze' is contingent upon the unmarked possibility of the bodies of men.' (Phelan 1997: 40)

[24] It is not easy to derive from Gilpin's text a more or less clear-cut conclusion that could serve as a guideline. This comes very close to what Phelan meant by 'performative writing': 'To name this performative writing is redundant since all good critical writing enacts something in excess of the thing that motivates it. But I am invoking that redundancy here because I want to mark the mimetic echo of what I 'wish all the same to say'. (I want you to hear my wish as well as my miss). The mimicry (…) is an imitation that knows both that it is too late and that is 'off', that in the very energy of its imaginative making it destroys what it most wants to save. In that mistake, I hope to find another mistake that demands to be remade, repeated.' (Phelan 1997: 12)

[26] The term appropriation is borrowed from the works of Michel de Certeau, where it refers partly to the double game of the people within a rational system like Foucault's. Because of individualisation and the great social alternatives being lost, people are forced to handle standardised goods, ideas and rules in creative ways, i.e. to make an immanent re-use of the system, which also turns the depiction of it into a highly paradoxical business. Cf. Rudi Laermans. 'Geloven, Handelen, Weten. Michel de Certeau en de Moderne Cultuur', in: Koen Geldof, Rudi Laermans (eds). *Sluipwegen van het Denken: Over Michel de Certeau*. Nijmegen: SUN, 1996, 16–71; also in Willem Frijhoff. 'Foucault reformed by Certeau: Historical Strategies of Discipline and Everyday Tactics of Appropriation', in: *Arcadia: Zeitschrift für Allgemeine und Vergleichende Literaturwissenschaft*, 33, 1 (1998), 92–108. Concerning the double game, see also Michel Maffesoli. *La Transfiguration du Politique: La Tribalisation du Monde*. Paris: Grasset, 1992.

[27] The advertising actions of Benetton occupy this ambivalence in a sharp and sometimes shocking fashion. Obviously societal contents (racism, AIDS, sexism, etc.) that simultaneously oppose the plastic esthetical fantasy world of fashion are linked to the advertising campaign of a product (even more, a sheer brand name, for mostly there are no Benetton trousers and jumpers included) in a shameless and purely heteronomous way.

[28] This text has only been made possible with the generous support, good advice, corrections and critical remarks of Kaat Debo, Koen Tachelet, Luk Van den Dries, Annemie Vanhoof, Kurt Vanhoutte, Myriam Van Imschoot and, most of all, Joke Rous. Also thanks to Claire Tarring for proofreading this text.

Eric Raeves, *1 Wereld*, Photo: Bart Michielsen

Luk Van den Dries

The Sublime Body

Performance theory has never paid as much attention to the body as in the present day. The body continues to fascinate us in its impermeability and intangibility. From the abject body to the cyborg, from the ideal body to the Aids infected body, a diverse discourse around representations of the body tries to invade an essential and elusive domain of the performing arts. Without attempting to be comprehensive, this text will explore some entries into this discourse. In order to circumvent adversative discussions concerning the body, this text will try to locate what is feasible within the category of the 'sublime body'.

When we talk about the body in the arts today it is usually in an antithetical manner. On the one hand, the body is discussed as an essence, a kind of 'prima causa', which is modified by diverse layers of cultural encoding. But this body can still be approached as an entity surviving those layers, or a state which precedes the body's entry into ideology. On the other hand, it is argued, the body is always already immersed in culture and thus marked by signs of the environment in which it emerges. In the performing arts, the latter area of body research concentrates primarily on the force of representation. The body always comes to represent something else, an aspect of power, an ideological position, a sexual principle, or an infringement of this principle. In this vision, the body is always conceived as an historical construct. The body is 'actively and currently conceived of and produced by ideological encoding, which it cannot simply transcend'. (Auslander 1997: 92)

Auslander considers this contradiction to be the result of a paradigm shift.[1] The modernist discourse around the body starts with a 'holy body' – a body rooted in the tradition of Artaud, Grotowski and Brook. The body transcends its own boundedness through the collective ritual of theatre, or it reaches a transcendental elevation of this boundedness by means of ecstasy, exhaustion or pain. Both states presuppose the existence of a 'universal' body and an archetypal condition. The body incorporates a primary mode of experience, which is situated in the anteroom of language; a domain which is believed to precede forms of cultural differentiation:

> The primary object of *The Theatre and its Double* is this truth, which, situated before language, must circulate not from mind to mind, but

from body to body. As Artaud said, 'in the state of degeneration we are
in, it is through the skin that the metaphysical will re-enter the mind'.
(Robert 1996: 28)

Framed within a different type of communality, the body is initiated into
a ritual dimension that emphasises the existence of collective mythology.
All these conditions (archetype, ritual, myth) situate the body within a
modernist set of ideas.

    Postmodern discourses view the body as a cultural and ideological
biotope. It is a construction site for the assemblage of identity, which will
consist of many foundational layers. It is a gathering place for projections,
which anchor themselves inside skin tissue and are connected with the body
through diverse genetic, familial or societal agents. Herbert Blau rightfully
proposes that 'there is nothing more coded than the body'.[2] Philip Auslander
denounces the modernist concept of the body, and explains the need for
postmodern encoding as follows:

> The problem is not that modernist performance theorists, especially
> Grotowski, fail to acknowledge that the body is encoded by social
> discourses, but rather that they suggest that these codes are only an
> overlay of the body, that there is an essential body that can shortcircuit
> social discourses. This essential body is a metaphysical, even a mystical
> concept: it is asocial, undifferentiated, raceless, genderless, and there-
> fore, neutralised and quietist. (Auslander 1997: 91–92)

The theory of Grotowski and his collaborators totally denies the social-
discursive body, which is marked by gender, class, and race. Moreover, the
materiality of the body itself is thought to prevent the experience of ecstasy.
The routine body must be transcended in order to merge with the essential
body and to reach a metaphysical dimension. Grotowski's emphasis on
training the body in order to reach a primary state enables the actor to leave
behind the routine body and to 'open up in a kind of translumination'.
(Grotowski 1967: 267)

> I have seen for a very long time now that a theatre with tangible,
> corporeal and physiological characteristics is an ideal medium for
> *provocation*, a pestering of oneself and the audience through the actor
> (the actor who actually challenges himself when he challenges the
> audience).
>   The theatre has to combat our stereotypical world vision, our con-
> ventional feelings, our preconceived notions as they are anchored in
> the body, in respiration, the inner reflexes, in short, in the entire
> human organism.
>   The theatre has to break these sorts of taboos.

> Through this *transgression* the theatre will enable us to engage ourselves, 'naked' and entirely agitated, in something which cannot be easily defined and which consists of Eros and Charitas.
> (Grotowski 1967: 273, italics in original)

Grotowski viewed the physical body as an entity that could transcend boundedness by means of a collective and ritualistic gesture. The routine body is thus viewed as a temporary phase, which can be discarded through rigorous self-disciplining in order to transform into a holy body.

Since the 1960s this state of 'working one's body' through a process-ual transformation of limits has been central in Grotowski's work, but even more so in the artistic experiments of so-called 'performance art' or 'live-art'. In a more explicit manner, artists started to use a physical materiality within the process of making art. Performance art and body art research actively and radically challenge the textures of the body. The artist places his/her body on display at the intersection between the theatre and the gallery, between the theatre and the other arts – altering the body, mutilating it and offering it to the viewer as a live act.

This area of performance art, consisting of extremely radical and provocative actions, is the ultimate terrain for the renewal of discourses around the body. The artist's infringement upon his/her body requires an appropriately radical response from the viewer and his/her statements. Indeed, discussions of the live-art spectacle have become prominent in cultural studies and theatre research. As important topics of cultural inquiry,[3] they have also expanded into the fields of ethnology, psychology, and anthropology. Text-based theatre, which for decades has been a prominent model for theatre studies and performance research, has been moved onto the back-burner to be replaced with the body-based research of perform-ance artists. As Erika Fischer-Lichte shows in a recent theatre history analysis, this entails some important shifts, because the referential aspects of theatre become less important than the performative ones. This also means that the referential aspects are no longer crucial to the experience of the audience, becoming less important than the experiential aspects of the performance: 'The dominant vision of "world as text" has been replaced by the vision of "world as performance" '.[4] The central ontological measure of performance is strongly situated in its 'live' character. Even the antiquated assumption that the 'live' character of theatre differentiates it from other media, seems to hold a central position in performance discourses. Presence, reality, and the live happening, all become very important components in theorising performance art. In this respect, Peggy Phelan talks about the immediate and total consumption of the work of art, whereby a referential surplus is replaced by the here-and-now experience:

> Performance implicates the real through the presence of living bodies. In performance art spectatorship there is no element of consumption: there are no left-overs, the gazing spectator must try to take everything in. Without a copy, live performance plunges into visibility – in a maniacally charged present – and disappears into memory, into the realm of invisibility and the unconscious where it eludes regulation and control. (Peggy Phelan 1993: 148)

However, any consensus about the ontological foundations of performance[5] and the importance of its experential qualities is shattered when we enter the mode of conceptualising the body. Once again, we come across the collision of paradigms, which was mentioned at the beginning of this article. In texts and statements that accompany performance art events, we can see a similar rift between those who view the body as an essence and those who emphasise forms of cultural encoding. This is, by the way, not only the case in contemporary studies of the history of performance art, but is also evident in statements of legitimation that performance art has produced since its inception. The theoretical contradictions between natural and cultural bodies take shape inside a vast number of historical performance documents, of which I will only cite a few.

In many statements we can find the rigid formulation of an attachment to and belief in the body-as-presence, a body which can resist forms of cultural encoding and ideological inscription. These ideas are inundated in liberation theology, that is, a belief in the ability to 'purify' the body. An important condition for purification is the necessity to place the body outside the cultural order:

> In its entirety, the body still presents the non-revealed part of mankind; despite every possible classification it seems to still slip away from the most severe restrictions, the most absurd manipulations, and the censured practises that are continuously imposed. (Inga-Pin 1978: 4)

The body disappears as though into a cosmic black hole, remaining present there as an energetic black-box, invisible to the analytical gaze. This present and invisible body no longer belongs to the linguistic order and is, therefore, in its pure essence undefinable. If the essential body is untouchable and out of reach, the layers around the body can be peeled away, making it perfectly possible to locate an existential foundation through the mass of cultural growth:

> The over-riding desire is to live collective *ethos* and *pathos*, to grasp the *existent* in all of its brutal physicality, to communicate something that has been previously felt but that is lived in the very moment of

> communication, to return to the origins without leaving the present, (…) to lead the individual, in short, back to his specific mode of existence (…).
>
> The accent is placed on *nature*, the desire to go beyond the values of current morality, (…) in order to be able to step back away from the artificial conventions of society. All of this is an attempt to eliminate culture – which is to say the whole nexus of cultivated ways of living, the concept of encyclopedism as opposed to the concept of consciousness, the collective formation of social groups within institutions that define and condition them, crystallization as opposed to evolution. (Vergine 1974: 3, italics in original)

The binary logic of this argument will inevitably end up in the dichotomy of nature-as-essence versus culture-as-trauma. Moreover, one can often find the image of culture as illness in performance discourses. The artist is considered to be a shaman, his/her theatre 'an instrument for healing the sick community; either through therapy or metaphysical ceremony'. (Wardle in Kultermann 1972: 13)

Several writings have appeared simultaneously that emphasise the cultural–ideological framework of performance, making it clear that the shift from modern to postmodern theories of the body does not have an historical but an epistemological foundation.[6] The actions upon and inside the body make us aware of the ideological DNA which constitutes the body and from which it cannot escape. On the contrary:

> No one can escape this oppression imposed by all on all which decides the morphological course and the formal statement of the condition of the body, which is always ready to be invested with new ideologies, the impregnation of which is so much deeper the more one wants to escape, resist, and control them. (Pluchart 1974: 52)

This conclusion is not very different from Phelan's diagnosis several decades later that '(t)he actor's body cannot forget its gender (…), cannot shake off the referential frame imposed by text, mode of productions, and spectator's narrativity'. (Phelan 1993: 365) Ever since the performing body itself began to beg for attention and recognition, it has been discussed in terms of binary oppositions. Theories of the body are dominated by binaries such as nature/culture, essence/inscription, 'orifical/artificial',[7] etc. Such binaries emerge regardless of the period in which the bodies and their discourses have taken shape. In other words, by theorising a virulent presence for the performer's body we have taken recourse to an antithetical model of analysis. This has been going on for quite a while now, how do we put an end to it?

The Body and Signification

Without attempting to be comprehensive, I would like to clarify the body and its analytical concepts and draw attention to large movements in theatre research that have emerged in recent decades. At each instance, the theme of the body has been dealt with quite differently. But time and again, researchers seem to stumble upon limiting values, which would prevent one from erecting discourses around the body. The field of semiotics, which since the seventies has manifested itself as a key theory for theatre analysis, does not have a problem analysing the body as long as it is located within the boundaries of representation. The body on the stage always and ultimately represents another body, which is mediated through an entire corporeal range of significations. This seems to happen automatically since the *scène par excellence* is the scene of signification; every element on stage can become part of the process of signification. Hence a gesture and movement on stage will stand for a gesture and movement in a fictional space of interpretation – a sign for something else. As we learned from Peirce, signs are 'interpretants' from the viewpoint of the spectator. Within the field of semiotics, the body is considered to be present, but mostly as a signifying force, as a tool for the creation of an imaginary other, the character.

The body compels the attention of semioticians. Here we can apprehend belief in the performance happening, but this attention is only geared toward the construction of the character. The body of the actor is, in other words, a transparent layer of tissue through which the spectator can look at a newly created body, which is evoked by the actor. The body is always slave to the new and implicit body of signification, whether this happens through a detached or an engaging performance mode.

Semiotics apprehends the purely performing body or the body without a referential function as an obscure other. It has a hard time understanding the pure category of the experiential. Sometimes it seems that semiotics is only suitable with respect to the cognitive aspects of the performing body and that the very domain of libidinality, corporeality, and sensuality has to be situated outside the field of semiotics.[8] In the body of literature, which constitutes theatre semiotics, little attention is given to emotional-affective elements. A semiotician such as Ruffini makes use of anthropological concepts for a description of pre-cognitive dimensions, which include the seductive forces of theatre and the energy radiated by the presence of the actor.[9] Durand also detects semiotic problems with the theatre, which seems to forget:

> [the] place of gesture, the place where a primary text could be seized, which would owe nothing to spoken language, the underground place

> which is also the place of fantasy and which one could call *the body*.
> (Durand 1975: 118, italics in original)

Other theatre researchers have suggested that semiotics is limited to the zone of consciousness and cognitive signification, that it loses its grip in the hinterlands.[10] Obviously one cannot be satisfied with a semiotics that can only capture the cognitive aspects of the body, as this would seriously amputate the totality of a theatrical experience, neither would it do justice to the responses and pleasures of the spectator. This point of view is also argued by De Marinis:

> It must be clear, however, that this agency, this acting of the theatre, this complex network of passion transformation (in addition to cognitive ones) which it produces, cannot be considered a purely and simply extra-semiotic phenomenon and, as such, would be pushed in the sphere of the unspeakable and unanalysable. (De Marinis 1981: 77)

It was the semiotician C.S. Peirce who made room for this extra-cognitive territory of semiotics. As we know, Peirce based his definition of the sign in a triadic structure, which differs from the signifier/signified concept of de Saussure, the continental founding father of semiotics. Peirce designed the universal categories of Firstness, Secondness, and Thirdness, which became the basis for an entire series of triadic relations in semiotics. Peirce described these categories differently in different places, established different types of categories, and provided them with different sets of examples:[11]

> Firstness is the mode of being of that which is such as it is, positively and without reference to anything else.
>   Secondness is the mode of being of that which is such as it is, with respect to a second but regardless of any third.
>   Thirdness is the mode of being of that which is such as it is, in bringing a second and third into relation to each other. (Peirce 1931/1974–1979: 8.328)

The mode of approaching the first category can be described as presentness, possibility or quality, the second as a reaction, the third as a mediation. In other words we are closer to positioning the emotional-affective moment: as a feeling or emotional quality (Firstness), as experiential category (Secondness), as representation or thought (Thirdness). These three categories are not autonomous, independent modes of existence, but touch upon each other through a principle of continuity, which requires that the third category infers the other two. These universal categories can also be applied on the level of the 'interpretant' (that which realises the sign), so that it is possible to make a distinction between an emotional, energetic and a logical interpretant. The emotional moment can be considered to be a form of Firstness in the sign-effect, which, if followed by an effort, becomes an energetic interpretant. It is only in the third interpretant-phase that the 'sensual meaning' can be transcended; the logical interpretant is a thought or a concept, it is a sign-effect, which Peirce considered to be the highest form of semiosis. It is the conceptual effect that we strive toward in interpretative analyses, but it is always built upon the previous sign-effects: emotion and reaction.

In other words, through the homogeneous semiotics of Peirce, it is perfectly possible to consider goose bumps, excitement, or chaos to be the effects of semiosis. It is possible to consider the pure presence of the body in similar way. However, there is still the urge to look for the stabilisation of meaning, because the logical conceptualisation is seen as a third elevating phase that finalises signification. Therefore, the extra-cognitive territory is still hard to reach within cognitive limits. The fluid territory of the libidinal body does not provide interpretation with a strong grip. In order to enter this territory, post-structuralist theory offers a more promising approach as it is geared around 'flux' rather than focus, the unrest of an endless trace rather than the final 'rest' quality of signification.

The Body as Untameable Other

Lyotard introduced the term 'somatography' (1977: 88) in order to investigate the inscription of performance on the body. Lyotard conceives the work of theatre not as a mediation of signs, but in terms of energy streams and libidinal forces. The body stands outside signification in order to be a stream of energy in an endless, elusive series of flows. A central figure for this desiring body is Artaud's 'Body without Organs', a body which withdraws itself from every possible occupation by an organism, from every possible colonisation by forms of representation. According to Deleuze, such a 'Body without Organs' is a continuous transformation of energy, which time and again takes the body to a limit. It is a perpetual fight against the downsizing and occupation of the body. It is a 'body without image' (Deleuze, Guattari 1972: 14) on a nomadic journey.[12] The Body without organs cannot be considered to be an emptiness, because the opposition between 'inside' and 'outside' no longer exists. Detached from the fixating subject, it is a body without ego-experience. It consists of pulsations and is both hypersensitive and extremely opened-up.

Post-structuralism offers a solution for a static, deterministic concept of the body. Here, the limit of the concept of the body is not situated within linguistic structures, but exists as a negative border that escapes the fixations of ideological indoctrinations through a fluid play with potential antibodies. Deleuze foresees the destruction of ideologically constructed bodies and enumerates countless 'outside' bodies – hypochondriac, paranoid, schizoid, drugged, masochist, ... bodies. These are bodies that are found outside the symbolical order and that explicitly refuse to be circumscribed by regulating and dominating societal conditions. The Body without Organs is thus a liberated body, as Artaud explicitly says:

> When you make him into a body without organs, you will free him of his routines, and return his freedom to him.
>   Then you will teach him to dance backwards again. (Artaud 1947/ 1974: 104)

But these sorts of external positions also reproduce the symbolic order. Everything that is removed, or mentioned in a negative mode, is also reconstituted in a new form. Once one accepts the principle of a discursive network, it is hard to escape from this network.

The antibodies described by Deleuze thus constitute the flipside of a coin that is marked by ideologically constructed bodies. This ideological marking strongly determines contemporary theories of the body. As I mentioned at the beginning of this article, the influence of cultural studies as a dominant discourse on the body corroborates this trend towards the body-as-trace paradigm. Today when we talk about the body in the arts, we talk about the body as it stands for something else. The body is a carrier of traces, the biological product of hereditary components, which gives away all its secrets through bio-technology. Ideologically, the body is a kind of a sponge, every hollow filled out with conditioned behaviour, culturally enriched formulas and all kinds of signs of cultivated traffic. We can explore the body as an archaeological site, where the remains of our civilisation are buried. The body is the product of a dominant mode of being in a particular culture.

Within a diverse array of cultural studies, the body is placed at the heart of a field of societal forces. The body resembles a discursive tower of babel, a gathering place of different ideological markings (nationality, ethnicity, gender, class, ...). In her study *Bodies that Matter: On the Discursive Limits of Sex*, Judith Butler emphasises the gendered branches of the body as a construct. Not only the matter of the body, but also the image of the body is inundated by notions of gender.[13] The body is constructed amidst these notions, only emerging as a result of ideological formations. According to Butler, there is no entity that precedes this construction. Everything outside the construction is situated outside a specific kind of discursitivity

that is its sign-post. That which is excluded from this area, at the border
regions of ideological formation, is still part of the construct itself. Any
extra-linguistic alterity pertaining to the material body can be considered
a pure projection.[14]

Following Lacan, Butler calls the body (or rather morphology) an
imaginary formation constituted in language. In the crucial stage of naming
('le nom du père', Lacan), the child is accepted into the Symbolic order of
language, which guarantees the integrity of the body:

> To be named is thus to be incalculated into that law and to be formed,
> bodily, in accordance with that law. (Butler 1993: 72)

As a true feminist, Butler is annoyed that the position of the Lacanian phallus is given as a 'privileged signifier' in this morphological process. She
replaces this phallus with the famous and more versatile 'lesbian phallus',
but this does not take away from the fact the body is still susceptible to
gendered, discursive practices.

Lacanian ideas concerning the relationship between the Symbolic
Order and the formation of the body have become more pronounced in
recent decades. Within cultural studies the field of gender studies has been
especially nurtured and stimulated by these ideas. The explosion of a group
of Lacanian feminists was aided by radical gender-oriented performance
works by artists such as Annie Sprinkle, Claude Wampler, Orlan, Carolee
Schneemann, and many others. Goldberg (1998: 131) concludes that '(a)s
a result, feminist scholars and writers, have for the past decade, been confronted by performance material of a kind so startling, so disturbing and
prescient, and so driven by a fierce and energetic sexuality, that feminist
theory has taken off in entirely new directions'.

These 'new' directions entail a new critical interpretation of Lacanian
subject formation. Entry into the Symbolical Order as final recognition of
the self by the other, and entry into the linguistic order through naming,
does not exclude the possibility of critically questioning this symbolical
network. As I have shown, such questioning cannot occur by departing
from or standing outside this order. Even if the body fights against discursive practices, it is still included within the normative field. Cracks within
the dominant Symbolical Order emerge when one tries to expand this
order, when one inflates it so as to turn it hyperbolically against itself:

> Where the uniformity of the subject is expected, where the behavioral
> conformity of the subject is commanded, there might be produced the
> refusal of the law in the form of the parodic inhabiting of confirmity
> that subtly calls into question the legitimacy of the command, a

repetition of the law into hyperbole, a rearticulation of the law against
the authority of the one who delivers it. (Butler 1993: 122)

The potential for violation and subversion is situated within the reproduction of the symbolical law, within it's 'critical mimicry'.[15] The fixating
violence of the 'nom du père' is, apparently, not so definite that it prevents
a critical distance. According to Butler, there is a border region between the
symbolical determining of the sexual position and the imaginary formation
of the ego. There is an in-between moment of crisis that can manifest itself
as a crisis of the symbolical definition of sexual orientation and the failure
of a morphology of the body, which results in a loss of 'its sure footing – its
cultural gravity'. (Butler 1993: 139)

It is very interesting to note that, with her specific definition of
gender, Butler's radical-feminist reading of Lacan dissolves binary oppositions. Her Foucault-inspired critique of discourses of power is not meant to
overturn power or to operate anarchistically outside power. Butler accepts
the symbolical limits of gender in order to shape them from within the
dominant network. There is no longer an attempt to transcend binaries or to
accept a kind of third gender, rather, 'it is an internal subversion in which
the binary is both presupposed and proliferated to the point where it no
longer makes sense'. (Butler 1990: 127) This strategy could also be used in
order to overturn the absolute opposition between essentialist and ideological concepts of the body.

The Category of the Sublime

I suggest we leave the trail of Lacan and the field of cultural studies for a
moment in order to investigate the body from the radically different field of
aesthetics. I will push against the stream of dominant discourses concerning the representation of the body, and submit the body to the aesthetic category of the sublime. My discussion will proceed by following the notion
of the sublime as it occurs in diverse domains. Firstly, I will discuss the
sublime as it is conceived in an old text written by Longinus. I will move
from this reading to an examination of Kant's famous treatise, followed by
Lyotard's critique of Kant's notion of the sublime.

Because of its long history, it is a risky business to talk about the
sublime. From Longinus' *On the Sublime*, written in the 3rd century AD, to
contemporary applications of the term, it has been used in diverse fields
of signification and has provoked diverse implications. In order to give a
sketch of this diversity, I would like to expand on some brief discussions of
the body to be found in classical texts concerning the sublime. If we read

the most famous texts, written by Kant and Longinus, the body is rarely mentioned as a carrier or a receiver of the affect of the sublime. In *On the Sublime*, Longinus mostly talks about the force of the sublime as a rhetorical strategy used to enchant the audience. The sublime, in other words, is a construction of language and presupposes an adequate dosage of symbolism, metaphor, a successful composition, deeply felt emotions, and inspired speech. It also requires the presence of a noble soul, who manages to elevate great ideas to sublime heights. Longinus shows the intricate quality of the sublime with examples from diverse sources (*Iliad*, *Odyssey*, Plato's *Timaeus*, Cicero, Demosthenes), arguing that it cannot be reduced to a formula, but requires a right mixture of qualities to induce in the spectators an enticing state of trance, and a burst of energy sufficient to cause a bolt of lightning.

In one passage of this rather badly preserved text, Longinus talks about the body as one of the many sublime paths in order to illustrate a complex constellation of diverse feelings. According to Longinus, the sublime emerges when several details are combined in order to constitute a whole. He quotes a poem by Sappho – a poem which has, by the way, only been delivered through Longinus – where she describes how her lover's gaze pierces her body and makes it crack:

> Yea, my tongue is broken, and through and through me
> 'Neath the flesh, impalpable fire runs tingling;
> Nothing see mine eyes, and a noise of roaring
> Waves in my ears sounds;
>
> Sweat runs down in rivers, a tremor seizes
> All my limbs and paler than grass in autumn,
> Caught by pains of menacing death, I falter,
> Lost in the love trance. (Sappho in Longinus 1957: 17)

Sappho evokes a desiring body as a body on fire, one which falters and breaks once exposed to the gaze of the beloved. The body falls into sensory pieces of localised pain, and then disintegrates into an act of incoherent stuttering. Nevertheless, Longinus uses this exact example in order to point to the rhetorical coherence of Sappho's poem: 'How does she excel? In her skilful choice of the most important and intense details and in relating them to one another'. (Longinus 1957: 17) For this pioneering theoretician of the sublime, the organic whole is superior: 'The beauty of the body depends on the way in which the limbs are joined together, each one severed from the other has nothing remarkable about it, but the whole together forming a perfect unity'.

The body has an equally marginal presence in Kant's work *Kritik der Urteilskraft* (*Critique of Judgement*). In this work, Kant primarily wants to demonstrate the superiority of reason. As we know, he makes a distinction in his aesthetic categories between the beautiful and the sublime. When one is in touch with the beautiful, a harmonious link between image and cognition arises. Beauty then delivers satisfaction: 'Such delight is determined not merely by the representation of the object, but also by the represented bond of connection between the subject and the real existence of the object' (Kant 1974: 122),[16] while the sublime causes a short-circuit of energy. The sublime takes your breath away, your imagination comes to a halt in confrontation with an excess. It is beauty with a razor sharp edge.

In confrontation with the sublime or with the intangible that escapes the imagination, Kant believes that harmony is destroyed. The revelation of boundless totality provokes a moment of obstruction in the imagination that is experienced as an impossibility. Though it is experienced as an impossibility the paradoxical totality appears; the imagination sacrifices itself in favour of reason, which clears the moment of obstruction and establishes a quiet contemplation. In confrontation with a formless infinity, a small moment of crisis emerges, a moment of perplexity that fills the spectator with pain and anxiety. This vision supersedes our imagination and becomes impalpable. After experiencing a time lag between perception and understanding, reason takes over and installs a distance through which it can establish its superiority. Reason stands in opposition to the perception of infinity, which is reduced to a tangible entity. As Paul de Man shows, there is a displacement between the 'Verwunderung' (shocked surprise) and the 'Bewunderung' (tranquil admiration). (De Man 1990: 102) Finally, this crisis leads to an affirmation of the quiet superiority of ethics: 'The feeling of the sublime in the end affirms – in the true Kantian spirit – the victory of reason over the senses'. (Verstraete 1998: 38)

The sublime titillation aroused across the skin tissue of rational morality is primarily caused by the force of nature images. But it is nature presented in its most chaotic form ('in its wildest and most irregular disorder and desolation', Kant 1974: 167), which throws the spectator back onto himself/herself. Here, Kant pictures gigantic rock formations, or a roaring thunderstorm, the spilling earth, rampaging hurricanes, frightening volcanoes.[16] In order to illustrate in his text the quality and agency of sublime confrontation, he refers back to the corporeal domain:

> The like is to be said of the sublime and beautiful in the human body. We must not regard as the determining grounds of our judgment the concepts of the purposes which all our limbs serve and we must not

allow this unity of purpose to influence our aesthetic judgement. (Kant 1974: 197)[18]

With this comparison, Kant primarily wants to ban the utility factor or the teleological perspective from aesthetic judgement. So as to create the impression of the sublime, the limbs are torn from their organic unity, the biological functions are out of order. Just as the rock masses, earth, ocean and heaven are torn from their geographical unity and become an amorphous unity of sublime matter, limbs are torn from their morphological structure, rendered formless, and that, as such, is a sublime experience. In other words, the organic utilitarian body makes room for an inorganic sublime body. We are now in a position, with respect to the representation of the sublime body, that is diametrically opposed to Longinus' notion of 'perfect unity'.

If Kant considered his category of the sublime to be 'a mere appendix' in his analysis of aesthetic judgement, it is definitely more interesting and useful than his theory of beauty. Kant wants to demonstrate that it is possible to experience aesthetic pleasure, and that it consists of reason finding finality in the absence of form 'the sublime is to be found in an object even devoid of form'. (Kant 1974: 165) It is, therefore, a form of negative aesthetics. This is probably why a postmodern philosopher such as Lyotard devotes so much attention to this particular text written by the most rational of thinkers – the sublime establishes a gap in Kant's thought; as Lyotard suggests: 'The teleological machine leaps'. (Lyotard 1991: 74) A moment of hesitation becomes visible, a sort of black-out of the consciousness. The gap between imagination and idea is created by means of a sensation of having 'too much'. Our potential for imagination is cluttered by the impression of something excessive, something that is enormous or appears to be infinite. An excess which expands infinitely and effectively becomes formless.

As mentioned previously, Kant's theory describes this obstruction as temporary. The obstruction of the imagination is followed by radical change, one could say a moment of conversion, which results in a 'reassuringly operative notion of the self'. (Herz 1985: 48) Following Weiskel's Freudian application of the sublime, Neil Herz analyses the moment of hindrance as a confirmation of the integrity of 'self'. The self, which was in threat of becoming absorbed into an infinite excess, is recuperated, as discrepancies are found between image and cognition. In Kant's terminology, it is again reason that makes this a possibility. And thus reason's supremacy over the other faculties is restored. What seemed to be purposeless or a 'counter-goal' (Lyotard 1991: 73) in the sublime apparition, will finally have the purpose of fortifying the triumph of reason. The teleological moment in the experience of the sublime becomes a thinking 'which becomes action: It actualises, subjectively, its all-knowingness'. (Lyotard 1991: 75)

Today we frequently hear echoes of the Kantian notion of the sublime, for example, through the application of the 'sublime' in the visual arts. Paul Crowther, one of the most important theorists exploring this tendency, posits the sublime as a position from which to counteract postmodern confusion. In the diverse work of assemblage and installation artists, we can detect a 'sensory and imaginative excess'. (Crowther 1995: 11) As an example he mentions a work by Cornelia Parker, entitled *Cold Dark Matter – An Exploded View*. This work consists of an installation comprising a wooden house which is subsequently exploded with dynamite. A photograph of the explosion is then carefully reconstructed as an 'overload' of fragments and diverse materials. The installation disintegrates in total fragmentation. According to Crowther, the sublime moment consists in the fact that we can project meaning onto it: 'It is this primal urge into meaning which is made vivid in the experience of the sublime'. (id. 17) The sublime work of art confirms, once again, our rational superiority and stabilises the 'self' as operator of signification. The semiotic determination of meaning operates like a dam that prevents one from being carried away by the infinity of the sublime effect. It constructs a point of rest and certainty.

How is it possible to skip Kant, the weight of reason, and meaning as the instrument of reason, without also leaving behind the experience of the sublime? Lyotard opened up this path in his interpretation of Kant's *Kritik der Urteilskraft* (*Critique of Judgement*). For Lyotard, the essence of the sublime experience lies in the confrontation with the unimaginable, what he calls elsewhere 'the unrepresentable within representation itself'. (Lyotard 1984: 81) Indeed, the sublime represents a picture of totality, which is at once an unattainable totality. Hence the sublime is simultaneously pleasurable and miserable. The sublime thwarts the evocation of a totality; it is a representation which at once fails as a representation. The perception of the unimaginable is, for Kant, a cause for its rational correction, its domination and destruction. But Lyotard brings the momentary eclipse of reason to a full force. The sublime, so conceived by Lyotard, is no longer characterised by its appeal to reason, but by the terror of the unknown. There is, therefore, a sort of regression: the detached gaze, instrument of human over-viewing and superiority, starts to compete with the other senses. The gap created in confronting the sublime is no longer bridged with rational evaluation, but expresses itself as a kind of hesitation. A currency breakdown places the entire house of rationality in the dark.

In the space of the unknown we find the possibility of breaking with everything that ties us to institutions, categories, and conventions. The break with representation, with an aesthetics of representation, is Lyotard's condition for the creation of libidinal energy. In this way, the sublime is directly related to Lyotard's notion of the 'event'. In the event we are confronted with a paradox, an impossible collision, which cannot resolve oppositions. Faced with this collision or short-circuit in mental consciousness, reason, unable to think through the resulting paradox, proves insufficient. Thinking encounters the limits of representation at which point the unknown can move around freely and make an appeal to the other sensitive faculties. This also means that there is a crisis in the intellect's capacity to bridge certain faculties, to make comparisons between oppositions, attitudes, aesthetic judgements or tastes; the subject cannot get a grasp on the complexity of the world as it manifests itself to him/her and ends up in a crisis from which he/she has to withdraw. The 'comparison', which is always an attempt to control the uncontrollable, fails to make room for 'le différend' or that which escapes from mental inclusion.

Unlike Kant, Lyotard situates the encounter with the sublime within artistic avant-garde practices. This encounter is geared towards putting the viewer in touch with 'le différend'. The sublime is thus ultimately threatening, frightening and irritating because it deprives us of certainty, it dismantles our consciousness, and opens up the shock of the new. The sublime looks within perception at a point where perception begins to slide, searching for 'new presentations, not to be enjoyed, but in order to sharpen a sensibility for the existence of the unrepresentable'. (Lyotard 1984: 81) The working of the sublime does not only entail a break or derangement of known modes of perception, but also opens up (in the sense of anticipation) new possibilities.

The Negative-Sublime

Lyotard's reassessment of the classical concept of the sublime that dominated 18th and 19th century aesthetics, places full emphasis on the force of the unrepresentable, which, like a 'crowbar', breaks open the quiet contemplation emanating from the Kantian sublime. I have previously shown the implications of the usage of such an instrument, which can thrust into one's face whatever it was that required prying open. Nevertheless, Lyotard's own wording 'the unrepresentable within represenation' creates an opening. Then, if the negative gap is viewed as emptiness, the binary opposition can be sidestepped. This path was taken by Slavoj Zizek in his amendment of the sublime. Here we can rejoin the Lacanian trail, which was temporarily left behind.

In his reading of Kant, Zizek cannot but notice the failure of the sublime. There is the foreboding of a formless and infinite totality, which he compares with the also unreachable Lacanian sublime object.[19] The gap between a phenomenological, empirical representation and a 'Thing-in-itself' cannot be bridged. We can call this a 'sublime lack', in that the sublime clarifies the ultimate impossibility, 'this very impossibility to reach after the Thing'. (Zizek 1989: 203) In the sublime a perfect paradox manifests itself, it makes present what is absent: 'the place of the Thing is indicated through the very failure of its representation'. (id. 204) The diagnosis of failure, however, is dependent on a positioning of oneself within the tension of the paradox. Zizek shows how Kant is imprisoned by the field of representation. If the sublime is defined as the 'transcendent surplus beyond what can be represented', it can only be known as negative, as that which escapes representation. When we leave behind the Kantian need for representation, we no longer have to speak of failure. If we know that there is nothing but the universe of representation, then one does not need a negative of representation.[19] Following the insights of Slavoj Zizek, it becomes possible to define the sublime in a different manner:

> the sublime is no longer an (empirical) object indicating through its very inadequacy the dimension of a transcendent Thing-in-itself (Idea) but an object which occupies the place, replaces, fills out the empty place of the Thing as the void, as the pure Nothing of absolute negativity – the Sublime is an object whose positive body is just an embodiment of Nothing. (Zizek 1989: 206)

We can exchange the field of representation for an emptiness-in-being. Thus, the sublime body is not a body doomed to failure by representing a subject, but one that fills emptiness with its presence. Zizek illustrates this point by means of a reference to Hegel's *Phenomenology of the Spirit* and his distinction between physiognomy and phrenology. Physiognomy always functions within a semiotic framework, it belongs to the order of representation and language and expresses the interior, even though the interior can never be translated into a sign. This is because 'there is no "proper" signifier of the subject'. (id. 208) Phrenology on the other hand, is purely a filling of emptiness, without the need for reference or representation:

> the bone, the skull, is thus an object which, by means of its *presence*, fills out the void, the impossibility of the signifying *representation* of the subject. (Zizek 1989: 208, italics in original)

The sublime body leaves behind the field of representation. It does not aim to be an amendment to the impossibility to represent the subject. Neither does it want to be an instrument for taming the uncontrollable nor a negative for a rational determination. These are all scenarios and extensions of the texts of Longinus and Kant and the way in which they have applied the concept of the sublime to the body. The sublime body, which we have constructed here, takes its strength from the acceptance of the paradox of the 'unrepresentable within representation' and looks for emptiness in that very space. Not as a melancholic memory about the loss of totality but as a draining of emptiness, which is inherent in presence. In this way, the collision between traditional views regarding the discourse of the body is destroyed, to be turned into an applause for the paradox, which cannot be resolved.

The Practice of the Sublime

Having discussed the theory of the sublime, let us make these insights more productive with a few examples that illustrate different facets of the sublime body.

The Belgian theatre director Eric Raeves has long been obsessed by images of the body. He started out as an actor with Jan Fabre, and developed his career as a choreographer to investigate the theme of the visible/invisible body. We can see a clear development in his work from the category of representation to the experience of the sublime body. His first big work, *Interesting Bodies* (1996) produced in collaboration with De Beweeging, consists of a series of living images presented in a museum. These images enable spectators to devote different time-spans to each installation. The work is not concerned with ideological formulations of the body (such tropes do not interest this choreographer), but with liberating the body as carrier of an image of the body. Raeves aims toward dismantling representation by searching for the limits of the body's representation.

In one set of images, Raeves, wanting to work on the skin and the structure of the body itself, undresses the dancers and actors he employs. He deprives them of their most individual characteristics, such as the face, the sex and hair, which are made invisible. The normal bodily functions, with which the subject manifests itself as an individual, are suppressed. This is not in order to construct an ideal body, as, for instance, hair is frequently removed in our culture. Neither is it about a process of de-individualisation, as, for instance, is the objectification of camp prisoners when their hair is shaved. What remains is an open surface of skin describing different shapes, measures, and sizes. Raeves uses the contours of the body in order to make a sort of moving installation. But he also looks for the most 'uncommon' movements, and positions bodies in such a way that they can hardly be recognised. One perceives fragments of bodies, discovering corporeal parts that move differently from what one usually expects. The choreography is driven by distortion, depriving the organic, natural body of its functional form. A twisted shoulder thus becomes a kind of abstract sculpture. Pieces taken from legs fit together, creating a new corporeal form. The body is pulled out of its own morphology in order to be reassembled as a new sculpture. In his research around the body, Raeves also tests the limits of the human imagination. He is interested in the limits of physiognomy. Things which normally express the presence of the body are silenced in order to give voice to other parts of the body – the spine, the shoulder blade, the pelvis. Fragments of the body are investigated because of their autonomous 'imaging' quality. In the perception of these strange isolated pieces of skin, which can be folded and moved around in remarkable ways, the physiognomical image of the body remains intact. This image is even fortified by the otherwise unsuspected expressive force of the silent pieces of flesh.

In the installation entitled *I Wereld* (*One World*), Raeves takes his ideas a step further. The installation consists of four images, four 'worlds', constructed next to one another, but separated by boards so that the autonomy of each image is not disturbed. It is again up to the initiative of the spectator to change 'worlds'. I will concentrate here on the installation called *Insect*. Every possible reminiscence of bodies, bodily functions, body parts, is avoided in this image. In the previous installation one could still see fragments of bodies, which were indeed behaving strangely, but were still recognisable as a 'corps morcelé' (Lacan). Bodies without subject, bodies-in-presence, with no other quality but skin and bones. In this new work even the body is formless, removing itself totally from any fixation, it disappears beyond the limit of representation. The image of the body flows into a kind of 'liquefaction' in which every meaning disappears in an infinite avalanche. The phase of the body is left behind, the unrecognisable body, the body in its emptiness is put on display. The title 'Insect' is a weak and useless attempt to give this image a metaphorical existence and lend it some kind of representation. The combination of darkness, the reflection of paint on the body, the slow motor nerves, the position on a pedestal, are intended to convey a continuous uncertainty about substance, form, apparition. The body image disappears as a form, not in order to transform itself into another form, but in order to stop existing within the formless itself. The body behaves like a black hole absorbing all energy. It has withdrawn itself from every form of representation. This regression from the teleological world can be viewed as a sort of infinite avalanche. Here the sublime is a form of emptiness within the form. The perception of it is at once confusing and fascinating.

In the theatre works of Romeo Castellucci and his company Societas Raffaelo Sanzio, we can see the workings of other aspects of the sublime body. In his interpretation of Shakespeare's *Julius Caesar*, the director cuts every tie with the characters. Actors no longer make references to characters, they do not incarnate roles, but are purely chosen as 'regressive bodies' who speak certain lines from Shakespeare's text, *Julius Caesar*. What strikes us in the bodies which appear on the stage, in each and every aspect, is their corporeal excess. The text of Marcus Antonius is delivered by an actor without vocal chords. He delivers the famous monologue through a perforation in his throat. The role of Caesar is played by an extremely old figure whose body is laid out in a hyper-real scene. We also see an extremely obese actor in the role of Cicero. Opposed to this concrete weight, two anorexic bodies are chosen who take care of the parts of Brutus and Cassius. The suicide of Cassius becomes a nightmare, wavering between fascination and disgust. The bodily excess that is shown here does not simply achieve its force from a pure demonstration of deformed, deviant or inadequate bodily images. The painful staring at 'deformed flesh' would only inform the spectator that socially molded bodily images are dominant and compulsive in our society, and s/he would therefore only detect a negative to acceptable bodily representation. Castellucci's *Giulio Cesare* goes beyond such a representation. The production is predominantly concerned with rhetoric, a central theme in Shakespeare's piece. It is not concerned with a deconstruction of political speeches or an ultimate revelation of discourse and power. Instead, the director brings the theme of rhetoric to a point where it no longer has a linguistic function, but becomes a bodily action whereby rhetoric is literally housed inside the body. The opening images made this point very clear: the performance opened with a figure who puts a medical camera in his throat while delivering his speech so that one can see the workings of the larynx. The public screening of emptiness in which the voice is constructed, the view of an opening and closing larynx, these elements reveal the corporeal quality of rhetoric. This corporeal quality is revealed not in order to indicate an origin or source to speech, but in order to demonstrate an emptiness, the hole in the body, the hole which makes discourse and presence possible. Other bodily images have been chosen with a similar obsession, and they all have to do with rhetoric. There is the speech of Cicero who manipulates his voice by means of helium gas and the speech of Marcus Antonious, given by the figure of a man afflicted with throat cancer.

These images brought my consciousness to a halt, because they touched upon this space that we have called the 'sublime'. Following the theoretical path of this article, we can now explain this reaction. In *Giulio Cesare* we can see an almost literal application of Zizek's theory of the negative-sublime as that which escapes representation and appears as 'the pure Nothing of absolute Negativity'. (Zizek 1989: 206) The image of the talking channel causes a pure presence of nothingness, which is fortified in the speech by Antonius, the actor without vocal cords, who speaks through his trachea. The formlessness of Nothingness is what touches us so deeply, and what creates a sublime moment of anxiety; the excess of infinity. Furthermore, it can be compared to an important motif of the sublime used in the 18th century, the view of a volcano. That smoking deep hole in the earth has, for several authors from Hölderlin to de Sade, provided a means for describing the sublime affect. The hole opens an area of nothingness and operates as a dizzying force of suction. It is the fall into the crater, into this bottomless hole, which is evoked in *Giulio Cesare*'s staging of that which is usually not admitted, speaking openings.

The use of anorexic bodies is another almost literal illustration of the negative-sublime. Brutus and Cassius are reduced to the final human form, the skeleton. These skeletons are no longer physiognomical bodies nor 'flesh of the world', but only emptiness within presence itself, the 'unrepresentable within representation'. This body which is about to vanish, this anorexic shortage of corporeality, results in an excessive consciousness of presence and bodily emptiness. Faced with these sublime affects, Kant can only drown in his rational faculties. Neither do we see a liberated Body without Organs that catalyses itself in a libidinal stream of energy. It is the unavoidable presentation of the hole in presentness that causes a sinking feeling and a feeling of loss, which is a typical reaction given a confrontation with the sublime.

The sublime body, which we have witnessed above in many examples, situates itself at the juncture between presence and unrecognisability. Reason no longer comes to the rescue, it cannot give an answer to the fluidity of bodily images, because reason could not help but make a choice and establish a reduction. Instead, the sublime floats around like a paradox, provoking in us a feeling of the unknown; a sublime full/ emptiness, which can carry everything. Fascination mixes itself with anxiety,

Romeo Castellucci, *Giulio Cesare – Bruto E Cassio IIe Atto.*,
Photo: San Giovanni Silva, agenzia contrasto
(Courtesy of Societas Raffaello Sanzio)

satisfaction with pain. These are sublime moments in the experience of the spectator.

Translated by Katrien Jacobs

Bibliography

Alvaro, Egidio. *Performances*. Strasbourg: Diagonale, 1981.

Auslander, Philip. *From Acting to Performance*. London and New York: Routledge, 1997.

Bolla de, Peter. *The Discourse of the Sublime*. New York: Basil Blackwell, 1989.

Brooks, Laura Wixley. 'Damien Hurst and the Sensibility of Shock', in *Art and Design*, Nr 40: 54–77.

Butler, Judith. *Gender Trouble: Feminism and the Subversion of Identity*. New York and London: Routledge, 1990.

Butler, Judith. *Bodies that Matter: On the Discursive Limits of Sex*. London and New York: Routledge, 1993.

Crowther, Paul. 'The Postmodern Sublime: Installations and Assemblage Art', in *Art and Design*, Vol. 10, Nr 40: 9–17, 1995.

Deleuze, Gilles, Guattari, Felix. *L'anti-Oedipe*. Paris: Editions de Minuit, 1972.

De Marinis, Marco. 'Vers une pragmatique de la communication théâtrale', in *Versus* 309: 71–86, 1981.

Diamond, Elin. *Unmaking Mimesis*. London and New York: Routledge, 1997.

Durand, Regis. 'Problèmes de l'analyse structurale et sémiotique de la forme théâtrale', in Helbo, André, *Sémiologie de la Représentation*. Paris: Complexe, 1975, 112–120.

Feral, Josette. 'Performance and Theatricality: The subject demystified', in *Modern Drama* 251: 170–181, 1982.

Fischer-Lichte, Erika *et al.* (eds). *Theater seit den 60er Jahren*. Tübingen and Basel: Francke Verlag, 1998.

Gache, Rodolphe. 'On Mere Sight: A Response to Paul De Man', in Silverman *et al.* (eds). 1990, 109–115.

Goldberg, RoseLee. *Performance: Live Art since the 60s*. London: Thames and Hudson, 1998.

Grotowski, Jerzy. 'Gesprek met Grotowski', in *Nieuw Vlaams Tijdschrift* 203: 265–277, 1967.

Grotowski, Jerzy. *Towards a Poor Theatre*. London: Methuen & Co Ltd, 1969.

Hart, Lynda; Phelan, Peggy (ed.). *Acting Out: Feminist Performances*. Michigan, Ann Arbor: University of Michigan Press, 1993.

Hertz, Neil. *The End of the Line: Essays on Psychoanalysis and the Sublime*. New York: Columbia University Press, 1985.

Inga-Pin, Luciano. *Performances*. Padova: Mastrogiacomo Editore, 1978.

Jones, Amelia; Stephenson, Andrew (ed.). *Performing the Body: Performing the Text*. London and New York: Routledge, 1999.

Kant, Immanuel. *Kritik der Urteilskraft*. Frankfurt am Main: Suhrkamp, 1974 (1793).

Kirby, Michael. 'Nonsemiotic Performance', in *Modern Drama* 251: 105–111, 1982.

Kultermann, Udo. *Art-Events and Happenings*. London: Mathews Miller Dunmar Ltd, 1971.

Lehmann, Hans-Thies. 'Die Inszenierung: Probleme ihrer Analyse', in *Zeitschrift für Semiotik* 11(1989)1: 29–49.

Longinus. *On Great Writing (On the Sublime)*. New York: The Library of Liberal Arts, 1957.

Lyotard, Jean-François. 'The Unconsciousness as Mise-en-scène', in Benamou, M. and Caramello, C. (eds). *Performance in Postmodern Culture*. Center for Twentieth Century Studies, University of Wisconsin, Milwaukee, 1977.

Lyotard, Jean-François. *Leçons sur l'Analytique du Sublime*. Galilee, 1991.

Lyotard, Jean-François. *The Postmodern Condition*. Translated by Feoff Bennington and Brian Massumi. Manchester: Manchester University Press, 1984.

Man de, Paul. 'Phenomenality and Materiality in Kant', in Silverman *et al.* (eds). 1990, 87–108.

O'Dell, Kathy. *Contract with the Skin: Masochism, Performance and the 1970s*. Minneapolis and London: University of Minnesota Press, 1998.

Peirce, Charles Sanders. *Collected Papers*. Cambridge: Harvard University Press, 1931/1974.

Phelan, Peggy. *Unmarked: The Politics of Performance*. London and New York: Routledge, 1993.

Phelan, Peggy. *Morning Sex: Performing Public Memories*. London and New York: Routledge, 1997.

Pluchart, François. *L'Art Corporel*, sd, sl.

Robert, Marthe. 'I am the body's insurgent', in Rowell Margit (ed.). *Antonin Artaud. Works on Paper*. New York: Museum of Modern Art, 1996.

Ruffini, Franco. 'Anthropologie', in Helbo, André *et al.* (eds). *Théâtre. Modes d'Approche*. Bruxelles: Labor, 1987.

Silverman, Hugh J. and Aylesworth, Gary E. (ed.). *The Textual Sublime: Deconstruction and Its Differences*. New York: State University of New York Press, 1990.

States, Bert O. *Great Reckonings in Littele Rooms. On the Phenomenology of Theater*. Berckeley: University of California Press, 1985.

Thusen Von der, Joachim. *Het Verlangen naar Huivering*. Amsterdam: Querido, 1997.

Vergine, Lea. *Il Corpo Come Liguaggio*. Milano: Giampolo Prearo Editore, 1974.

Verstraete, Ginette. *Fragments of the Feminine Sublime*. New York: State University of New York Press, 1998.

Zizek, Slavoj. *The Sublime Object of Ideology*. London and New York: Verso, 1989.

Zizek, Slavoj. *Het Subject en Zijn Onbehagen*. Amsterdam: Boom, 1997.

Notes

[1] Philip Auslander (1997: 92).

[2] Blau in Auslander (1997: 91).

[3] For instance, in the work of Philip Auslander, Peggy Phelan, RoseLee Goldberg, Kathy O'Dell, Nick Kaye, Erika Fischer-Lichte, Amelia Jones and Andrew Stephenson, etc.

[4] Fischer-Lichte (1998: 14–15) bases this finding on research of the ethnologist Conquergood.

[5] This consensus is only violated by the writings of Auslander who questions the difference between the live quality of theatre and the reproductive quality of other types of communication.

[6] See Auslander (1997: 93).

[7] See Elin Diamond (1997: 84).

[8] See Lehmann (1989: 47–48).

[9] Ruffini in Helbo *et al.* (1987: 91–112).

[10] See a.o. Féral (1982), Kirby (1982).

[11] See Peirce (1978: 1304, 1324, 1337, 8329–8331).

[12] The sensory experience, the most typical quality of the theatrical experience, is also for phenomenology a reason to leave behind the semiotic project in favor of a phenomenological reading of a work of theatre. See a.o. Bert O' States (1985: 25).

[13] Judith Butler does not consider the matter of the body to be located outside language, on the contrary: 'In this sense, then, language and materiality are not opposed, for language, both is and refers to that which is material, and what is material never fully escapes from the process by which it is signified'. (Butler, 1993: 68)

[14] Judith Butler (1993: 70) here points to Kristeva who envisions a pre-symbolic order where a synthesis with the maternal takes place. Kristeva calls this pre-discursive area the 'semiotic' area or the 'chora'.

[15] See Judith Butler (1993: 47).

[16] All quotations from Kant are translated by James Creed Meredith.

[17] The volcano together with the sublime are popular themes in the 18th century. There is a strange mixture of disgust and attraction in front of the volcano which coincides with the perception of the sublime. Sade for example uses the image of the volcano as a space where all things useless, excremental, and sensual assemble (see e.g. Von der Thusen, 1997).

[18] Translation from J.H. Bernard. New York: Haffnes Press, 1951.

[19] 'an object raised to the level of the (impossible-real)Thing'. (Zizek, 1989: 203)

[20] Zizek similarly shows in his theory of the subject that there is no 'outside' to the symbolical order. Even in the most intimate fantasies, the subject is tied to a public symbolical order, because it possesses an inherent transgression, 'an obscene superego-supplement of the symbolical law'. (Zizek, 1997: 13)

Thierry Smits, *CyberChrist*, Photo: Pieter Kers

Kurt Vanhoutte

Allegories of the Fall:
Corporeality and the Technological Condition in Theatre

The Ghost in the Shell

Early in the twentieth century, theatre started to account for the emergence of modern technologies. Relatively soon certain famous theatre makers acknowledged that new information and communication technologies, and the process of industrialisation in general, had a drastic effect on traditional views of reality. The technological apparatus – consisting of film and radio but also cars, trains and aeroplanes – left a determining mark on the relationship between humanity and the environment and on a socio-political and aesthetic consciousness. Artists such as Laslov Moholy-Nagy, Oskar Schlemmer, Wsewolod Meyerhold, Sergei Eisenstein, Erwin Piscator and, later, Bertolt Brecht all tried to turn a new technological consciousness into fertile ground for the stage. By integrating a new disposition of montage, shock and interruption, they hoped that the theatre would find a way to merge with the industrial revolution. But this 'rejuvenation cure' was not only a reflection on the technological appearance of reality. It was also part of a political strategy. The bond with technology intended to sharpen the instrumental function of the theatre, transforming it into a tool which could be used to pull apart the bourgeois institution and force the entry of the masses (read 'the proletariat'). At the zenith of such a socialist utopia, a future image of the new human being emerged who would master himself, and the means of production, in accordance with a humanistic ideal.[1]

Even prior to the Marxist-oriented avant-garde, the scene of pre-WWI Futurism was inspired by technological innovations; it is known that the enthusiastic welcome of the new industrial age did not occur out of humanistic motives. Unlike the explicitly leftist artists, supporters of Marinetti considered technology to be a goal rather than a method and, in this respect, the prophetic melting of man and machine was less of a political strategy than an anarchistic provocation. 'We must introduce to the scene the reign of the machine'; such radical claims of the first theatre manifesto in 1911 were already geared towards provoking the moral majority by declaring bankrupt the existing artistic conventions. The contempt in the Futurist credo for anything established or accepted led to an affirmation of a future which would be spectacular and stunning. We can assume that this attitude, which eventually led some of its supporters into the trap of fascism, explains the fact that there is relatively less literature available about this movement than about the socially engaged avant-garde. Anyhow, the almost blind rage with which countless Futurist manifestos and reviews nurtured the myth of the post-human machine did not make it any less interesting. On the contrary, the excessive character of its techno-optimism made Futurism a most discernible movement in theatre, causing an increase in internal tensions and aberrations.

In hindsight, it is easy to envisage the loss of strength and eventual death of the historical avant-garde against an environment of changing socio-cultural conditions in the twentieth century. One could argue that the exponential evolution of a post-war culture has replaced and assimilated the avant-garde. The promotional and mediated technologies of late capitalism have rendered revolutionary formalist and ideological inspirations obsolete. An entire range of societal conditions that were decisive for the avant-garde have imploded in this phase.[2] As for the relation to technologies, the dissident quality of the machine-metaphor has declined with the growing impact of technologies on everyday life. As I will show later, the euphoria in the 1970s of media prophets such as McLuhan has largely dwindled, with the ecstatic endorsement of technologies giving way to cynicism and doubt. It is, moreover, interesting to note that such insights are not only the privilege of generations for which the avant-garde – both pre-war and the aftermath in the 1960s – is to be 'historical'. Partisans of Marinetti were themselves soon aware of the paradoxes inherent in their experiments – as if the internalised speed of the modern era caused a heightened self-awareness. Giovanni Lista shows in his study of the development of Futurist theatre that a fundamental change of consciousness emerged in the epicentre of the movement, starting from the mid-1920s. It is assumed that the dramatic works of the Futurist Ruggero Vasari, more particularly his allegorical play in three parts *L'Angoscia delle Machine* (*The Fear of the Machine*) written in 1921 and performed in 1925, were the seismograph of this internal rift.

In Futurist circles, Vasari's was the first piece to suggest a voice that struggled with a deeply rooted fear about the mechanisation of humanity, a fear that Futurism had previously sublimated forcefully with the myth of the anarchic-Nietzschean super-hero. Marinetti's ideal appears in Vasari's plot through the words of a triumvirate ruling over the empire of robots with an iron fist. The machines have programmed themselves for a time of rampant progress and victory. Thus far their ideas seem to be in accordance with the worldview propagated by orthodox Futurism. The turning point in

Vasari's scenario, however, is the moment when one of the three despots, and not coincidentally the one who invented the empire of machines, changes his mind and starts to acknowledge the vanity of the entire operation. His existential doubt becomes visible throughout Vasari's text and is an allegorical way of affirming the ideological disposition of Futurism as an unsteady oscillation between 'the mechanical spirit and the human soul'. (Lista 1989: 279) The man-machine symbiosis, which previously coincided with the fundamental premise of Futurism, breaks into two incompatible parts. In the text of the drama, the tyrant concerned gets destroyed by this schism and also drags the entire empire into annihilation. To put it in a broader context, Vasari's *magnum opus* paves the way for a generation of Futurist authors who start using stereotypical expressions to attack a triumphant disposition towards technology.[3] The main motif of their tragedies is the fall of man:

> The nostalgia of the Flesh and the Fall, the idea of a return to the Tenebrae and to the Earth as protecting and reassuring spaces, were from now on opposed to the crystalline but too cold purity of the mechanical world, to the ascending motive of the Rise. (Artioli in Lista 1989: 282)

Nevertheless, the author of *L'Angoscia delle Machine*, even in his negation of the Futurist utopia, still owed a lot to Futurism. The protagonist was still the irrational, mechanical super-hero as conceived by Marinetti and others, and his catastrophe that of a tragic hero doomed by a surplus of consciousness. Vasari takes this idea a step further in his next play *Raun*, which ended with the rejection of the destroyed machine and a return to primitive nature. According to Lista, a third play was meant to display a human being liberated from all feelings of guilt, who would be able to establish a harmonious relationship with the machine. With this reference, Lista suggests that Vasari seems to have written himself out of the Futurist avant-garde completely with this text. The text was meant to have the title 'The Antichrist' and was supposed to be a culmination in the dramatic cycle. Vasari's end piece, however, was never completed.

So why am I telling you this? Obviously because of the narrative of the Fall, as it manifests itself in theatre and technology, unfolding itself explicitly for the first time and announcing the downfall of the historical avant-garde. But, that aside, there is also a more concrete reason. More than half a century later, the figure of the anti-Christ will re-appear in the final scene of a performance which, just like its historical precedent, referred explicitly to the status of technology. The performance under discussion is entitled *CyberChrist* and was performed by the company Thor and the Belgian director Thierry Smits. For obvious reasons, Smits' performance cannot be viewed as a close match of Vasari's play. Even if we ignore the divergent time periods, there are generic differences. *CyberChrist* was a thirty-five minute solo dance independent of a text. It is thus impossible to make a comparative analysis in the strict sense of the term, but I do believe the thematic similarities between both works to be significant enough to make a link.

The starting point in *CyberChrist* at first seems to be a surprising combination of visual themes, such as the crucifixion of Christ, anatomical etchings of the Renaissance doctor André Vesalius and references to a contemporary technological state. The result of this was formulated in the programme as:

> a study of mutations of the body today. In this body, just as in the songs of Madonna, we find traces of Christianity and some transient images of Vesalius, but for the most part the muscles, the nerves and the bones revealed in this anatomical research, drift away from a humanist model of the Renaissance. The body shown here contains, helter-skelter, technology and nature, sex and the sacred, tradition and innovation, without a preferential order.[4]

CyberChrist announces itself explicitly as an allegory of the human condition, situated on the crossroads between transcendence and technology. And it is even more significant that the allegories of technology point to the myth of the Fall. It is the Fall in technologies which allows me to see a connection between *CyberChrist* and *L'Angoscia delle Machina*.

The respective titles reflect the changing historical conditions, which I have alluded to before. The transition from the era of the machine to cybertechnology has caused a change in our (self)perception, which has had consequences for everyday life as well as the field of art. Without anticipating an analysis of the actual performance, I want to state here that *CyberChrist* did not contain direct references to contemporary technologies. The historical avant-garde body was utterly semiotic in that its setting and language of movement contained clear references to the machine. This would be in sharp contrast with the minimalist style of *CyberChrist*, in which a half-naked body dances in light diffused around a big black stone. The stone is the only object in the set-design, and it makes the audience think of a tombstone or a dissection table. It forms a semantic anchor for a bodily language, which depicts the human body's surrender to science and technology by incarnating historical and contemporary icons. The muscular and utterly flexible body of the dancer is a medium for a continuous merging of religious and profane bodily poses, from popular to elevated ones, from Vesalius to the crucifixion of Francis Bacon, from Robert Mapplethorpe to contemporary video-clip-icons such as Madonna. In other words, science and technology seem to go underground in order to become an integrated image-reservoir for a corporeal language that includes references to contemporary television culture. Within this kaleidoscopic plurality of corporeal images, the anatomy of the individual takes centre stage. The image of the Fall in Smits' performance becomes the disintegration of the human body. More than human agony in front of the machine, the human robot's neurosis (Vasari's *L'Angoscia*), *CyberChrist* represents the decline of human physicality as such. The somewhat surprising absence of multimedia projections makes this performance, in my view, more unique and intriguing.

Even though *CyberChrist* is characterised by appearing sober when compared to other productions, the view on the theme of technology nonetheless carries some degree of similarity. It is striking that significant productions of this kind often construct a metaphysical frame that alludes to the diabolical and the Fall of man. The story of Faust, the scientist who fell from grace because he sold his soul to the devil, has for several years been a source text for pioneering multimedia performances. The Faust-motif was one of the central discourses in *House/Lights*, a production that the Wooster Group brought to Belgium in 1998. In the same year, The Builders Association introduced *JumpCut (Faust)*, a staging which lingered between a digital film and a play, between Murnau's *Faust* and a staged actualisation of this text. In the Dutch-speaking arena, Guy Cassiers and Het Zuidelijk Toneel changed the tack of multimedia performance with their Goethe-based *Faust*. On a smaller scale, but also worth mentioning, is *Kaufhaus-Inferno*, an experimental theatre project which simulated Vergilius's descent into hell as a computerised exploration of a consumerist society and its technological media. With these examples in mind, we can ask ourselves why the theatre seems to be such an adequate scene for the narrative of the Fall, especially when it comes to staging the state of technology. More particularly, the question arises whether there has been an essential shift in emphasis since Vasari's (planned) version. Is it meaningful that the anti-Christ appears within an actual performance, whereas Vasari in his time did not (yet) manage to put this character on stage? In an attempt to answer this question, I would like to throw some light on the conceptual links between the Fall, the medium of theatre, and the notion of technology. After outlining this triadic connection, I will try to show how it is articulated in *CyberChrist*.

However, the reader of this article should not expect a semiotic-axiomatic analysis of this performance. I do not intend to explain the art form in its times, but the times within the art form. The general starting point in my work, the relationship between theatre and technology, presupposes a perspective that removes the absolute boundaries between disciplines. The aim is to expand on this premise with a study of the artwork, to see how it manifests an integral construction of socio-political tendencies at the end of this century. In this view, the term 'technology' denotes the late capitalist dynamic of our culture. The contents of technology are not technology itself, as Heidegger already wrote in 1954.[5] My essay shows similarly that the machine is a concept in which speculations about the technological condition are crystallised. In this essay, diverse ideas about the technological condition are constructed through the magnifying glass of the arts. The theory presents itself as a constellation of texts, old and new, each of which are read in the reflection of the other. They are positioned in such a way as to deliver relevant insights about the disposition of the Fall.

Allegories of (Post)-Modernity: Walter Benjamin

The conceptual scheme of the Fall can be found in the writings of Walter Benjamin on the allegory as work of art. It is known that the German philosopher/cultural theorist was a key figure in the debate about the historical avant-garde. In his time he made clear statements about the non-committal 'art for art's sake' credo with a view to the social aspects of art. Benjamin's affinity with the project of the avant-garde functioned undoubtedly as an important motivation for his study of allegory. Consequently, whereas allegory had brought to light the ideological crisis of the avant-garde, one can read it today as a blueprint of a historical conflict of paradigms. But more than that, Benjamin's theological reflections and meditations about the transcendental permeate his cultural and political thoughts and anchor themselves in the figure of the allegory. I want to use these reflections to find a way into my argument. For clarification, the allegory is a rhetorical form that enables me to articulate more clearly the inter-relationship between the Fall, theatre and technology. My aim is to elucidate previously mentioned tropes within the allegorical.

Even though allegory is a central element of Benjamin's thought, he did not present a systematic theory. Ideas on this subject are spread throughout his texts and show up in curious places, only to disappear from sight as quickly as they appear. *Ursprung des deutschen Trauerspiels*

(*The Origin of German Tragic Drama*), a document which Benjamin intended as his dissertation, is the most significant and richest source of all these fragments – at least as far as my purposes are concerned.[6] In this study, Benjamin tries to think historically about theatre using allegory, more particularly about German Baroque tragic drama. He pushes aside the prevalent ideas about the tragic that had been the norm since Friedrich Nietzsche's *Geburt der Tragödie* (*Birth of Tragedy*). It is known that Nietzsche saw in the mythical, timeless essence of Greek tragedy a perpetual reconciliation between a protagonist who is always guilty and the cosmic order. Thus tragedy always integrates the theme of guilt and debt on a metaphysical plane. According to Benjamin, Baroque tragedy lacks this transcendence in the first instance. Whereas tragedy ends up in catharsis and the eventual absolution of earthly misery, 'the German tragedy is taken up entirely with the hopelessness of the earthly condition'. (Benjamin 1974: 260, tr. 81) Earthly suffering is absolutely distinct from salvation. With this viewpoint, the mindset of Baroque theatre is less driven by myth, the close connection between the earthly and the supernatural, than by history as it is actually experienced by people in their time.

In many ways, Benjamin saw the spirit of the Baroque age torn apart. Politically speaking, the tensions between the upper class and the rest could no longer be resolved other than with violence. Furthermore, natural catastrophes and wars had extended the gap between disconsolate earthly existence and eternal life, so that the promise of salvation had become unbelievable. The fading of a transcendental horizon forced people to fall back onto bare existence, so that a consciousness of transience (*Memento mori*) and insignificance (*Vanitas vanitatum*) became prevalent. In this vein, Benjamin believed that the Baroque allegory translated the sensibility of an epoch that experienced the history of the world as a process of degeneration and disintegration. The pressure of historical experience, more than a desire for sublimation, existed in the author of tragedy:

> This is the heart of the allegorical way of seeing, of the Baroque,
> secular explanation of history as Passion of the world; its importance
> resides solely in the stations of its decline. The greater the signifi-
> cance, the greater the subjection to death, because death digs most
> deeply the jagged line of demarcation between physical nature and
> significance. (334, tr. 166)

In other words, allegorical art intensified an emerging secularisation of a traditional worldview. In Benjamin's view, it announced a vision of the world as God-forsaken and a senseless universe which humanity had to fill with meaning from its own individual initiative. For these reasons, he

describes Baroque tragedy as 'the new drama' which distinguishes itself
through 'the rejection of the eschatology of religious drama', as a theatre
where the modern individual comes face to face with his own image for the
first time. (Benjamin 1974: 260, tr. 81)

One could wrongly conclude from this that Benjamin's concept of
allegory is tied to a historical-linear narrative. The secularising tendencies of
the Baroque mindset did not oppose dominant metaphysical ideas, as they
were in themselves the result of opposing force fields. In his first thesis,
Über den Begriff der Geschichte (*Theses on the Philosophy of History*),
Benjamin talks about an automatic chess player, shaped like a puppet wearing
a Turkish costume and with a waterpipe in its mouth, destined to beat his
opponent in every game. This puppet, according to Benjamin, is historical
materialism: 'It can easily be a match for anyone if it enlists the services of
theology, which today, as we know, is wizened and has to keep out of sight'.
(Benjamin 1974: 693, tr. 245) A similar belief in the power of theology as a
hidden catalyst already permeates his tragic drama-book, where metaphysics develops into a narrative frame for the allegorical. In addition to the
passage quoted above from the tragic drama-book, the author views the intru-
sion of time into the allegorical work of art as a 'cipher' for the Fall of man:

> But if nature has always been subject to the power of death, it is also
> true that it has always been allegorical. Significance and death both
> come to fruition in historical development, just as they are closely
> linked as seeds in the creature's graceless state of sin. (343, tr. 166)

The interplay between the profane and the transcendental in the Baroque
mimics the flexible diaphragm of the researcher. The writings of Benjamin
are not intended to construct a frame of reference that can fully resolve
oppositions. Irving Wohlfarth has pointed out that a (strategic) deviation
from a closed narrative is a recurring motif in his entire *oeuvre*. Within this
logic of extremes, the tension between conceptual poles is important, not
the choice of one above the other (Wohlfarth 1985). I will show that this
certainly holds for the Fall, an image of the author's concept in which the
extremes (transcendence/paradise versus history/fall) constantly collide
into each other. It is this fundamental ambivalence which provides the link
between a theory of the Baroque and contemporary theories. In order to
clarify this point, we have to return to Benjamin's tragic drama-book and
the dialectical opposition established between allegory and symbol.

Benjamin sees the cause for the disdain of allegory in art history
in the idealised theological concept of symbol. He believes that symbolical art subjugates the material object to a spiritual enlightenment that

illuminates it from the inside. Because it embodies the transcendental order in which it participates, it suggests the appeasing unity of the sensory and supernatural, earthly and godly, the factual work of art and its spiritual meaning. This totalitarian thinking is so ingrained in the symbolical work of art that we can no longer even speak of a form of representation. According to the nature of the word, representation presupposes a certain split between signifier (representation) and signified (represented). This is not the case for the symbolic, which according to Benjamin claims to *be* presence rather than represent it. The appeal to the immediate rather than the mediated, to presence rather than representation, turns this symbol into a closed category of art. The geometrical symbol of the sign exchange is a circle, as it were, because a transcendental frame of interpretation is always already embedded in the process of constituting meaning. Thus on the level of perception, the symbolical urges for a moment of revelation, 'the mystical instant' (342, tr. 165), when the viewer opens up a process of signification in the artwork where this move had been anticipated. The empirical and the transcendental fuse into a meaningful, harmonious moment when the artwork also reveals the sensible coherence of the cosmic order.

I already pointed out that the writer of tragic drama opposes the view that 'the beautiful is supposed to merge with the divine in an unbroken whole' (337, tr. 160) as this view was thwarted by a desolate reality no longer clarified or illuminated by transcendence. If symbolical art kept the earthly and heavenly united, this unity fell apart in the individual's experience of the world. The Baroque individual is no longer empowered to read an immanent meaning from the book of life. He falls prone to melancholy and loses himself contemplating incoherent fragments of meaning. The Fall of the melancholic could be endless but for the fact that he can slow down depression by temporarily being elevated by the new and unexpected. Benjamin indicates this almost fatal craving for the new, when the melancholic gaze becomes allegorical, as a decisive turning point: 'for the only pleasure the melancholic permits himself, and it is a powerful one, is allegory'. (361, tr. 185) At that moment destruction becomes creation. Faced with a meaningless world, the melancholic has no other choice but to project subjective meaning onto a world which has lost objectivity. In a gesture of randomness, the allegorist will whisper meaning into a dumbfounded world that will listen to his individual logic. The world disintegrates into a plurality of viewpoints, which initiate the essentially Baroque stream of images.[7]

Symbol and allegory are both amendments to natural history in the end. While symbol idealises and is founded on an illusion of totality, allegory is witness to the naivety of this enterprise. The romantic narrative of an organic totality is shattered, the fragments fixated in *nature morte*: 'In the field of allegorical intuition the image is a fragment, a rune. Its beauty as a symbol evaporates when the light of divine learning falls upon it'. (352, tr. 176) Unlike the symbol, the allegorical perception does not make an effort (nor does it have the power) to hide the gaps between sign and signification but, according to Benjamin, sinks 'into the depths which separate visual being from meaning'. (342, tr. 165) As soon as the text breaks free from the normative codex of theological vision, it is exposed to the allegorist's manipulation, in whose power 'any person, any object, any relationship can mean absolutely anything else'. (350, tr. 175) Allegorising is most of all a cerebral activity, which corrects the absence of direct, accessible knowledge (symbol) through a second, intellectual meaning which is dependent on the object of perception. The allegory literally speaks about something else (in Greek: *allos* + *agoreuein*). Polysemy is its primary intention.

Following the above characterisation, it is no surprise that postmodern thought is equally enchanted by allegory. Already in the 1970s, Fredric Jameson signals the upsurge of this topos as 'a pathology with which in the modern world we are only too familiar'. (Jameson 1971: 72) The growing interest in allegory is, in this case, a symptom of an epistemological crisis that has become known now as the 'death of great narratives'. Even though Jameson's perception of the allegorical is initially melancholic and pessimistic,[8] he will later present post-modern affinities in a much more positive light. In his influential study, *Postmodernism or the Cultural Logic of Late Capitalism*, the author believes that the upsurge of allegory is due to:

> a generalized sensitivity, in our own time, to breaks and continuities, to the heterogeneous (not merely in works of art), to Difference rather than Identity, to gaps and holes rather than seamless webs and triumphant narrative progression, to social differentiation rather than to Society as such and its 'totality', in which older doctrines of the monumental work and the 'concrete universal' bathed and reflected themselves. The allegorical, then (...) can be minimally formulated as the question posed to thinking by the awareness of incommensurable distances within its object of thought, and as the various new interpretive answers devised to encompass phenomena about which we are at least minimally agreed that no single thought or theory encompasses all of them. (Jameson 1996: 167–168)

Jameson shows adequately how allegory today is used to articulate the supposed fracture in (theories of) history. The post-modern scenario seems to suggest nothing less than a paradigmatic murder of the father. The question, however, is whether such post-modern reading does not run the risk of reducing the ambiguity that resides in Benjamin's interpretation.

There is, of course, no doubt that the Benjaminian allegory is intended to carry out a reconstruction of myth and the appearance of myth in symbol. In this process of allegorising, the version of natural history that presents history as a natural given remains unmasked. Upon careful consideration, it is exactly this historical-materialist argument which forms the stepping stone between Benjamin and the neo-Marxist wing of post-modernism. But despite this important connection, we have to be aware of the dangers of a post-modern recuperation. In order to escape recuperation, we have to keep in mind the Janus face of allegory. In any demystification of 'natural history', allegory is still tied to a remarkable belief in truth as a hidden metaphysical principle. Benjamin's critique of ideology cannot be isolated from the position that a certain configuration of nature and history can actually illuminate the essence of the world. Benjamin remarks in his tragic drama-book that allegory is 'ontological rather than psychological' (359, tr. 184), due to the fact that it keeps a hidden connection with the symbol. In order to understand the complex relation between allegory and that which it opposes, it is necessary to look into Benjamin's theory of language. Of this I can only give a brief summary.[9]

Allegory resembles language after the Fall of man. Harmony existed in the order of 'the paradisiacal language of the Name' (Benjamin 1977: 155), which established the identity of things in nature with words coming out of God's mouth. But in a gesture similar to plucking fruit from the tree of knowledge, man leaves harmony behind. Conscious of notions of Good and Evil, he develops an abstract intellect according to which the world can be divided into self-made categories. Language from now on expresses something other than a divine essence in language itself, which is the Fall of man. The allegorical will now emphasise the fracture between language and nature by overtly affirming the role of randomness and subjectivity in the construction of meaning. The allegorist himself starts to embody the role of God by suggesting meanings where God has omitted to do so. The inflation of signification which results from allegorical activity leads to 'drivel', 'nonsense' and 'language confusion', in short, to the mythical 'design of the tower of Babel' (Ibid. 154), where subjects display their vanity. Allegory is aware of this burden of guilt. Whereas symbol expresses the idyllic story of a state of paradise, allegory's preference for death and decay reveals the mourning of nature. But it is exactly this melancholy, the main register of the allegorical, which emphasises painfully and clearly what is lacking. Even the sign-dynamic of allegorising, which posits a random relation between sign and thing, reconstructs in this way a subjective and momentary identity of language versus objects. From this perspective, history falls apart into randomly cited histories that, just like the monad structure, always possess a meta-narrative. Benjamin made it very clear in his theory of translation that we can catch a glimpse of a lost Eden, because a Babylonian plurality of languages enables the return to 'pure language'. (Benjamin 1972: 13, tr. 74) In transposing signs from one language to another, a space emerges which closes as soon as it opens up, but which momentarily reveals the 'adamic' origins of all languages. According to Benjamin, the perfect language is the one that has knowledge of that hidden essence.

In the theology of this philosopher of culture, a lost paradise reflects itself in a messianic redemption at the end of times. Allegory is art born on the edge between paradise and the historical world. This art is the bastard child of transcendence and historicising, and writes the story of decay that can be read in many different ways, as a narrative of a lost unity or one of future redemption.

Tekhne

In view of what we have seen before, it is a short way from the 'language of overnaming'[10] and the allegorical 'eruption of images'[11] to 'mechanical reproduction'.[12] To what extent does Benjamin's vision of technology offer a constructive perspective on the world today? In order to answer this question, we have to consult with the texts about industrial modernity, in which the writer shows a strong interest in the age of the machine. The undeniable protagonist in these articles is Charles Baudelaire, the French poet whom Benjamin considered to be the only real inheritor of Baroque allegory. The work of the *poète maudit* is the map that the philosopher used to trace a change in perception and experience at the end of the nineteenth century. The technological inventions of that time mark intersections on this map between aspiring humanity and the changing environment. In other words, the machine is, for Benjamin, a concrete image onto which a capitalist dynamic anchors itself. Baudelaire's sense of perception turns this image into an allegorical constellation.

The allegorising of modern capitalism is closely tied to the experience of shock, which results from the confrontation of humanity and technology. In *Über Einige Motive bei Baudelaire* (*On some Motifs in Baudelaire*) Benjamin suggests that the machine gives a concrete answer to the needs of the modern bourgeois individual. In so far as technological media perfect human aspirations, they grow into extensions of the body in its conquest of the environment.[13] At the same time, the technological product exerts a regressive influence on its user. Even though a simple gesture is sufficient to start most machines, this 'abrupt movement of the hand' (Benjamin 1974: 630, tr. 171) results in an almost unnoticeable but intensive shock for the user. With this perspective in mind, Benjamin makes a rough outline of technology, which starts with the invention of the match in the mid-nineteenth century and ends with modern inventions such as the telephone, the printing press, the factory machine, photography and, last but not least, film. The combination of all these actualisations delivers allegorical images of modern city life as 'a reservoir of electric energy'. (Ibid.) The inhabitants of this forcefield are compelled to adapt to the effects of their inventions. According to Benjamin, who appeals to Freudian traumatology for his findings, a total re-organisation of human sense-perceptions is involved. The machine penetrates the human mental landscape and lays the foundations for a new sensory perception and 'thus technology has subjected the human sensorium to a complex kind of training'. (Ibid.)

The outcome of this practical exercise is apparently as unpredictable and uncertain in the technological universe as the human reflex itself. In *Über Einige Motive bei Baudelaire*, Benjamin evokes Karl Marx to complain about the alienating aspects of technology: 'All machine work (…) requires early drilling of the worker'. (Marx in Ibid. 631, tr. 172) The Marxist concept of *tekhnè* is then fortified with his reading of Freud, which posits that the nervous system, through its resistance to shock, excludes the quality of experience. Benjamin concludes that technology numbs the sense-perception – the immune system saves us from trauma – and anaesthetises us before new experiences. On the other side of Marxism, Benjamin calls on Baudelaire as a sensitive and receptive poet who takes the other position. Overall, Baudelaire manages to conjure up the chaos of modern city life by making it aesthetically productive. The French writer could thus be called a 'traumatophile type', for whom the quality of experience rules over self-protection: 'Baudelaire made it his business to parry the shocks, no matter where they might come from, with his spiritual and his physical self'. (616, tr. 160) It is Baudelaire's contribution to the stalemate of technology to have 'placed the shock experience at the very centre of his artistic work'. (Ibid., tr. 159)

In the essay of the same time, *Das Kunstwerk im Zeitalter seiner Reproduzierbarkeit* (*The Work of Art in the Age of Mechanical Reproduction*), Benjamin extrapolates the case study of Baudelaire to the status of art.

It seems at first that he places emphasis on what is lost in the age of technology: the craftsmanship, the cult status, the bond with nature, the ritualistic dimension of the work of art in general, and theatre in particular, or 'the auratic being of the work of art'. (Benjamin 1974: 441) But despite this impression, the text can hardly be viewed as an elegy written on the grave of the auratic experience. It is significant that Benjamin again evokes Freudian psycho-analysis to clarify the working of technology on the human psyche. Only this time the comparison does not result in a poverty of experience, but in a richness in which perception does not numb but rather sharpens the human being. For Benjamin, film is typical in this respect – as if it were a technology with an allegorical shape – as a deepening of a sensibility that opens the eyes to the 'unconscious optics'.[14] The cinematographic medium just enables a new and unexpected experience to be felt. The author also compares the camera here to a surgical instrument that penetrates the unseen depths of the object. Benjamin's self-pronounced admiration for the 'cautiousness with which his hand moves among the organs' (458) illustrates for that matter how the author occasionally evaluates the machine through the lens of technology.

But despite this fresh astonishment, the writer keeps in mind the risk of anaesthesia on the patient. Far from falling into technological determinism, his famous last closing paragraph warns of the socio-political dangers which potentially bubble up from a 'therapeutic explosion of the unconscious' (462) within the dreamlike state of technology:

> '*Fiat ars – pereat mundus*,' says Fascism, and, as Marinetti admits, expects war to supply the artistic gratification of a sense perception that has been changed by technology. This is evidently the consummation of '*l'art pour l'art*.' Mankind, which in Homer's time was an object of contemplation for the Olympian gods, now is one for itself. Its self-alienation has reached such a degree that it can experience its own destruction as an aesthetic pleasure of the first order. This is the situation of politics that Fascism is rendering aesthetic. Communism responds by politicizing the art. (508, tr. 235, italics in original)

The 'dreamt-of metallisation of the human body' (Marinetti in Benjamin 1974: 468, tr. 234) of a movement such as Futurism ends up in a delirium of devastation and destruction. In light of Benjamin's reprimand, it is even more remarkable that Benjamin in *Das Kunstwerk im Zeitalter seiner Reproduzierbarkeit* sides with technology on the brink of a new war, or rather the fusion of art and technology. Strengthened by his admiration for Bertolt Brecht (who inspired Benjamin in writing this essay) and the Russian cinematography of, among others, Eisenstein (not long before Benjamin had returned from Russia), he remains loyal to the belief of the historical avant-garde in the emancipatory potential of this fusion. He seems to position himself as it were between the Fall narrative of the dissident futurist Vasari and the utopian Enlightenment ideas with which a lot of (theatre) artists were familiar.[15]

However, with this ambiguous statement I did not elucidate sufficiently Benjamin's attitude towards technology, and less so how this attitude can be fruitful for the contemporary configuration of art and technology. It is true that Walter Benjamin manifests himself within opposing positions and ideas that influence each other. His writings describe the enchantment and disenchantment of the world through technology as two sides of the same event. In Benjamin's bizarre theory of aura, the imaginary and scientific melt into a new quality. Susan Buck-Morss in her book, *The Dialectics of Seeing*, asks herself the question, 'Is This Philosophy?' More specifically, she brings under discussion the methodological premises of the German philosopher of culture, which consists of a mixture of Kabbalism (a mystical wing of Judaism), historical materialism, and anarchism. As a key figure of modern thought, Benjamin resides on the edge, between the conflicting positions of his contemporaries and his friends Scholem, Brecht and Adorno. In one sense, one could say that his writings do not emanate from the heart of modernity but from the area around it. As much as Benjamin's thought is apt to trace the crisis of modernity, this crisis has grown into the heart of his thinking. The life-work of the philosopher of culture consists of compiling streams of concrete images, which each time contain a deadlock of the experience of his time. 'Allegories are in the realm of thoughts what ruins are in the realm of things' (354, tr. 178): the famous dictum of the tragic drama-book can thus be applied to the person who wrote it down. Ever since the modern era started to crumble underneath its own weight, Benjamin opted resolutely for the fragment. Just like the admired Baudelaire, he looked into the eye of the storm, not in a hesitant manner, but with the conviction that 'where there is danger, there is also salvation' (Hölderlin).

An indication from Irving Wohlfarth suggests that Benjamin's *tekhne* is drenched in the radical speculative side of his philosophy. This expert on Benjamin points to the fact that a second version of *Das Kunstwerk* makes a subtle but important distinction between first and second technology. Technology engages the human being on a first level, whereas it tries to do this as little as possible in second technology. In the metaphorical words of Benjamin, 'the main technological achievement of the first technology is in a way the human sacrifice, that of the second is in line with remote controlled aeroplanes, which have no further need of a flying crew'. (Benjamin in Wohlfarth 1998: 195)[16] There is little doubt that Benjamin has high hopes for second technology. In the second order the machine secretly possesses a fire of redemption, which scorches the human being in war in the first order. The difference in emphasis falls on the instrumental-isation of the human being by the environment. Whereas traditional tech-nology is meant to conquer nature, the utopian version 'rather entails a combined action of nature and humanity'. (Ibid.) Is it an exaggeration to say that this technology paves the way to paradise? Wohlfarth seems to think in that direction, when he reads the quotations from *Das Kunstwerk* as an extension of *Zum Planetarium* (*To the Planetarium*), the piece of prose that ends Benjamin's *Einbahnstrasse* (*One Way Street*). This obscure, but utterly rich fragment pushes technology forward as the condition of a mythical, quasi pre-modern unity with an original nature:

> In technology a physis is being organised whereby contact with the Cosmos takes on new and different forms from those it had within the nation and the family. (1972: 147)

'New and different', that is of course on a higher plane than the one envis-aged by first technology. It is only possible to save the state of paradise within technology, when its destructive potential is detached from the instrumentalist inclination of bourgeois capitalism, the artistic extension of which is fascist imperialism and Futurist art. However, I believe that one could wrongly conclude that Benjamin wants to channel the destructive force of technology by installing the machine in a neutral and pacifying position. Second technology would then push itself away from first tech-nology in a pacifist gesture. Although this is part of the story, the goals of Benjamin are equally situated on a different plane. The inclination towards a purely non-destructive use of the machine would entail an instrumental-isation that places technology between humanity and nature. And it is exactly this split between object and subject which is, for Benjamin, a Fall of man. A Marxist recovery of the machine would thus be located on the level of first technology, and would inevitably reiterate the Fall of man. Second tech-nology is metaphysical in the sense that it is put on a higher plane than the physical, *before* the so-called victory over nature and *before* the subject-ivising of objectivity. In other words, second technology is the state of the art before humanity's exit from paradise.

Technology is for Benjamin a centrifugal force in a field that holds a remarkable balance between paradise and the Fall. In this messianic dynamic, doubt and hope regarding new technological modalities are continuously interwoven without solidifying into one uniform position. Therefore, a consciousness of destruction and decay for Benjamin can be a source of creativity and hope. This is applied to the allegorist and his creation, to the allegory as well as to the figure of technology as it manifests itself to humanity as a medium for enchanting and disenchanting the world. This paradox cannot easily be reduced – I cannot emphasise this too many times – to a materialistic utopia of a socially correct application of technology, but it has something of an almost magical conjuration of forces which unfold themselves within the machine. This is the point where Marxism and theology melt together in order to provide new material. Benjamin does not so much want to *circumvent* the machine and destruction in order to reach utopia, but wants to reach for salvation by *going through* the machine and destruction.[17]

Aporia

Walter Benjamin's pattern of thought opens up to a 'dialectics of arrestation', which follows the law of ambiguity and does so without a synthesis of opposites. The extreme opposites collide into one another without causing the emergence of an encompassing third category. Nevertheless, one could argue, the dynamic cannot be neutral as long as activities go in a certain direction. Even if we can state that the paradox generates time, because it makes thoughts travel back and forth endlessly, the question is in what direction does the arrow of time point? One could state that Benjamin – who also happens to be a fan of Proust – uses a compass containing past measures to look for traces in the present world. The mythical pre-history of modernity, paradise, is indeed at the same time the spark and conductor of a dialectical curve of current outlined above. In this way the area in which his concept *tekhne* operates is paradise, which posits that technology could be a utopian resurgence of nature. It is finally a known fact that Benjamin's texts, whether they deal with topics of art or history, can be read as a philosophy of history that aims to rescue an experiential factor from the past towards the present. For the same reason, the mode of working of the paradox for Benjamin is history. And one could thus wrongly conclude that his thoughts are nostalgic or regressive. But the driving force is not so much the desire for a golden century, but the agony of the modern experience itself. Benjamin's fragmented work does not want to reconstruct the ruins from the past in order to live there, but wants to detect the skeleton of a new kind of living. However, the architectural plan is missing, and this fact is compensated for by the (Judaic) predicament from *Über den Begriff der*

Geschichte that 'every second of time was the strait gate through which the Messiah might enter'. (1974: 704, tr. 255)

Whoever makes use of Benjamin's ideas needs to know that this author is inclined to think beyond the boundaries of rationality. But he may also be assured that the way will not lead to the darkness of irrationalism, the path will neither be marked by the signs of 'Anything Goes' which are more typical of a certain type of post-modernism. Benjamin's movement of thinking opens a gap in the act of thinking. Following Jacques Derrida, it is perhaps possible to call this opening the 'desert within the desert'. In *La Religion*,[18] Jacques Derrida poses the question of how we can speak today in a justified manner about religion and, more specifically, about the widely anticipated return of religions. Even if this question invites first of all an argument about God and religion, this text is equally interesting to sketch the actuality of Benjamin's reflection for contemporary technologies. One might think that the state of technology has changed a lot since Benjamin's time, that his reflections are due for a fundamental revision. The first part of that statement is correct. Even if the technological images of film used to exist in the margins of society, today we live in a mediated society in which moving images infiltrate all units and technological pros-theses are the backbone of our culture. The quantitative distribution of the image cannot be dissociated from its new quality, grounded in digital tech-nologies whose seriality and endless potential of combinations creates new paradigms. Contemporary discourses about technology have replaced repro-duction, the image which refers to an original, by simulacrum, the spectre without origin except technology itself. In view of the expansive reign of technology, the concept of simulation has replaced that of reproduction to capture today's mimetic processes, and this also in the cultural sphere. But despite this change, Benjamin's *tekhne* concept and by extension his concept of allegory are, for me, important 'habits of thought' which could take a legitimate place in post-modern discourses. I hope therefore to interest the reader in an analysis of Derrida's text which will end this section and makes a bridge to the performance analysis of the next section, where a theoretical amalgam of technology and transcendence get a unique theatrical extension.

Derrida's experimental thoughts look for an impulse beyond the strict binary opposition between Religion and Reason, belief and knowledge. This duality is, according to the philosopher, a heritage from a dominant stream within Enlightenment thinking, and is thus part of the problem. It blurs what can no longer be denied in today's technological globalisation of capital, that science and religion develop from one and the same source.

It is a characteristic of this communal source that it splits in two streams which place themselves in opposition to one another. Based on this apparent dichotomy, the philosopher pronounces his main thesis. This is that religion and what he calls 'techno-science' (contemporary knowledge as a performative gesture) relate to each other as 'reactive antagonism and a reaffirming offer' (10). In a perverse sort of way, religion today props up, carries and presupposes technological knowledge. Or the other way around, religion can find no place outside the development of critical reason, which today is equipped with the qualities of the machine (efficiency, production, practical intervention, etc.). Moreover, the stage of religion is a techno-stage without which it cannot exist. Belief and knowledge are conditions of each other, the holy and mechanical are apparitions of the same condition. Derrida wants to make this paradox apparent, by thinking about it within Kant's 'boundaries of pure reason'.

The essence of this double movement, the point where the two streams flow into one another to be joined forever, obeys, according to the author, the 'terrible but fatal logic of *the auto-immunity of the unharmed*' (66). This means that religion and techno-science, critique and belief, start a relationship to which both partners react in full force. Like Siamese twins they generate poison for the other, but they also supply each other with the necessary antidote. They protect each other in their global orientation, but at the same time they ban what protects them. This strange liaison leads to a deadly spiral in which the violence 'of a hyper sophistication of the military tele-technology of the "digital" and cyber-spatial culture' on the one hand, and the revenge of the 'new archaic violence' (e.g. religious fanaticism) of the phantasmic pre-modern body on the other hand, relieve each other (80). The same movement, which stems from the double origin of religion and machine, repeats each time the machine-reflex 'of abstraction and attraction which *alienates and unites* (…), that what simultaneously dis-possesses and re-possesses, uproots and makes roots, *what brings a halt to re-possession* (…)' (63).

The contemporary hegemony of religion and science within and by means of technology is, according to Derrida, strongly contained, indissoluble and without alternative. The philosopher thus makes a plea for an attitude of deferral which structures the problem without erecting a utopian horizon (this would reiterate the reason/religion opposition). The only space which Derrida's thinking can create is 'aporia' (space of indeterminacy), the abstract space and '*place itself (…) of an endless resistance*' (29), which does not have anything to do with the oppositions mentioned above. Such a topos is the 'desert within the desert'. Derrida's description of this 'extreme abstraction' could also be used to denote Benjamin's line of thinking: *The Messianic, or the Messianity without Messianism.* (Ibid.) It thus concerns a possibility which precedes every dialectic and which positions itself *before* the intervention of the social and political, *before* the emergence of community, even *before the opposition between the sacred (holy) and the profane* (28). This place of impossibility enables us to wait without anticipation, to hope without programme or factual expectation. Because it exists in the indeterminate wavering between happening and potential virtuality, 'between the order of "revelation" and that of "potential for revelation" '(34), this waiting entails a big risk. By becoming vulnerable to absolute surprises, the Messianic has no certainty, except for the abstract idea that it has to take into account *'the good and evil, one never without the possibility of the other'* (30). The essential indeterminacy of the Messianic on the flipside of every imaginable position creates in Derrida's thought a kind of joint-thinking of religion and techno-science. This creation is just like Benjamin's thought characterised by paradox, which precludes a dialectical *alter*native (another route) but sees salvation in overstraining the actual dialectic:

> In this sense, technology offers the potential for a new chance for religion. This chance has to include the highest risk, even the threatening of *radical evil*. Otherwise it would be a potential of program and evidence, rather than belief, and that means the annihilation of the future. Instead of positioning them against each other, as is usually the case, we need a joint-thinking as one and the same possibility: the mechanical and belief (71).

It does not take a long discourse to make the link between Derrida's interpretation of technology and Benjamin's speculations around the industrial revolution. I would call the central point in this web of connections the homeopathy of evil. In this line of thought, there is no alternative, no resistance imaginable, except in the idea of negativity which holds a potential for the future. According to this logic, one approaches a positive regularity through the formulation of its impossibility, the same way thinking an absent horizon may cause a flicker on the condition of the horizon. The no man's land between first and second technology, the double enchantment and disenchantment, the crisis of modernity – these are all descriptions of incommensurability which cause reflection today. So we will leave behind the trail of strict oppositions (nature/technology; original/reproduction; good/evil) in order to explore the paradox. Here we take, with Benjamin in *Über den Begriff der Geschichte*, the absolute risk of 'a tiger's leap into the past'. (701, tr. 253)

Anatomy of Myth

La grâce du tombeur (*The Grace of Falling*) the first choreography of Thierry Smits, was produced in 1990.[19] After a nine-month period of contemplation about the movement of falling, the young dancer obviously came to the story of Icarus, the mythical figure whose *hybris* takes him too close to the sun and causes him to crash to earth with burned wings. The fate of the winged human being who is the symbol *par excellence* of earthly aspiration and limitation, was developed in three stages. The first part of the performance takes place around a labyrinth and expresses a boundedness to earthly limits. In the second movement, Icarus appeals to the souls of birds in order to prepare his flight from the human condition, which will eventually bring him to his fall in the last part. *La grâce du tombeur*, however, is not a story of defeat. The tragedy of chaos found its counterpart in a glorification of human self-exaltation. This conviction was translated into movements resembling dervishes, whose rotating, spiralling dance with mystical overtones erased the differences between falling and rising. The fall of the body is also its elevation, that is its grace. Smits himself performed this solo dance.

Looking back, we can see that the idealistic debut of the 26-year old choreographer carried the seeds of his later work. Right from the start, the makers of *La grâce du tombeur* staged a protest against what they called 'post-modern poetics'. In press coverage, they took every occasion to assert their differences from the so-called Flemish Wave of choreographers such as Anne Teresa De Keersmaeker, Wim Vandekeybus and Jan Fabre. Smits and his company positioned themselves against this 'garde' in provocative ways, which in their view had developed into a narcissistic investigation of their own dance patterns. Their dance would explicitly embody an idea, or even a philosophical statement, which made them into the 'ugly ducks' of the dance world. Central to their disposition was the focus on myth. 'Compagnie Thor' – it is no coincidence that Smits took the name of a Germanic god of thunder for the company that performed his second dance piece, *Eros délètere* (*Deadly Eros*) (1991). Later productions such as *Sang de Chêne* (*Oak's Blood*) (1993) or *L'âme au diable* (*The Soul in the Devil*) (1994) would add to this mythographic preoccupation with archetypes from Greek, eastern and Celtic traditions. This reservoir of images found an extension in formal eclecticism. Without reservation the choreographer integrated old and new registers of dance and taps from the reservoir of images of kitsch and the arts. No doubt, Smits' marked interest in gay and rock-culture also entered into these art combinations. Probably because of the excessive surplus of images, the performance for that matter used to elicit references to the proverbial Baroque aesthetics.

Performances which were initially narrative-driven have in recent years gradually made space for more popular performances such as *Soirée Dansante* (*Dancing Party*) (1995) or *Corps(e)* (1998), shows that develop a new equilibrium between form and content. In hindsight, one can say that this change had already taken place in *Vesalii Icones* (1994), a solo dance created for a new production with three musical compositions by the renowned contemporary composer Peter Maxwell Davies and performed by the Belgian Kameropera Transparant. It is this same *Vesalii Icones*, a central piece in Transparant's so-called *Triptych of Madness and Loneliness*, which Smits himself turned into the performance entitled *CyberChrist*. It is striking that the initial structural principle of Maxwell Davies' source production, the idea of grafting the stations of the cross on to fourteen etchings by Vesalius, was retained in both Flemish adaptations. The dramaturgical concept of *CyberChrist*, in other words, is as old as the 1969 performance of *Vesalii Icones* on the stage of the Queen Elisabeth Hall in London. Reputedly, the ballet solo of the British composer-choreographer caused a big fuss then, due to Maxwell Davies' experimental musical composition and especially the suggestive dance solo which attracted a lot of attention.[20] Not only did he present the martyrdom of Christ in a series of scientific images of a dissected body, gradually stripped down to the primary figure of the skeleton. He also modified the passion of Christ in order to represent the resurrection of the Lord in the shape of the Devil. I will show later that Smits' *CyberChrist*-version of 1995 will place even greater emphasis on this poisonous tale of *Vesalii Icones*.

Moreover, Vesalius' sketches of the body were as recognisable throughout the dance positions of Smits' *CyberChrist* as they were in Maxwell Davis's piece. They indicated the successive stations of the cross without alteration, except this time they also evoked a context of technology. The loud, overt musical decor of the Belgian formation Noise-Maker's Fifes, which immersed the solo in a collage of industrial and electronic sounds, played a crucial part. As I have said before, the choreographer also made use of images from video-clip-culture, which merged throughout the performance with the completely winding body language of Romeo-Fromm, carried out in slow-motion and with full control over the details. In one extensive movement of 35 min, the dance unfolded itself as a panorama of almost invisible and interchangeable bodily icons. The audience only saw short interruptions in this stream through the flashing, spastic muscular vibrations. The contrasting quality of these abrupt moments of chaos

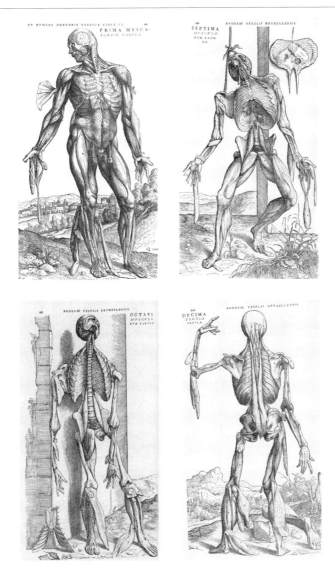

Anatomical etchings of Andreas Vesalius

strongly evoked the sufferings of the body, which evoked a body on a dissection table as well as Christ's body on its way to crucifixion.

It is interesting to note today how (Flemish) critics were disturbed by the so-called superficiality and false attempts at depth in this production.[21] In a certain sense, these negative reviews mistakenly see Smits' general evolution as a particular shortcoming. But otherwise it is definitely true that the plurality of images complicates a uniform reading. The alchemy of different layers of meaning generates a 'text' which actually leaves behind a linear symbolism and manifests itself rather as an allegorical *tableau*. In the Benjaminian perspective, this allegorising leads to a field of contradictions and ambiguities. Since it is impossible to capture this diversity in a totalising and ordered picture, it can be stated that allegory frustrates attempts at interpretation. The non-reducible opposition between the sacred and the profane, the epistemological basis of the Benjaminian allegory, also separates the two levels of *CyberChrist*. There is on the one hand the metaphysical *corpus* of the *imitatio christi* in the stations of the cross, and on the other hand the scientific research of the human body in Vesalius' *De Human Corporis Fabrica* (1543). The dialectical turning of transcendence and secularisation leads to an emotional *scripture,* in the work of Smits, i.e. the melancholic mourning for a body in decay, its pain and transience, which Benjamin deemed a necessary ingredient of the Baroque spirit. Semiotically speaking, *CyberChrist* represents the gap between signifier and signified and hereby the perspective of the Fall becomes central. In order to elucidate this point, we have to look at the actuality of *CyberChrist* as a performance, as an actual exponent of the age-old and powerful dramatic genre of the dance of death.

Death and dance, two extremes of human endings and movements unified in a phenomenon as old as man himself. Putting aside our guesses at the origins of this macabre ritual, it is sure that Christianity marked this type of dance with a clear sign. Pictorial and literary remainders of this medieval genre traditionally show a round dance in which the living and the dead join hands. The morbid master of ceremony takes the shape of a human cadaver or a moving skeleton. In the allegory-saturated consciousness of the old Christian, the symbolical exchangeability of the figure of the dead and the human being is obvious. Thus, in his study of the death-dance motif Helmut Rosenfeld mentions a door sculpture near Rouen (France), where death cuts its throat with a razor blade with the inscription *Ego mors hominem jogulo corripio*: 'I, death, take the human being by the throat.' (24). In the same way the dance solo *CyberChrist* unites the living and the dead in one body, and the typical circular dance is condensed into one figure. We all have to die; the sub-text of the allegory is no less clear. *Sic transit gloria mundi*. The example of Rosenfeld illustrates the repulsive ways of representing the message in the twelfth century. But the triumph of death over the body seldom took such horrifying forms as in Baroque tragedy with its obsession for processes of rotting and decomposition, as Benjamin mentions.

One could ask oneself if the secularising tendency which Benjamin attributed to the Baroque equally motivated the dance of death. It is striking anyhow that death was not choosy in its selection of dance partners: king, nobility, clergy, farmer, and beggar – all were shown in traditional representations without distinction between class or rank. In addition, the dance of death was known to most classes of society and was widespread in times of political (or other) trouble. One could therefore conclude that it answered a latent feeling of dissatisfaction with existing hierarchies. The question whether this was a case of subversion from the people or repressive tolerance of the state can be left out of the equation. Erwin Koller notes in *Totentanz* that in every way the official artistic expression since the French revolution has promoted worldly (read 'political') matters and thus gained status (87). In the field of dance, Luuk Utrecht shows that death as a secularised persona shows up especially in dances of the Romantic period, when it becomes prone to more individualistic interpretations of the artists. In the twentieth century, this estrangement from the orthodox Catholic Church spread itself through expressionistic dance pieces. The closing remark of Utrecht's essay is that the *Butoh*-dance is the most legitimate heir of the medieval dance of death. The simulated death throes of Japanese Butoh is a plastic meditation about actual death in Hiroshima, one of the most fatal consequences of the Devil's pact between technology and political madness. In fact a more striking example of a worldly version of the dance of death in the twentieth century could not be imagined.

Contemporary technologies have a predecessor in the anatomical dissections of the body. In his notations about Vesalius, Maxwell Davies narrates with a certain sensationalism how the Belgian doctor obtained his specimens from the corpses of criminals, which he would dig from graveyards at night.[22] Nearly ten years later, Vesalius became professor of anatomy at the University of Padua, and his fame turned planned executions into public lectures. In the following years, the method of dissection was institutionalised in theatres of anatomy in big cities like Paris, Leiden and Bologna, where they were assured an elite audience elbowing its way through the crowd to catch a glimpse of the internal truth of the human body. The anecdotes of Maxwell Davies find a scientific extension in the studies of Michel Foucault. In *Naissance de la Clinique* (*Birth of the Clinic*), the French philosopher sketches an impressive archaeology of the medical gaze which, since the invention of pathological anatomy, announces a new epistemological and anthropological paradigm.[23] Modernity as the triumph of analytical explanation of the body turns into a new configuration of power which, according to Foucault, is the immediate result of a professionalisation and refinement of anatomical dissection methods. This is the power of the norm of the dead above the living organism. Previously, in pre-modern medicine, the illness of the patient could only be identified when the dead body was prepared for inspection. The diagnosis of the illness followed *a posteriori* scientific study of the symptoms and the traces of it carried by the dead body, which were organised, classified and deduced from living processes. This changes with the arrival of pathological anatomy, which finds in the dead body what had mistakenly been searched for in books: 'an unsupersedable model, prescribed by nature'. (147, tr. 144)[24] From now on the landscape of death is *a priori* the map of the scientist, the norm according to which healthy bodies can be measured:

> Knowledge of life finds its origin in the destruction of life and its extreme opposite; it is at death that disease and life speak their truth: a specific, irreducible truth, protected by the circle of death that designates them for what they are from all assimilations to the inorganic. (148, tr. 145)

Death is the ultimate truth of living, which embodies death beforehand. The medical gaze is 'no longer that of a living eye, but the gaze of an eye that has seen death – a great white eye that unties the knot of life'. (147, tr. 144)

Foucault's historical study ends where contemporary technologies start to exert their influence. The great merit of the philosopher is still valid today. It reveals the paradox inherent in the medical gaze, i.e. the preventive mastering of the end of life as an obsessional fixation on death is an extension of Enlightenment thinking. On a medical level, nuclear technology has managed to penetrate the basic components of the organism itself, so-called genetic engineering constituting the data-structure of the human body, and is a discursive model of the same technology. Here we can see a consolidation of the precession of abstract forms to concrete ones, of the map to the environment. 'And now', Barbara Maria Stafford can add:

> in the age of electronic imagery, endless streams of lopped and laminated *pictures are further falsely allegorized*. Surreptitiously manipulated, excised, patched in or out of a specific time or place, they coldly molecularize experience without seeming to do so. Television, in particular, doses us with a computerized and crazed dermatology of

'spots', 'snippets', and 'bits'. (...) Denatured by a hectic pace and severed from a thought-provoking simultaneity, images lose their difference. (339, my italics)

The tone of this quotation must remind the reader of the loss of aura and the consequential poverty of experience that Benjamin detected in emerging technologies – the metaphor of the surgeon perfects this analogy. Stafford for her part seems to have followed the insights of Foucault in her analysis of digital technologies which – at least in Stafford's reading – does not offer a space for a Benjaminian reversal (technology as a marriage with the cosmos). However, her description would not be misplaced as a general outline for *CyberChrist*, where the dissected corpus of science recognises itself as an assemblage of images from past and future, technology and corporeality. The dance of Romeo-Fromm wakes the body from the anatomy table in order to find the new dispersed totality of the dreamed multi-sensorial cyber-body. As I pointed out before, the impossibility of self-identity manifests itself immediately within a stream of incorporated images. The crisis of the body underneath the surgeon's scalpel resembles the crisis in front of the penetrating gaze of the technological scanner.

Yet, is the production not too much carried away in this respect by a vision of technology leaving little room for ambivalence? What about the unconditional sensuality that *CyberChrist* displays? Thierry Smits' brief statement from the artist, 'I have wanted to show the solitude of the body. A dancer's body in a space much too large. The solitude of the human being who stands in front of the block in the hour of truth' (Smits in Bollinger). Nonetheless publicist Michiel Bollinger, in an essay about the Triple X festival, presents *CyberChrist* as a 'comforting production'. Is this a casual indication that the production could be more than an expression of a now classical technophobia, or is it an emotional outburst *en passant* and of little significance? Does the allegory hold up as an art form and as a method of interpretation? Or does the allegory implode at last in the truth of the symbol, which reads the essence of a technologised modernity in the irreversible apocalypse of human experience? I invite the reader for the last time to read the tragic drama to see where an ultimate dialectical turning in *CyberChrist* leads us.

The last pages of *Ursprung des deutschen Trauerspiels* belong to the most obscure ones Benjamin ever wrote. In condensed, allegorising prose, the author gropes for the actual essence and ultimate destination of allegory. The starting point is the vision that the body cannot make an exception to the law of allegory which tends to destroy the organic and mummify it into a sign of death. Evidence of this are the numerous bodies that tragedy uses as one of the most important stage props, cut up 'in the manner of anatomical dissection, and with an unmistakable delight in cruelty' (392, tr. 218); 'seen from the point of view of death, the product of the corpse is life'. (Ibid., tr. 218) Benjamin relates this morbid orientation towards death of the Baroque artists to 'Cartesian dualism' (391, tr. 271), the foundational distinction between body and spirit which is a product of the Enlightenment and responsible for the devaluation of the body. But unlike Foucault, Benjamin shows little concern for the modern victory of technology over nature. After a short reference to Descartes, the author covers his reflections about the allegorical in purely theological terms. Regardless of insight into the body's allegorisation as a most productive expression of the penetrating gaze of reason, Benjamin is concerned with the roots of the allegorical *attitude*. And this reaches much further back into the distant past. The destructive impulse of allegory ignites through a confrontation of the guilt-ridden body of Christianity and the natural body of an Hellenical pantheon. Christianity's monotheistic ban on pagan gods is, for Benjamin, the main allegorical impulse.

Christian allegories deprive the old gods of their signification, cut them down to bloodless shadows of themselves, hollow signifiers which are then exposed to the violence of allegorical randomness. From the Middle-Ages until the Baroque, Christianity practices the substitute of the aura, the innocent incarnation of the divine within the body through the martyrdom of the suffering body. Whatever remains from the antique gods is demonised into the allegory of Evil inside the human being. Benjamin does point out that this pietist starvation of the pagan body also, and paradoxically, entails its only delivery. Investment in the perpetually new and hostile meanings fishes the gods out of the well of history, even though the price to pay is their transformation into abstract schemes. In the desolate allegorical landscape of the Baroque they are spread out like monumental empty shells:

> the gods project into the alien world, they become evil, and they become creatures. The attire of the Olympians is left behind, and in the course of time the emblems collect around it. And this attire is as creaturely as a devil's body. (399, tr. 225)

Herein lies the redemptive destruction of allegory. As long as the gods are deprived of their power, they become available to the artistic image manipulation in which they exist. In Christianity's fight against the gnosticism of deviant movements such as the Rosicrucians, alchemists or astrologers, the lights are momentarily lit up. Superstition nurtures itself in the vision that magical powers are retained in the smouldering remains of the cult. It is exactly this demonic nature, which is the mark of Christian damnation and which Christianity tried to expel, that keeps the interest in the occult alive.

The representation of the body in *CyberChrist* displays, in my view, a similar logic. This is the double movement of allegory. On the one hand, we have the devaluation of the cult-sensual body when it is deprived of its aura and turned into fetishising fragments, in anatomy as well as technology. On the other hand, there is a survival in front of the spectator's inner eye of a body unified in senses and nature. That body appears as a fictive *after-image* at its moment of erosion in modernity, its disintegration prompts an imagined reconstruction. The allegory of *CyberChrist* thus speaks truly of 'something other' than it first appears. Only by integrating the duality experience-technology in one image, that of the dancing Romeo-Fromm, can the original beauty of the body emerge. Therefore the sensuality and starvation of the flesh, the becoming-object of human hedonism, appear in one movement. Smits is looking for the glowing embers of a holy, but extinguished, fire which can still set fire to the status quo in spite of everything. For the same reason, he filters the Christian iconography of Good and Evil through images whose diabolical qualities have paganistic overtones.

Presented with the technological condition in mind, the paradox enters this dance solo to clarify contemporary visions of the body in general. Whereas the body's disappearance in new technologies (virtual reality, cyberspace, etc.) is prophesied everywhere, the body is discursively more present than ever. Aura and technology are two poles within a negative affirmation, showing a similar dynamic. In a similar way, the mortification of the body in *CyberChrist* emphasises negatively, and with more intensity, its absence-in-presence. Here is the comforting gesture of the production; in the messianic view that paradise can only be perceived in the Fall of man, that the body's salvation from the intrusive technological apparatus does not exist outside technology. The allegorisation in *CyberChrist* leads to the place of aporia (indeterminacy) of the body in religion and science, myth and technology.

But the reader may perhaps remember Derrida's definition of 'aporia' as an 'extreme abstraction', a given without a name, programme, or performative gesture of any kind. For Thierry Smits, aporia does seem to carry a name in that it attributes signification where, strictly speaking, it is not desired. The allegorist who occupies the 'desert within the desert' is, for him, Satan. In the revealing final phase, after a series of distortions and contractions of the dancing body (the death and laying out of Christ), the Devil stands up. Bathing in blood-red light, he invites the spectator with masturbatory gestures to take a look at his personal garden of delights until he turns this scene into complete darkness. In the traditional dance of death it was not unusual that death assumed the properties of Satan. Erwin Koller has pointed out that the semantic field of the historical art form was explicitly moved to the economy of guilt and sin. The author shows that the theological foundation of the dance of death is turned into a structural principle of biblical history, which goes from the Fall and Judgement to Christ's victory over death. It is the Devil who seduces us to sin and brings death to mankind, but it is the same Devil who waits next to God for the human being at the end of time, when the living join the dead for the last judgement. This was precisely the warning of the dance of death – the virtuous human being will be accepted into the eternity of the resurrected God. 'What lives/Dies through Adam's need: What dies/Lives through Christ's death'. (Rusting in Koller 1980: 443)

In the last pages of the tragic drama-book, one can similarly hear a diabolical jeer. We already know that knowledge, the knowledge of Good and Evil of the allegorical subject, applies to the material world after the Fall of man and is the Devil's territory. However, through an obscure and intellectual descent into dead matter, it does not reach an ideal but a limit. The meandering gaze of the allegorist is thus arrested within the ultimate emblem of death and decay; Satan, the phantasmagorical impersonation of transience and the diabolical which Baroque artists so desperately searched for. At that moment, allegory finds its perfection in the antipode of aspirations for sovereignty, manifesting itself as self-illusion in the clear demarcation of the Christian icon of Evil. The endless streams of signifiers fall back on themselves and show the emptiness of their own gesture. Where the allegorist thought he signified something, in fact he carried signs which were imposed from the outside. What follows is the ultimate dialectical reversal; the allegory itself becomes allegory: 'The absolute spirituality, which is what Satan means, destroys itself in its emancipation from what is sacred'. (404, tr. 230) At the height of its workings, allegory loses its naivety and gets to know the limitation of the circular form of representation. The consequence is turning around mortality, which was buried before, to eternity or heavenly salvation. Resurrection shines through the image of decay. It is this big turn which powerfully erases the former profane powers of the allegorical to the benefit of an orthodox message of salvation: 'The seven years of its immersion are but a day'. The author says,

> For even this time of hell is secularised in space, and that world, which abandoned itself to the deep spirit of Satan and betrays itself, is God's world. In God's world the allegorist awakens.

> And this is the essence of melancholy immersion: that its ultimate
> objects, in which it believes it can most fully secure that which is vile,
> turn into allegories, and that these allegories fill out and deny this void
> in which they are represented, just as, ultimately, the intention does
> not faithfully rest in the contemplation of bones, but faithlessly leaps
> forward to the idea of resurrection. (406, tr. 232)

Betrayal and repudiation – Benjamin's judgement finds its expression in
bitter words. It is up to the reader to find out if the apotheosis of *Cyber-
Christ* in his consciousness erases equally the effect of what preceded it.

Translated by Katrien Jacobs

Bibliography

Benjamin, Walter. *Gesammelte Schriften*. Eds. Tiedemann, Rolf & Schweppenhäuser,
Hermann unter Mitwirkung von Adorno, Theodor W. und Scholem, Gershom.
Frankfurt am Main: Suhrkamp Verlag, 1974–1989.
(—. *The Origin of German Tragic Drama*. Translation Osborne, John. London,
New York: Verso, 1994.)
(—. *Illuminations*. Translation Zohn, Harry. London: Fontana Press, 1992.)
Bollinger, Michiel. 'Dat duivelse Lichaam.' *Notes* (September 1996), 17–18.
Buck-Morss, Susan. *The Dialectics of Seeing: Walter Benjamin and the Arcades
Project*. Cambridge: MIT Press, 1989.
Bürger, Peter. *Theorie der Avant-Garde*. Frankfurt am Main: Suhrkamp Verlag, 1974.
Derrida, Jacques. 'Geloof en Weten: De Twee Bronnen van de Religie Binnen de
Grenzen van de Zuivere Rede.' Derrida, Jacques *et al. God en Godsdienst:
Gesprekken op Capri*. Vert. Herman Note. Kampen: Kok Agora, 1997, 9–100.
Fiebach, Joachim. *Von Craig bis Brecht: Studien zu Künstlertheorien in der ersten
Hälfte des 20. Jahrhunderts*. Berlin: Henschel Verlag, 1975.
Foster, Hall. *The Return of the Real: The Avant-Garde at the End of the Century*.
London: MIT Press, 1996.
Foucault, Michel. *La Naissance de la Clinique*. Paris: Presses universitaires de France,
1963.
(—. *The Birth of the Clinic: An Archaeology of Medical Perception*. Translation Smith,
A.M. Sheridan. London: Tavistock Publications Limited, 1973.)
Heidegger, Martin. 'Die Frage nach der Technik.' *Vorträge und Aufsätze: Teil I*. Tübingen:
Verlag Günther Neske, 1967 (Dritte Auflage), 5–37.
Jameson, Fredric: *Marxism and Form: Twentieth-Century Dialectical Theories of
Literature*. Princeton: University Press, 1971.
—. *Post-Modernism, or: The Cultural Logic of Late Capitalism*. London: Verso, 1996
(4th edition).
Koller, Erwin. *Totentanz*. Innsbruck: Innsbrucker Beiträge zur Kulturwissenschaft, 1980.
Lista, Giovanni. *La Scène Futuriste*. Paris: CNRS Editions, 1989.
Maxwell Davies, Peter. *Maxopus: The Official Web Site of Sir Peter Maxwell Davies*.
Online. www.maxopus.com Ed. Arnold, Judy. Virtual Cyberspace Computer
Company, 20 July 1999.
Opsomer, Geert; Van Kerkhoven, Marianne, Eds. *Van Brecht tot Bernadetje: Wat maakt
Theater en Dramaturgie Politiek in onze Tijd?* Brussel: Vlaams Theater Instituut, 1997.

Rosenfeld, Hellmut. *Der Mittelalterliche Totentanz.* Köln: Böhlau Verlag, 1974.
Stafford, Barbara Maria. *Body Criticism: Imaging the Unseen in Enlightenment Art and Medicine.* Cambridge: MIT Press, 1991.
Utrecht, Luuk. 'De Eeuwige Rondedans van Doodsangst en Doodsdrift: De Dood in de Dans.' Ed. Peter Grijp, Loius *et al. De Dodendans in de Kunsten.* Utrecht: HES Uitgevers, 1989, 74–83.
Wohlfarth, Irving. 'Der "destruktive Charakter": Benjamin zwischen den Fronten.' Ed. Lindner, Burkhardt. *Walter Benjamin im Kontext.* Frankfurt am Main: Atheneum Verlag, 1985, 65–100.
—. 'Der Zauberlehrling oder die Entfesselung der Produktivkräfte: Zu einem Motiv bei Goethe, Marx und Benjamin.' Eds. Raulet, Gérard & Steiner, Uwe. *Walter Benjamin: Ästhetik und Geschichtsphilosophie.* Bern: Peter Lang, 1998, 165–199.

Notes

[1] For a well researched overview of historical avant-garde theatre and its social context, see the work of Joachim Fiebach. It is also known that Antonin Artaud borrowed aesthetic strategies from film. His poetics, however, were geared towards overwhelming the senses rather than social consciousness, and did not carry the signature of socialist conviction.

[2] The foundation for the Hegelian view that the historical avant-garde was integrated and dissolved in the realisation of late capitalist mass culture was laid down by the German literary historian, Peter Bürger, in his famous *Theory of the Avantgarde.* It is not a coincidence that Bürger is a much cited source for post-modern theories of the avant-garde. In this respect, one could look at the recent influential study by Hal Foster, *The Return of the Real: The Avant-garde at the End of the Century.* Similar ideas were a guiding light for theatre research in the essays for a conference at the Antwerp Theatre Festival of August 30, 1997, published as *Van Brecht tot Bernadetje: Wat maakt Theater en Dramaturgie Politiek in onze Tijd?* (*From Brecht to Bernadetje: What makes Theatre and Dramaturgy Political in Our Times?*), especially the texts by the editors and the contribution by Hans Thies Lehmann.

[3] Lista on the futurist crisis of consciousness: '(…) the partisans of Marinetti had now another consciousness than modernity since they took for granted the patrimony of the ideas and experiences of the avant-garde. Anyway, their research corresponded with a mitigated experimentalism which wouldn't stand for either the will of rupture, or true formal originality, which have always been a motivation for the avant-garde.' (279).

[4] This text served as a press release and also appeared in the Kaaitheater brochure in Brussels (Studiowerk – 30 October–2 November 1996).

[5] This is a reference to *Die Frage nach der Technik.*

[6] In this early work (begun in 1916 and finished in 1925) Benjamin gathers all aspects of his previous intellectual development into a theory which draws the outlines for his later insights into the allegorical. Another would be his longer essay about *Goethes Wahlverwandtschaften* (1921–1922) in which Benjamin tests out his early ideas about

allegory in an allegorical reading of Goethe's short novel. Later, allegory will reappear in the writing of Baudelaire, more particularly the unfinished *Passagen-Werk*, in which two comprehensive sections, *Das Paris der Second Empire bei Baudelaire* (1937–1938) and *Über Einige Motive bei Baudelaire* were preserved next to a useful collection of loose fragments with the (allegorical) titel *Zentralpark* (1938–1939). The tragic drama-book is a starting point in my text because of its explicitly metaphysical tendency.

[7]   'With every idea the moment of expression coincides with a veritable explosion of images, which gives rise to a chaotic mass of metaphors'. (Benjamin 1974: 349, tr. 173)

[8]   'Allegory is (…) the privileged mode of our own life in time, a clumsy deciphering of meaning from moment to moment, the painful attempt to restore a continuity to het-erogeneous, disconnected instants'. (Jameson 1971: 72)

[9]   I will mostly use the language essays from 1916, *Die Bedeutung der Sprache in Trauerspiel und Tragödie* (Benjamin 1977) and *Über Sprache überhaupt und über die Sprache der Menschen* (Ibid.), and also the essay he wrote in 1921, *Die Aufgabe des Übersetzers* (Benjamin 1972).

[10]   From *Über Sprache überhaupt und über die Sprache des Menschen* (*On Language in General and on the Language of Mankind*): 'The language of overnaming is the essence of human language after the fall of man'. (Benjamin 1977: 155)

[11]   See footnote 7 above.

[12]   I am, of course, alluding to Benjamin's essay *Das Kunstwerk im Zeitalter seiner technischen Reproduzierbarkeit* (*The Work of Art in the Age of Mechanical Reproduction*) which I will discuss later.

[13]   Benjamin's *tekhnè* here anticipates the vision of Marshall McLuhan, the author of *Understanding Media: The Extensions of Man* (1964), even though the ideological agenda of both thinkers differs radically.

[14]   'The camera introduces us to unconscious optics as does psychoanalysis to uncon-scious impulses'. (Benjamin 1974: 461, tr. 230)

[15]   I wrote about this techno-optimism at the beginning of my text.

[16]   Thanks to Irving Wohlfarth and Vivian Liska, who gave an extensive manuscript written by Wohlfarth with the same theme entitled ' "Klages in their Knapsack": Walter Benjamin and the Idea of a Techno-Cosmological Eros: A Reading of "To the Planetarium".'

[17]   This insight is in accordance with the findings of Lieven De Cauter in his doctoral thesis *The Hunchback in the Chess Automaton: Walter Benjamin's Hidden Doctrine* (Katholieke Universiteit Leuven, 1996) where he posits that the 'genotext' at the source of Benjamin's thought is a messianic curve, where paradise and Fall are antithetically joined and redemption is found in the burning point where both extremes meet. I thank the author for this insight at a time his text was still unpublished.

[18] See Derrida 1997. I have used the Dutch translation of Herman Note, *Geloof en Weten,* of selected sections from *La Religion.* Paris: Editions du Seuil, 1996. Italics in original, also the quotations which follow.

[19] This production was the result of a close collaboration between set designer Damien De Lepeleire, musician Steven Brown and director Antoine Pickels.

[20] In 1969 the composer not only composed the music, but also made the choreography for *Vesalii Icones.* Recently some interesting facts and the composer's short notations about his pieces were revealed (<www.maxopus.com>). I also refer to the article by Paul Griffiths: *Davies as Dancer* (<www.maxopus.com/essays/dancer.htm>). The analysis by Michael White was also informative: *Maxwell Davies' shockers sprout again in Brussels* (*The Independent,* 10 April 1994).

[21] 'The systematic vagueness on the level of content leads to a half-mystical and some-what irritating results. Instead of revelations, we get clichés and hence kitsch.' (Sigrid Bousset, 4 March 1995, *De Morgen*); 'It does not become clear what is exactly the point, they are impressions which replace each other as equal possibilities. This kind of vagueness is nonetheless an open invitation to see deeper truths. But in actuality it only has to do with kitsch: the suggestion of a big effort which has shortcomings in actuality.' (Pieter T'Jonck, 2 November 1996, *De Standaard*).

[22] See 'Note on Vesalius' on <www.maxopus.com/works/vesalii.htm#review>

[23] It needs to be stated here that Foucault, in a similar way, deconstructed age-old stories about body snatchers. According to Foucault, they served to legitimise the start and growth of the official medical anatomy industry. (Foucault 125–127)

[24] The transformation can be summarised in the recommendation of Bichat, author of the famous *Anatomie Générale*: 'Open up a few corpses: you will dissipate at once the darkness that observation only could not dissipate.' (Bichat in Foucault 149).

Maaike Bleeker

Disorders That Consciousness Can Produce:
Bodies Seeing Bodies on Stage

In the theatre, people gather to see other people perform. The simultaneous presence of both performer and audience is usually considered to be a fundamental characteristic of the theatre event, and crucial to the strong effects it can produce. The performer is 'live' – is present right there – before the eyes of the audience; a living body, exposed to our look. On the contemporary stage, this body seems to be more present than ever. Breaking through theatre conventions, performers offer us glimpses (or more) of 'themselves' as living, breathing beings, by standing literally or figuratively naked before our very eyes. One is able to see all of them, or so it seems, to see right through them and even to feel what they feel, sensing the physical reactions of the body seen on stage as though they were one's own.

The body on stage draws a lot of attention, not only from the audience but also from theorists. What is more, the powerful and fascinating presence of bodies on stage appears to be capable of capturing the attention of both audience and theorist to such a degree that the other bodies present – those of the audience – are almost or completely forgotten. The theoretical attention paid to bodies seen on stage thus produces a corpus of knowledge which, while testifying to a growing awareness of the embodied character of meaning production on stage, and the ways the bodies seen there are products of culture rather than a natural presence, at the same time bears witness to a rather 'disembodied' notion of what it means to *see* these bodies. It is precisely such a disembodied notion of vision that allows for a conflation of what is seen and what is present 'over there'. That is, to take what is seen for what is 'over there', and to understand the strong effects experienced as resulting exclusively from the body present on stage. What is left out this way is the relation between the body seen and the body seeing. The latter is left in the dark, 'just looking'. Absorbed in the object of their attention, these bodies seeing and theorizing about the bodies on stage are conspicuous by their absence. It is this absent body that will be my concern, the body of the seer – the body that is the seer – and I will approach this body via a critique of vision.

At first sight, it appears that nothing could be easier than seeing: We simply focus our eyes and take in whatever is before us. A new or renewed focus on questions of vision in a wide variety of fields, however, has begun to open our eyes to the complexity of what is easily but mistakenly taken for granted as 'just looking'. Martin Jay suggests that the fascination with modes of seeing and the enigmas of visual experience may well token a paradigm shift in the cultural imagination of our age: 'What has been called the "pictorial turn" bids fair to succeed the "linguistic turn" so loudly trumpeted by twentieth-century philosophers'. (Jay 1996: 3) This does not imply, however, a simple reversal – i.e., the replacement of the linguistic and the discursive by the pictorial and the figurative – but rather the replacement of the word-image opposition with a more complicated account of the ways viewing and reading – the linguistic and the visual – are intertwined. The 'pictorial turn' reflects the lesson of the linguistic turn 'to attend to the constituted rather than the found quality of seemingly "natural" phenomena'. (Jay 1996: 3) As Stephen Melville observes, the interest in the visual typically has taken the form of a 'critique of vision' – 'a systematic suspicion of the apparent transparency and naturalness of vision'. (Melville 1996: 103) 'Just looking' appears to be far more complicated than the expression might first suggest. Seeing appears to be irrational, inconsistent, and undependable. It is caught up in the threads of the unconscious and entangled with the passions. Ways of seeing are historically determined and culturally mediated. More than that, seeing appears to alter the thing seen and to transform the seer. Not only are words and images intertwined in many ways, but so too are the seer and the seen.

In this paper, I will explore some implications of this intertwining of seer and seen, starting with a theatre performance that exposes the relation between bodies seeing and bodies seen on stage. This performance is *De Zieleweg van de Danser* (*The Path of the Dancer's Soul*[1]), which was co-created by theatre director Gerardjan Rijnders and choreographer Krisztina de Chatel, and performed by a dancer and an actor. Their performance blurs the boundary between dance and text-based theatre, a move typical of many experiments by Dutch and Flemish theatre makers in the 1980s and 1990s – including Gerardjan Rijnders himself. In search of new kinds of theatrical presence, dancers, actors, directors, and choreographers began to collaborate or to borrow techniques from other disciplines. Rijnders, for example, worked with the Dutch National Ballet for his version of *The Bacchae*,[2] and later used the experiences he gained from working with these dancers to create *Ballet*[3] with actors from his own company. *The Path of the Dancer's Soul* is a continuation of these explorations in what, at first sight, seems to be a paradoxical format. A theatre director, a choreographer, a dancer and an actor collaborate to come up with a performance in which an actor stands still and speaks a text on one side of the stage, while on the other side of the stage a silent dancer performs dance movements. The stage is thus divided into two in a way that seems to confirm rather than cross or dissolve the boundary between the disciplines. The title of the show is a quote taken from the text spoken by the actor. This text is Heinrich von Kleist's *On the Puppet Theatre*, which consists of three short stories about bodies seen, followed by a conclusion that turns the three stories into an argument about the relationship between self-consciousness and bodily grace. Von Kleist argues that self-awareness and bodily grace are antithetical. The less self-conscious living beings are, the more beautiful their bodily appearance is, thus relating grace and bodily beauty to a state of innocence that precedes the awakening of self-awareness. Typically, von Kleist's text directs all attention to the bodies seen, putting the seer, implicitly, in the position of objective observer of what is there to be seen. In their staging, however, Rijnders and de Chatel manage to redirect attention and also expose the body seeing. In this way, their performance presents a critique of von Kleist's text and the understanding of the relationship between vision, bodies, and self-awareness underlying it, a critique formulated in the artistic discourse of the theatre. Their staging exposes as a highly subjective account, von Kleist's narrator's objective observations on bodies seen. Rather than resulting from the consciousness of the bodies he sees, it seems to be his own consciousness that produces the disorders he observes in them. My paper is a theoretical response to both the performance and von Kleist's text, drawing on critiques of vision as formulated in the theoretical discourse of the academy. I read von Kleist's text and Rijnders/de Chatel's staging of it alongside Lacan's psychoanalytical account of the relation between bodies, self-awareness, and vision in his theory of the mirror stage. I turn to Kaja Silverman's elaboration on Lacan to further explore the relation between the Lacanian subject of vision and embodiment. Inspired by the performance, I also make an excursion to dance theory, and present John Martin's concept of *inner mimicry* as an alternative account of the relation between seeing and embodiment. Martin's concept has been subject to severe criticism, and not without reason. Silverman's re-reading of the Lacanian mirror stage, however, also seems to allow for a reconceptualization of inner mimicry. Finally, I will make a theoretical move analogous to the one proposed by the performance and look back at the subject speaking in *The Mirror Stage*, and wonder what might be the relationship between this subject as body and the bodies observed.

A Sense of Self

In von Kleist's *On the Puppet Theatre*, a first-person narrator tells about an encounter some years earlier with Mr. C, the chief dancer of the opera in the town of M. Much to his surprise, the narrator discovers that Mr. C is a great admirer of the puppet theatre. Mr. C appears to think that puppets make much better dancers than human beings, and he goes as far as stating that 'any dancer who wished to improve his art might learn all sorts of things from them'. (Von Kleist 1982: 211) The narrator sits down with him to listen to the grounds on which he bases this remarkable assertion.

According to Mr. C, the movements of the marionette are more beautiful because they are more natural, and he explains this beautiful naturalness or natural beauty in terms of a lack of self-awareness. He acknowledges that the range of movements that these mechanical bodies can produce is, of course, limited. But the lightness, grace, and serenity with which they are executed must, according to him, amaze every thinking person. These movements are produced by an operation that may seem simple from a mechanical point of view – consisting of a movement of the center of gravity in a straight or curved line – but which, from another point of view, is something very mysterious, 'for it is nothing less than *The Path of the Dancer's Soul'*. (Von Kleist 1982: 212, italics in text) In the mechanical puppet, this soul is located in the exact center of gravity of the puppet's body, and this is what makes their movements so graceful. Unlike living dancers, the puppets have the advantage of counter-gravity. 'They know nothing of the inertia of matter, which of all properties is the most obstructive to the dance: for the force that lifts them into the air is greater than that which pulls them to the ground'. (Von Kleist 1982: 214) This weight that grounds living dancers also appears to have a metaphorical meaning. Mr. C associates the disturbed relationship between movement and soul, which he observes in living dancers, with the Fall. The price living dancers paid for their bite from the tree of knowledge, was loss of grace. More than their material weight, it seems to be their conscious awareness of themselves as bodies seen that disturbs the relationship between their soul and their movements. As a result, their *vis motrix* – or soul – is usually located at any point other than the center of gravity, which results in the disturbance of natural grace and produces affectation, which Mr. C associates with baroque mannerism.

For Mr. C, the dancing body of the marionette represents a state of natural grace and innocence – a state that he, as a conscious being, has lost. The naturalness and truthfulness he perceives in the marionette's movement therefore do not result from a convincing representation of bodies as he knows them. It is not because he is able to recognize himself in these bodies that they are so attractive to him; on the contrary, the marionette's true and natural movements are more ideal than his own, and they therefore seem to promise fulfillment of what he lacks. Looking at the marionette's dance provides him with a link to a state of innocence he has lost. It provides him with a provisional, temporary, and of course – in the end – incomplete recourse to what he will never again be.

The narrator replies that he, too, knows only too well the 'disorders that consciousness can produce', and tells of an event that happened to him three years before. He had been swimming with a young man whose physical form seemed to radiate a marvelous grace, of which the young man was not yet aware. While the young man was drying himself, he unconsciously assumed the position of a famous statue called the Spinario, a statue they had admired in Paris shortly before. Looking at himself in a large mirror, the young man recognized the similarity and jubilantly pointed it out to the narrator. The narrator, however, although he had had to admit that he had noticed it, laughed, saying that the boy was seeing phantoms. The boy, confused, tried to re-create the jubilant moment, but was not able to do so. 'From this day on, as though from that very moment, an inconceivable transformation began in that young man. He would stand whole days before the mirror; one charm after the other fell from him. An invisible and incomprehensible force, like an iron net, seemed to spread over the free play of his gestures, and when one year had passed not a trace could be detected of that sweetness which had once so delighted the sight of all who surrounded him'. (Von Kleist 1982: 215)

In front of the mirror, the body seeing and the body seen, separated in the case of the marionette, merge into one, and it is exactly this merging that, according to Mr. C, produces the reprehensible condition of self-consciousness. The marionette's inability to see prevents it from making the discovery the boy made. The puppet will never become aware of itself as a visible body, and therefore will not lose its bodily grace. The boy, however, did recognize himself in the mirror; he recognized the Spinario's beauty as his own, which resulted in one jubilant moment; from that moment on, however, he was on a downgrade. Like Mr. C, nothing is left for him but to mirror himself in the ideal but unattainable grace of, for example, the marionette.

Von Kleist's story about the boy in front of the mirror shows remarkable similarities with Lacan's psychoanalytical account of the development of a sense of self in what he calls the mirror stage. The mirror stage describes the moment the young child is suddenly able to recognize the image of its body in the mirror, that is, to recognize an image of its body as its own. According to Lacan, it is at this moment that the ego comes into existence as a mental refraction of that image. The most psychical of agencies – the psyche – thus appears as the effect of the image of the body. Lacan founds his concept of the ego on Freud's remark that 'The ego is first and foremost a bodily ego: it is not merely a surface entity, but is itself the projection of a surface'. (Freud 1923: 26) With this statement, Freud acknowledges that our experience of self is always circumscribed by and derived from the body. In the Lacanian mirror stage, the role of vision in the inauguration of the self is given a hitherto unimagined prominence. Through the mirror stage vision, body and self are inextricably intertwined. It is through the mirror stage that one enters the scopic domain. Lacan calls it the 'threshold of the visible world'. (Lacan 1977: 3)

The moment the child recognizes itself in the mirror image is, according to Lacan, 'an identification in the full sense that analysis gives to the term', namely 'the transformation that takes place in the subject as he assumes an image'. (Lacan 1977: 2) It is a jubilant moment, for the visual imago of the body is more coherent than the organic disturbance and discord of the body as felt. However as Lacan points out, the jubilant moment of assuming an image is in fact a mis-recognition: it is an identification with something outside the self. Like the marionette, the mirror presents an image of a more ideal body, but unlike Mr. C, the child in front of the mirror does not see a more ideal *other* body. Instead, it recognizes the image as its own, and identifies with it as the form – or Gestalt – of the ego in a way that conceals its own lack. This conflation of self and other on the threshold of the visible world will remain an important ingredient of vision for the rest of the subject's life.

Dance as Re-creation

Lacan presented his idea on the mirror stage at a conference of the International Psychoanalytic Association in Marienbad in 1936. Three years later, John Martin published *Introduction to the Dance*. Like von Kleist, Martin believes that looking at dancing bodies is so attractive because – in the ideal case – it allows for direct contact with the moving force – or *vis motrix* – behind the movements seen. This way, dance can compensate for something lost, for a lack. 'All art, with the dance in the forefront, is a matter of compensation. It deals not with what we already have, but with what we lack,' (Martin 1939: 130) writes Martin. For him, as for von Kleist, this lack results from the loss of a more natural or original state. 'The oneness of all dance lies in the fact that in its every manifestation it consists of movement arranged in form to provide compensation for suppressions and unfulfillments in life experience'. (Martin 1939: 132) Modern life does not offer the opportunity to live one's inherent potentialities to the maximum; therefore, a set of circumstances must be set up to compensate for the denials and suppressions that occur in daily life. Dance is such a circumstance: it helps to restore the individual to what Martin calls 'normal and harmonious functioning', that is, to a more natural functioning which, according to him, we have lost during the process of ongoing civilization. This re-creational function of dance applies not only to dancing, but also to looking at dance. Looking is what Martin does.

For Martin, the *vis motrix* or soul of the dance does not reside in the center of gravity of the moving body, but consists of pan-human emotions. Through looking at dancing bodies, we have access to a universal layer of basic human feelings, and this is accomplished through what Martin calls the body's capacity for *inner mimicry*. Through inner mimicry, we 'cease to be mere spectators and become participants in the movement that is presented to us and though to all outward appearances we shall be sitting quietly in our chairs we shall nevertheless be dancing synthetically with all our musculature'. (Martin 1965: 53) Through a reaction of bodily responsiveness, we become aware of how it feels to make the movements seen without actually executing them. Much more, this bodily awareness allows us to feel not only the movements, but also the feelings of the body seen executing them, because – according to Martin – there is a natural connection between seeing movement and feeling it, and between feeling movement and emotions. In this way, dance provides us with a universal language that unites all mankind.

Martin writes not about marionettes, but about modern dance. With his explanation, he provided a rationale for the (then) new modern dance. His theory allows for a new understanding of the meaning of the bodies seen on stage, no longer explaining them in terms of Swans, Willis, or other ghosts within the representation of a narrative on stage, nor reducing them to sexualized appearances constructed to satisfy the desires of a male gaze. Nevertheless, his explanation also presents problems. As Susan Foster points out, Martin presupposes an intrinsic and mechanistic connection between seeing, movement, and feeling. He 'imagines movement to be the transparent vehicle of an innermost, and hence, pan-human emotional realm. In the same way that muscular action intrinsically links to emotion, so for Martin, the individual psyche replicates the tensile patterns of the universal human condition'. (Foster 1998) He builds his universalist claim on the presupposition that 'the body spontaneously maps the contours of the psyche, the veracity of its pronouncements a direct product of its intrinsic connection to interiority'. (Foster 1998) This would suggests that all human bodies have the capacity to feel what other bodies feel just by looking at them. Yet, notwithstanding the claimed universality of this pan-human realm of feelings, not all humans appear to have equal access to it, nor do all human bodies appear to be equally able to express these universal emotions through their movements. Martin's body willingly mimics some bodies, but refuses to mimic others. For, while his concept of inner mimicry serves to justify Martha Graham's impersonations of native American dances and Helen Tamiris' embodiment of the plight of the Negro, he also uses it to criticize black and native dancers for being too specific to represent the universal. Like von Kleist, he blames this difference on disorders perceived in the bodies seen, claiming that it is their racial and ethnic features that obstruct direct access to their *vis motrix*. They have to leave behind their racial and ethnic features in order to enter a realm Martha Graham and Helen Tamiris possess 'by nature'.

The Mirror Stage as Model

In Martin's model there are two bodies: that seeing and feeling in the auditorium, and that seen as a spectacle on stage. The gap separating them is bridged by an instantaneous mapping of one body onto the other within the act of looking. Although Martin does not refer to psychoanalysis, it is hard to miss the analogy of his theory of seeing dance with the Lacanian scenario of the mirror stage. And, surprisingly, Silverman's critique of the Lacanian mirror stage in *The Threshold of the Visible World* (1996) parallels Foster's critique of Martin on at least one crucial point, i.e., the presupposed instantaneous and natural character of the jump from the body felt to the body seen needed to support the claim for universality. In Lacan, this instantaneous (mis)recognition serves the constitution of the self. In Martin, it allows for a direct contact with the feelings of the other body seen on stage. In both cases, the automatic alignment of the visual and the corporeal as presupposed by the authors produces a mixing up of what is self and what is other. This mixing up is the core of Silverman's critical engagement with Lacan. Her project is not to undo this mixing up, but to 'space-out' the instant in which it is supposed to take place, in order to show it as a process of interaction taking place in time in which different positions are involved. A process, furthermore, that is not the result of natural or intrinsic mechanisms, but is mediated by culture.

Silverman turns to the work of Henri Wallon and Paul Schilder, two contemporaries of Lacan, for a slightly different account of the mirror stage, one focussing less exclusively on vision in the constitution of the self. According to Lacan, the mirror image itself – the image of the body seen in the mirror – is sufficient to induce the 'assuming of an image' that inaugurates the self. Silverman comes up with an alternative model, in which the bodily ego has a sensational as well as a visual dimension. A model, furthermore, in which the bodily ego is not unified but produced in an ongoing process of 'laborious stitching together of disparate parts'. (Silverman 1996: 17) Following Wallon, she calls these components the 'exteroceptive' ego and the 'proprioceptive' ego. The former is comparable to the mirror image; the latter refers to 'the egoic component to which concepts like "here", "there", and "my" are keyed'. (Silverman 1996: 16) Silverman points out the etymological roots of the term proprioceptivity as a combination of *proprius* – 'which includes among its central meanings, "personal", "individual", "characteristic", and "belonging"' – and *capere*, 'which means "to grasp," "to conceive," and to catch"'. She concludes that proprioception signifies 'something like "the apprehension on the part of the subject" of his or her "ownness"'. (Silverman 1996: 16, italics in text) It is bound up with the body's sensation of occupying a point in space, and with the terms under which it does so. It encompasses the muscular system in its totality, and involves a non-visual mapping of the bodily form on the basis of a gathering together and unification of otherwise disparate and scattered sensations provided by the various sense organs. And, finally, it 'provides something which the specular imago alone could never provide – something which Wallon elsewhere, in an unfortunate choice of words, designates "presence".' (Silverman 1996: 16)

Silverman calls Wallon's use of the term 'presence' unfortunate, because it does not correspond with the idea of presence as being non-relational and independent from cultural interference. The concept of proprioceptivity as Silverman develops it on the basis of Wallon, includes all the effects of physical interactions not only with the physical environment, but also with other bodies. These interactions take place 'within culture'. It is through these interactions that the subject comes to have a body that is sensationally marked by gender, race, and sexual preference. It is, furthermore, in relation to this sensationally marked part of the bodily ego that we perceive things as exterior to us, that the specular image might be said to be 'outside'. It is also this relationship that, in Silverman's re-reading of Lacan through Wallon, allows for the jubilant experience of 'here and nowness', in which the image outside and the bodily self as experienced from the inside seem to merge into one.

> As I have already suggested, the visual imago cannot by itself induce in the subject that *meconnaisance* about which Lacan writes. The experience which each of us at times has of being "ourselves" – the triumph of what I have been designating the *moi* part of the bodily ego – depends on the smooth integration of the visual imago with the proprioceptive or sensational ego. When the former seems unified with the latter, the subject experiences that mode of "altogetherness" generally synonymous with "presence". When these two bodies come apart, that "presence" is lost. (Silverman 1996: 17, italics in text)

'Presence' thus understood is not something given and observed to be over there, but an effect produced as a result of a particular relationship between visual imago and proprioceptive ego, one that suggests its own absence in a jubilant moment of (mis)recognition. It results from a relationship between a body seeing and the image of a body seen, and both sides of this relationship as well as what connects them are embedded in culture. Within this relationship, 'presence' is an experience of confirmation of the body seeing rather than a quality observed or present in a body seen. It is for these reasons that Silverman calls the term 'presence' unfortunate. However, it is for these very same reasons that I think such a relational notion of 'presence' might be a useful concept for rethinking the intense effects produced by the bodies seen on the contemporary stage.

'Theatre has long been celebrated as the stronghold of presence, embodiment and reciprocity – particularly by those working outside or at the margins of the discipline,' (Freedman 1991: 48) observes Barbara Freedman. She refers to film theorist Christian Metz stating that reality in the theatre 'is physically present, in the same space as the spectator'. Body seeing and body seen are both present as part of the theatrical event. In cinema, on the contrary, 'seeing and being seen are split. The cinema only gives the bodies seen in effigy, inaccessible from the outside in a primordial elsewhere'. (Metz in Freedman 1991: 49) At the same time, inside the discipline, theatrical presence is a much debated and contested issue, especially since the emergence of performance in the 1960s. Surprisingly, early performance artists and theorists accused the theatre of the very same split situation that, according to Metz, is typical of film, namely of being a representation of a primordial elsewhere, a split situation that prevents direct and immediate contact between audience and performer. Theatre 'was charged with obeisance to the playwright's authority which actors disciplined to the referential task of representing fictional entities,' (Diamond 1996: 3) as Elin Diamond (in a 1996 review) puts it. In the conventional theatre, instead of being fully here and now, actors have to submit to role-playing and deliver texts that are not their own, making themselves subservient to the representation of an absent meaning. Spectators are similarly disciplined, for they are 'duped into identifying with the psychological problems of individual egos and ensnared in a unique temporal-spatial world whose suspense, reversals, and deferrals they can more or less comfortably decode'. (Diamond 1996: 3) The construction of the event forces them into pre-given ways of looking and responding and, this way, free, direct contact with what is actually there present on stage is prevented. Performance, on the other hand, 'has been honored with dismantling textual authority, illusionism, and the canonical actor in favor of the polymorphous body of the performer. Refusing the conventions of role-playing, the performer presents herself/himself as a sexual, permeable, tactile body, scourging the audience narrativity along with the barrier between stage and spectator'. (Diamond 1996: 3) Performance is presented as the deconstruction or denial of theatre conventions in order to undo the obsessive disciplining of both audience and performer, and to open up to direct contact with what is actually present there. The rather ironic ring of Diamond's description already indicates that she now understands herself to be at a certain distance from this concept of performance as a celebration of presence. Still, a major concern of experimental practices in the 1960s and early 1970s, i.e. the presence of performance – and especially the ontological claims implied by this notion of presence – became subject to severe criticism shortly afterwards, and turned into a highly problematic concept. 'After Derrida', as Elinor Fuchs puts it, the avant-garde theatre of presence tended to give way to a theatre of absence that rejected 'the theatrical enterprise of spontaneous speech, with its logocentric claims to origination, authority, authenticity – in short, Presence', to seek instead performance that 'disperses the center, displaces the subject, destabilizes meaning'. (Fuchs in Carlson 1993: 165, 172) Diamond concludes that 'In line with poststructuralist claims of the death of the author, the focus in performance today has shifted from authority to effect, from text to body, to the spectator's freedom to make and transform meanings'. (Diamond 1996: 3) She calls performance nowadays a 'contested space' promoting heightened awareness of cultural difference, a space where meanings and desires are generated in multiple form.

Yet, notwithstanding the fact that presence's ontological claims have been successfully and convincingly deconstructed, the experience of intense 'here and now-ness' – the feeling that one is seeing it 'as it is' right before one's eyes – is still very much a part of the theatrical experience, and a much desired effect. It is an experience sought after by audiences, rewarded in critical reviews, and associated with the 'live' character of the theatrical event. It is associated, furthermore, with such qualities as immediateness, non-artificiality, credibility, and authenticity. The body – no longer understood as a natural given before or beyond meaning, but as a culturally inflected and multi-interpretable entity – more than any other element of the theatrical event seems to be capable of evoking these experiences. Here, I think Wallon's notion of 'presence' might help to turn it into a productive concept again, because it allows for a relocation of 'presence' in the eye of the beholder, turning it into an effect of culturally mediated vision and constituted within a relationship of seer and seen. Furthermore, Silverman's re-reading of the mirror stage through Wallon makes it possible to theorize about how the eye of the beholder is embodied, that is, about how the beholder as a body is involved in seeing bodies on stage. This way, 'presence' as a culturally inflected effect of seeing bodies might help us to become aware of some of the limitations of the spectator's freedom to make meaning. It might also contribute to a re-reading of John Martin's concept of inner mimicry, i.e. reading it as a way of making things one's own through a process of non-visual mapping of what is seen on a culturally inflected body. I will come back to this later. Yet, if the mirror stage is to be used as a model for the theatre, some questions have to be answered first. Is it possible to use the mirror image model of identification to describe the relationship with bodies other than one's own? Can the model of mirror stage identification describe what happens when bodies see bodies that are not comparable to a mirror image in the strict sense, like for example John Martin assuming the image of Martha Graham's body? This immediately brings up a second question: Why does his proprioceptive ego smoothly integrate with Martha Graham's white female body, but not with the image of a black dancer? What forms the limits of mirror stage identification?

Seeing and Being Seen

In Lacan's account of the mirror stage, the subject 'assumes an image' and as a result a transformation takes place, one that inaugurates the self as we know it. The image assumed differs from the body as felt in some important respects. Lacan puts it as follows:

> The fact is that the total form of the body by which the subject anticipates in a mirage the maturation of his power is given to him only as a Gestalt, that is to say, in an exteriority in which this form is certainly more constituent than constituted, but in which it appears to him

above all in a contrasting size (*un relief de stature*) that fixes it and in
a symmetry that inverts it, in contrast with the turbulent movements
that the subject feels are animating him. (Lacan 1977: 2)

The difference between the body as experienced from within and the image
perceived in the mirror, is of crucial importance for the assuming of the
image to take place. It is because the image is more attractive than the body
as felt, that the infant subject is prompted to recognize it as its own. At the
same time, Lacan's reliance on the mirror – that is, on a tableau in which
the visual image seems to be a direct extension of the physical body of
the child and naturally related to it – implicitly but strongly suggests the
importance of correspondence. The mirror as a model suggests that
the child recognizes itself in the image, because it is an image of its *own*
body and is recognized as such because it is the same. At this point, too,
Silverman argues for more 'space' in the Lacanian model. She sets out to
theorize about the possibility of a disjunctive relationship between visual
imago and sensational body, a relationship that is mediated by culture. She
therefore proposes to replace the mirror with another Lacanian concept:
that of the screen, as theorized by Lacan in *Seminar XI*.

In *Seminar XI*, Lacan repeats what he said before, i.e. that the subject
relies for his or her visual identity on an external representation. In his
explanation here, however, he does not refer to a mirror but to what he calls
'the screen'. The screen is not reflective like a mirror surface, but is
opaque. The images of the screen appear as a result not of mechanical
reflection, but of cultural intervention. The screen makes visible what the
culture admits, and blocks out the rest. In *Male Subjectivity at the Margins*
(1992), Silverman proposes imagining the screen as the repertoire of representations by means of which our culture figures all of those many var-
ieties of 'difference' through which social identity is inscribed. (Silverman
1992: 150) Von Kleist's story of the boy in front of the mirror offers an
example of the working of the screen. In this story, the boy does not recognize himself in a mere image of his body in the mirror. His jubilant moment
of (mis)recognition takes place at the moment that his mirror image resembles a classical statue he and the narrator had admired shortly before. The
classical statue represents an ideal of bodily beauty, especially at the time
von Kleist wrote this text. 'Copies are familiar and to be found in most
German collections', he says. The statue represents an ideal that belongs to
the cultural repertoire of images that makes up the screen.

There is no existential connection between the screen image and the
subject who is defined through it, and no necessarily analogy. The screen
can invite identification with images that are rather different from a mirror

image in the literal sense. This distance, however, does not imply freedom. To be able to successfully invite identification the image must possess a certain ideality. It must appeal to a desire, just as the mirror image appeals to the child who identifies with it. What can appear as ideal, is culturally mediated. Furthermore, what is culturally mediated is not only what can appear as an ideal image, but also who is allowed to identify with it. It is not enough that the subject (mis)recognizes him or herself within an image. In the Lacanian model of the field of vision, the (mis)recognition can only be successful if the subject is apprehended in that guise by an other. The alignment of the proprioceptive with the exterioceptive ego involves more than the look of the body seeing and feeling. It involves the look of others, the look of the other. Identification, it turns out, is a three-way rather than a two-way transaction. (Silverman 1996: 18)

The experience of being seen has a tremendous effect on our sense of self, and on how we experience the relation between self and world. It can both confirm our self-(mis)recognition and deny positive identification, as happens to the boy in von Kleist's story. The older man, being the authority, has introduced the boy to the culture represented by the Spinario, and to the notion of bodily ideality represented by it. He taught him how to see it, and – more important – taught to him to see 'through' it, and even to see himself 'through' it. Yet, in the end, what is decisive is not how the boy sees himself or would like to see himself, but how he is being seen. As soon as the boy recognizes himself in the mirror image, he turns to the man for confirmation of what he sees. The man, instead of providing such confirmation, destroys the self-image of the boy, leaving him in confusion. This negative possibility is implied by Lacan's account of the mirror stage, but is not theorized by him. This possibility, however, would become central to Silverman's elaboration on the Lacanian model. Silverman refers to Franz Fanon's *Black Skin White Masks* (1986) in order to illustrate the devastating effects of such a denial on the construction of a self-image. Fanon – a black man born in one of France's former colonies, and 'raised on a steady diet of Gaelic culture' (Silverman 1996: 27) – regards himself as 'French' rather than 'black'. At least, as long as he remains in the colony. When he moves to France, however, he is suddenly confronted with what he looks like in the eyes of those who are not black. He describes how he feels himself being addressed by the look of others in a very disconcerting way. He feels himself *being seen through images of blackness*. 'Assailed at various points, [my preexisting] corporeal schema crumble[s]', he recounts. 'I [subject] myself to an objective examination, I [discover] my blackness, my ethnic characteristics; and I [am] battered down by tom-toms, cannibalism, intellectual deficiency, fetichism [sic], racial defects, slave ships, and above all: "Sho' good eatin'''. (Fanon in Silverman 1996: 28) Through the look of others addressing him, he is forced to see himself as being, first and foremost, black. His awareness of being seen in this particular way forces him to identify with an imago that is abhorrent to him.

Von Kleist's and Fanon's stories demonstrate how we become aware of ourselves as bodies not only through reflections in mirrors, but also through the look of others seeing us. Through our awareness of being seen, we become aware of ourselves as a spectacle for others and as part of the spectacle of the world. This is not the result of the look of individual people projecting things onto one another. Fanon states how it is impossible for him to indicate the source from which he is seen through these images of blackness. Whenever he tries to point at where it comes from, the source seems to evaporate. His awareness of being seen results from an unlocalizable mechanism that makes him feel 'photographed' in an undesirable way. This is what Lacan theorizes as the mechanism of the gaze. Silverman describes the Lacanian gaze as something that impresses itself upon us through the sensation each of us at times has of being held within the field of vision, of being given over to specularity. (Silverman 1996: 167) The gaze is everywhere and nowhere at the same time, and manifests itself more through its effects than through its source. It has much in common with the Sartrean concept of *le regard*, as he theorizes it in his famous theoretical story of the voyeur peeping through a keyhole – has become deeply familiar in contemporary critical theory. Although Lacan engages himself with Sartre's text only once, his account of the gaze, according to Silverman, 'begs to be read in tandem with that text'. (Silverman 1996: 167) This is not only because of the similarities, but also because reading them in tandem can help to clarify the differences between them. Since these differences are crucial to the critique of vision as presented in *The Path of the Dancer's Soul*, I will follow Silverman's example and start with a brief look at the Sartrean model.

Relocating the Transcendental Eye

Sartre distinguishes between two different acts of looking, and illustrates the difference between them with the example of a voyeur peeping through a keyhole. The voyeur is absorbed in the spectacle in front of him to such an extent that his own embodied presence escapes his attention. In his condition as voyeur, he is devoid of self-consciousness, and paradoxically this is synonymous with a certain transcendence. But then, suddenly, something happens that reminds him of his 'being there', for example, the sound of footsteps behind him. The sound conjures him out of his state of 'nothingness' into existence. He becomes aware that he himself is part of the visual world as well as seen from the point of view of the other evoked by the footsteps. From having a pure consciousness of things, the voyeur now becomes aware of himself as a spectacle, and it is through this awareness that a consciousness of self is produced in him. This sense of self is inextricably bound up with an awareness of his own specularity, of his being visible to others, to the other. The voyeur suffers his specularity as the loss of transcendence. His transcendent position is transcended, and he feels himself no longer master of the field of vision. His mastery is unmasked as an illusion, as he suddenly realizes that he himself is also 'on view'. Like von Kleist's Mr. C before him, Sartre relates this falling into a state of self-awareness with the Fall. To function as a spectacle, and thus to exist for the other, is to lapse into a 'fallen' state. (Silverman 1996: 165)

Silverman points out how Sartre associates this experience of specularity with a whole series of psychic 'symptoms', all of which are somehow indicative of the condition of being in a relation of exteriority to one's self. These symptoms are then imaginarily converted into a list of antithetical values to produce *le regard*. (Silverman 1996: 164) She demonstrates how these oppositions contribute to a central opposition at work at the heart of Sartre's model of the field of vision: that of subject and object, or – to be more precise – the antithesis of a pure or absolute subject and an object that is its absolute opposite. As Silverman observes, Sartre characterizes this 'pure subject' in terms that are so in excess of human capacities that it ultimately becomes a phantom category, one that cannot be associated with an actual pair of eyes. She therefore calls this absolute subject a 'specular agency' fantasized into existence on the basis of the voyeur's apprehension of his emplacement within the field of vision. It is more a subjective effect than the result of actual situation. (Silverman 1996: 166) Yet, at the same time, Sartre consequently attributes to this agent, human (or at least anthropomorphically inflected) functions, as a result of which the absolute subject or other appears as an imaginary rival.

The Sartrean model of the field of vision informed what is now a strongly established line of feminist criticism that gained its fullest theoretical articulation in film studies. It helped to theorize the role of the camera in the construction of what is to be seen on film, how the camera mediates in the appearance of female bodies, and how this construction invites particular ways of looking at them. It helped to unmask the appearance of bodies on screen as product of subjective vision constructed in order to satisfy what is called 'the male gaze'. What otherwise might pass for a mechanical inscription of what bodies look like, thus becomes exposed as a construction implying a specific point of view. These developments in film theory in their turn proved to be productive for the theatre as a tool for analyzing the appearance of women within the scenarios on stage. However, the transposition of this model to the theatre proved to be not unproblematic. As Sue Ellen Case (1995) observes:

> The power relations of the Gaze in narrative cinema seemed homologous to operations of spectatorship in the theatre. Yet the obvious but astonishing fact that this construction of the Gaze helped to inscribe a role for the technology of the camera and the screen in the critical understanding of gender politics somehow eluded our attention. We neglected to comprehend fully how the power relations in the visual were necessarily cojoined with a mechanical apparatus for seeing. (Case 1995: 330)

Theatre lacks such an apparatus. It does make use of techniques to direct attention and to guide the look of the audience, yet it lacks a technique of vision comparable to the camera. Furthermore, although some theatre traditions and theatre practices do exploit the voyeuristic pleasure of peeping through a keyhole into another world while remaining invisible in the dark, a wide range of other theatrical practices demonstrate that this is not a necessary characteristic of the theatre event, nor a necessary pre-condition for the intense experience referred to as 'presence'. On the contrary, in many contemporary theatre practices, it is precisely the direct and explicit relationship with the audience that contributes to the intensity of the theatre as a 'live' experience, present over there.

The new theatre as it has developed since around the 1970s, can be defined largely by the fact that it privileges process, event, or situation over quality of work as representation of an absent subject matter. Hans-Thies Lehmann describes this development as the rediscovery of a space and speech without *telos*, hierarchy without structured meaning, and inner unity producing a new kind of architecture of the theatre. This architecture manifests itself in the construction of spaces and discourses liberated from the restraints of goals, hierarchy, and causal logic, and terminating in scenic poems, meandering narration, and fragmentation. In these practices, the theoretical and practical opposition of theatre and performance seems to dissolve. 'If theatre used to be defined as a kind of fictive cosmos presented to a public by means of theatre signs, theatre now tends more and more to be defined as a special and unique situation (…) in the sense of the construction of a theatrical moment where a kind of communication different from everyday talk could possibly, virtually, structurally happen'.

(Lehmann 1997a: 58) These new scenic discourses seriously affect the position of the various elements that make up the theatrical event, including that of the actor who plays in it. The appearance of bodies in this theatrical moment can be quite puzzling. For various reasons, it is often difficult to speak of dramatic players in the sense of actors. 'Performers' seems more to the point, performers who in the theatrical situation present something that in many cases seems to be very close to 'themselves'. Often these works are no longer concerned with fictive persons, except in rudimentary ways. What frequently emerges is what Lehmann has called 'a true "exhibition"' of the bodies of the players. (Lehmann 1997b: 45)

These bodies on stage are not objectified, like the female bodies turned into spectacle and criticized in feminist film theory. They do not necessarily capitalize on voyeuristic pleasures. On the contrary, often they are explicitly theatrical. They look back at the audience, showing that they know that they show. They present a challenge to the audience to make a distinction between the act of showing and what is actually there to be seen, in this way challenging the old anti-theatrical prejudice reflected in Mr. C's rejection of the self-conscious behavior of living dancers as being 'baroque mannerism'. That is, they challenge the use of theatricality as a pejorative term to refer to behavior that is false or inauthentic to the extent that its concern with being seen takes precedence over what it shows. Much more they challenge the presuppositions underlying this negative understanding of 'theatricality', namely that it would be possible to see things 'as they are', and that this 'givenness' becomes distorted in a self-conscious act of showing. In this way, these 'exhibitions' of bodies on stage point at some limitations of the Sartrean model for an analysis of vision in the theatre.

In Sartre's model, the point of view of the voyeur is transcended and exposed in its objectivity. The model thus tends to confirm rather than deconstruct the opposition of 'mere' representation and a true presence behind it. According to Silverman, in this way Sartre misses the crucial opportunity implicit in the concept of the 'looked at look' – i.e. the opportunity to theorize it in relation not to objectivity but to subjectivity. She acknowledges the value of his insistence upon the eye's embodiment and specularity for feminist attempts 'to divest the male look of its false claim to be the gaze', yet also points out that what happens this way is *not so much a deconstruction as a relocation of the notion of a transcendental eye*. (Silverman 1996: 166, my italics, MB) Von Kleist's story demonstrates what such a relocation involves, and how it helps restore a stable sense of self through the construction of a new, all-seeing point of view, that of the absolute subject.

In von Kleist's third story, Sartre's imaginary rival materializes into an actual body and literally becomes a rival in a fencing match. In this story, Mr. C recalls a visit he once paid to the estate of a Livonian nobleman. Mr. C, as well as being a very good dancer, appears to be a virtuoso fencer and is more than a match for all but one of his opponents. After he has defeated the sons of the nobleman, they challenge him to test his skills on a bear that their father was having raised on the estate. Much to his own surprise, Mr. C appears to be unable to beat the bear. The bear makes him feel highly uncomfortable. What appears to be most confronting is the way the bear looks at him and seems to be able to read his soul.

> The earnestness of the bear was robbing me of my composure, thrusts and feints followed on one another, I was dripping with sweat: in vain! It was not merely that the bear, like the world's leading fencer, parried every one of my thrusts, but to my feints he reacted not at all (a feat that no fencer anywhere could match). Eye to eye, as though he could read my very soul, he stood with his paw poised for the strike, and if my thrusts were not in earnest he simply did not move. (von Kleist 1982: 216)

Mr. C feels threatened by the bear, while in fact it is he who attacks the bear. The bear only defends itself. What is really threatening Mr. C is the look of the bear. This unexpected look undermines Mr. C's notion of himself not only as a master fencer, but also as master of the field of vision. Like the Sartrean voyeur, he is robbed of his sense of transcendence and mastery, and feels exposed as part of the visible world.

In von Kleist's story, Mr. C finally beats the bear in the conclusion, in which he puts the three stories in a broader, cosmological perspective. He himself produces a new point of view that allows him to transcend the threatening encounter with the bear, and to regain his sense of self as master of the field of vision. According to him, the three stories demonstrate how 'in the organic world, as reflection grows darker and weaker, grace emerges ever more radiant and supreme. But just as two intersecting lines, converging on one side of a point, reappear on the other after their passage through infinity, and just as our image as we approach a concave mirror, vanishes to infinity only to reappear before our very eyes, so will grace, having likewise traversed the infinite, return to us once more, and so appear most purely in that bodily form that has either no consciousness at all or an infinite one, which is to say, either in the puppet or in a God'. (Von Kleist 1982: 216) The conclusion exploits what Paul de Man describes as 'the idea of innocence recovered at the far side (...), of paradise regained after the fall into consciousness (...) of a teleological and apocalyptic history of consciousness'. This is a history in which the gap separating being and consciousness will finally be closed again in a state of immediate presence. As de Man observes, these powerful and seductive ideas of the romantic period make it easy to forget how little this pseudo-conclusion in fact has to do with the rest of the text. (De Man 1984: 267–268) The conclusion suggests a symmetry that is not supported by the stories it claims to be based upon. For, although it is not very hard to link the conclusion to the first story about the marionette owing its superior grace to its lack of consciousness, the question remains, how to consider the other possibility for the return of grace – God – a bodily form with infinite consciousness. None of the three stories gives a clue about the relation between infinite consciousness and bodily grace. On the contrary, again and again they stress the first part of Mr. C's conclusion that grace and reflection are to be understood as antagonistic. The second story – about the boy in front of the mirror – reads as an illustration of how self-consciousness hinders bodily grace. When the boy self-consciously tries to assume the image of the Spinario, he is not able to repeat the graceful attitude he unconsciously assumed a moment ago. No clue is given about how to overcome this repulsive situation again. The third story – about the bear – is even more puzzling in relation to the teleological and symmetrical history suggested in the conclusion. Where to position the bear in the teleological history of consciousness 'from puppet to God'? In the first and the second story, Mr. C and the narrator are the subjects observing grace – or the lack of it – in other bodies, and explaining it in terms of a relationship between consciousness and grace in the bodies observed. In the third story, however, Mr. C is the object of the sharp eye of the bear. Here, so it seems, it is the bear's lack of consciousness that allows him not to perform, but *to read* movements in a superior way. The bear sees right through Mr. C's attempts to fool him, and this gives Mr. C the feeling of being exposed.

The look of the bear undermines not only Mr. C's self-image, but also the Sartrean symmetrical model of the field of vision. Although the story of the bear is – as pointed out above – similar to the Sartrean scenario in some ways, it differs from it in important respects. For example, unlike the voyeur, Mr. C can hardly have been unaware that he was the object of the bear's vision, otherwise it would have made no sense to play a game of fencing with it. It cannot be his sudden realization that he is being seen by the bear that bothers him and undermines his sense of self as master of the situation. It is rather the way in which he feels exposed to *others*, just as it is *others* – and not the bear threatening him – that he has to convince of the truth of his conclusion, of his version of 'how it is' with the world. It is the narrator's confirmation that Mr. C seeks with this conclusion, and it is through the involvement of this third party that he sets out to regain his sense of self and of mastery. Mr. C's story about the bear thus indicates an asymmetry at work in the field of vision that Sartre's model does not account for and is better theorized with Lacan's.

Lacan stresses the asymmetry of the look with which the voyeur peers through the keyhole, and the gaze with which he is surprised. The Lacanian gaze is not the same as the look of a subject: the gaze escapes the category of the subject. At one point, he defines it as 'the presence of others as such', but is eager to make clear that it is a 'function of seeingness' and is not to be mistaken for the look of concrete other subjects. This 'function' precedes any individual act of looking, and is that out of which the look somehow emerges much as language might be said to preexist the subject and provide him or her with his or her signifying resources. For this reason, Silverman calls the gaze 'the manifestation of the symbolic within the field of vision'. (Lacan in Silverman 1996: 168) The Lacanian gaze is neither subjective nor objective. It appears as a third term mediating in the constitution of what is self and what is other. It points at interference of culture in the experience of 'just looking', of how we perceive the visual field. The gaze disrupts the symmetrical opposition of subject and object, of self and other, of body and mirror image. It is the cultural interference in the field of vision that is at work in John Martin's body mimicking the body of Martha Graham, perceiving the ideal image presented by her white, female body as 'naturalness', while rejecting the bodies of black and native American dancers as distortions of the natural essences he perceives in her. It is not only because Martin is white, like Martha Graham, that her body can appear to him as more natural and truthful, but also because within the culture in which Martin's observations take place, whiteness signifies this complex intertwining of the natural and the ideal. It is therefore also not only because Martin himself is not black or native American, that seeing native or black bodies does not produce that feeling of recognition, the feeling of being able to spontaneously feel the feelings of the bodies seen. As Silverman's example of Fanon demonstrates, recognition is not only based on sameness or similarities; it also involves a certain culturally specific ideality, as a result of which – within a particular cultural and historical context – some bodies can appear as 'how it is', that is, as the manifestation of a naturalness that other bodies lack.

Gestures of Exposure

In their staging of von Kleist's text, Rijnders and de Chatel foreground the asymmetry at work in the field of vision on stage through a perhaps not very spectacular, yet most effective *mise en scène*. They present von Kleist's text as an act of exposure, literally an exhibition of a body on stage, and a very specific one, too. Their staging resembles the gesture of showing, which according to Mieke Bal (1996) is typical of a museum. It is a gesture that points at things, saying 'look, this is how it is'. Bal deals with exhibitions, not with theatre performances. Nevertheless, her analysis of the exhibition as an act of exposure also proves to be useful for an analysis of the exhibition of bodies on stage.

In an act of exposure, something is made public and, according to Bal, this involves making public the deepest held views and beliefs of a subject. Exposition, therefore, is always also an argument. In publicizing these views, the subject exposes himself as much as the object. 'Such exposure is an act of producing meaning, a performance'. (Bal 1996: 2) This performative character of exposure, however, remains hidden in the typical constative gesture of exposure of the museum saying 'this is how it is'. In order to lay bare the performative aspects involved in constative gestures of exposure, Bal proposes to conceive of gestures of showing as discursive acts analogous to speech acts. In such acts, three positions or 'persons' are involved: The 'first person' – the exposer – who tells a 'second person' – the visitor – about a 'third person', the object on display. (Bal 1996: 3–4) In the Rijnders/de Chatel performance, the actor represents the first person. He stands on the left-hand side of the stage and recites von Kleist's text *On the Puppet Theatre*. He acts as though he is giving a lecture, addressing the audience that represents the second person. On the right-hand side of the stage, there is the dancer making simple dance movements. He does not speak; he is just there, acknowledging the presence of the audience through his look. He represents the third person, the object on display, a true exhibition of a body on stage. The object is put within a frame that enables the statement to come across. An important part of framing in this performance is the change of title, from von Kleist's *On the Puppet Theatre* to Rijnders and de Chatel's *The Path of the Dancer's Soul*, which is a quote from the text. This new title turns the dancer into the object of the argument. This object does not participate in the conversation. It is there to substantiate the statement. However, unlike the case in the speech acts that make up von Kleist's text, the object, although mute, is present. This is important, for it allows for the critical move the performance will make.

When the speaker is near the end of the text, the dancer makes an unexpected move: he leaves his position on the right-hand side of the stage, walks toward the speaker, and looks at him. This move appears to be highly uncomfortable for the speaker: he tries to avoid the dancer's eyes, tries to ignore his presence near him, and instead focuses his attention on the audience; he repeats the entire text at double speed, and also repeats his demonstrative gestures. The unexpected move by the dancer resembles that of the bear in Mr. C's story. Like Mr. C, the speaker tries to counter the threat by attempting to impose his story – his vision of 'how it is' – on the audience, and to deny the disturbing look of the object of his vision. He literally ignores the dancer and repeats what he has already said, as though to stress that this is 'how it is'. However, the dancer, who is visually present before the eyes of audience, prevents him from accomplishing what Mr. C in the text manages to accomplish. On stage, the speaker loses his authority, and his demonstration of how it is with the object of his attention turns into an exposition of himself as an embodied subject.

The unexpected move by the dancer offers a second point of view, i.e. an invitation to the audience to look in a different way. It is what Mieke Bal (1991), using a beautiful bodily metaphor, has called the 'navel' of the performance text. The navel 'is a metaphor for an element, often a tiny detail, that hits the viewer, is processed by her or him, and textualizes the image on its own terms'. Like the human navel, it is 'a center without meaning, yet it is a meaningful pointer'. (Bal 1991: 22) The navel allows the viewer to propose new readings in order to meet his or her needs. The move by the dancer that makes up the navel of the performance causes an actual re-reading of the entire text by von Kleist in a different way, exposing it not as a demonstration of truth, but as a nervous attempt by the speaker to keep going. By redirecting attention, the move by the dancer turns the demonstration of 'how it is' with the dancer – with bodies seen – into a performance that exposes the observer as subject. His critical move turns the demonstration of 'how it is' with the body of the dancer seen, into an exhibition of the speaker as body seeing. He is exposed as a desiring subject to himself, and also to the 'presence of others as such'. In this process, the look of the audience represents the Lacanian gaze. This is not to say that the audience is gazing, nor that their look is the gaze: the Lacanian gaze refers to being conscious of one's visibility. It is a mechanism internalized in a way analogous to the way Foucauldian Panopticon is internalized in his account of the psychological construction of the modern subject. *The Path of the Dancer's Soul* uses the theatre situation to externalize the mechanism and this way expose its functioning.

Relocating Lacan

In *The Path of the Dancer's Soul*, the desiring subject exposed is a body on stage. Lacan's account of the field of vision, however, allows for an analysis of how the look of the body seeing in the auditorium is also under cultural and psychological pressure. Here, moments of 'presence' prove to be particularly instructive. With a Lacanian model of the construction of the field of vision, it is possible to understand the feeling of intense closeness to bodies directly 'present' on stage, not in terms of the characteristics of the object, nor as the result of the immediateness of the presentation, but as the effect of a culturally mediated way of looking.

Even before we become conscious of having seen something, perception has been processed in all kinds of ways. The look is exhorted from many sides to perceive and affirm only what generally passes for 'reality'. In *Male Subjectivity at the Margins* (1992), Silverman therefore proposes to replace 'reality' with 'dominant fiction'. The 'fiction' in 'dominant fiction' foregrounds the constructed nature of what passes for reality. The 'dominant' points at the fact that there is more than one fiction possible, but also that these different possibilities do not have equal access to the 'reality' status. Calling reality a fiction undermines its ontological claims of truth, and opens it up to change and cultural difference. However, here again, it is important to notice that this does not imply unlimited freedom. The dominant fiction is not a story told by the self, nor can it be changed by an individual. It is the story within which both world and the self are produced, and it is at work at levels we do not consciously control. Von Kleist's version of the mirror stage moment can be read as a demonstration of the dominant fiction at work. What is needed in order to expose this fiction at work, is to redirect attention analogous to the critical move performed by the dancer in *The Path of the Dancer's Soul*. Von Kleist's narrator tells a story about a boy in front of a mirror. Yet, this story is not that of nor that told by the boy: it is the story of the older man observing the boy. It is as much about him as about the boy observed. Interesting in this respect is the account the narrator gives of his own reaction to what happens to the boy. Recalling the moment the boy pointed out that he looked like the Spinario, the man says: 'I indeed had noticed it too in the very same instant, but either to test the self-assurance of the grace with which he was endowed, or to challenge his vanity in a salutary way, I laughed and said he was seeing phantoms'. (Von Kleist 1982: 215) His denial of the boy's discovery is not the correction of a mistake. It is not an exposure of 'how it is', confronting the boy's subjective point of view with the objective truth seen from a transcendental point of view. On the contrary, it is a denial of what he, too, has seen, but does not or cannot believe. It is a subjective reaction dictated by cultural values and psychic pressure, dictated perhaps by the same cultural presupposition that was already at stake in the first story, namely that a living and self-conscious being can never approach the beauty and grace of a marionette. Seen this way, the older man's reaction is an aggressive one toward someone who seems capable of approximating what he himself cannot. His reaction demonstrates how he translates a threat to his own ego into a disorder perceived in the boy.

In the same way, to expose the audience as a desiring subject, what is needed is an explanation of the appearance of bodies on stage as the product of a cultural and psychological determined look, rather than as simply being there to be seen. Here again, moments of 'presence' can provide a point of entrance for they present a kind of audience variant of the constative gesture of 'this is how it is'. 'Presence' – understood in terms of Silverman/Wallon as a successful stitching together of an image of a body seen and the proprioceptive ego of the body seeing – can function as a meaningful pointer, indicating that the body seen appeals to a desire of the body seeing. It appeals to a specific desire, namely that to recognize the body seen as natural, as 'how it is'. This desire is not a deformation of reality, but constitutive of what is perceived as reality. To demonstrate what such an exposure of the subject of vision could mean, I propose to end my paper with a little thought experiment, and to understand the mirror stage as described by Lacan as a staged situation like the Rijnders/de Chatel performance. In order to 'look back' at the subject of vision, I will perform a move analogous to the one proposed by the performance, and expand Bal's analysis of the act of exposure as a discursive gesture to this academic demonstration of 'how it is'.

Like von Kleist's story about the boy in front of the mirror, the Lacanian account of the mirror stage is a story about a child, and not that of or by this child. It is the story of Lacan seeing and observing the child, and it is therefore as much about the subject 'Lacan' as it is about the child. By the subject 'Lacan', I do not mean Jacques Lacan as a historical person, but the subject of vision as it is produced in his text. I wonder what his text about the mirror stage can tell me about this subject of vision as a body. What could it mean to understand Lacan's observations as the product of an embodied look under cultural pressure to perceive the world from a pre-assigned point of view? As I will show, especially the jubilant recognition is telling in this respect, provided that it is approached as proposed by the performance, that is, starting from the question to whom this bodily image appears as more ideal, and what desire this image appeals to.

According to Lacan, it is the 'organic disturbance and discord' of the body as experienced from the inside that prompts the child to seek out the 'whole body-image' in the mirror. Lacan acknowledges the possibility of moments of collapse of the alignment with the ideal image, moments that result in what he calls 'the fantasy of the body in bits and pieces'. However, as Silverman points out, this explanation in terms of disintegration and failure is only one way of apprehending the heterogeneity of the corporeal ego, and a very particular one, too. It is a way of apprehending that is inextricably tied to the aspiration toward wholeness and unity. Silverman proposes to reverse Lacan's argument, and argues that the opposite is actually true. It is not that the child seeks wholeness because it experiences itself as fragmented. According to her 'it is the cultural premium placed on the notion of a coherent bodily ego that results in such a dystopic apprehension of corporeal multiplicity'. (Silverman 1996: 21) It is because of the cultural appreciation of bodily wholeness that the child experiences its bodily fragmentation as dystopic. Both the identification with the unitary image of a body in the mirror, and the fantasy of the body in bits and pieces are the result of the cultural premium placed on unity that informs the Lacanian subject. This way, Silverman again draws attention to the constructed nature of what can appear as ideal image. Again, she points to the fact that the relation between the image the subject identifies with and the body as felt, has to be understood as a product of culture, rather than as naturally given. Yet at this point, Silverman's elaboration on Lacan seems to open itself up to a more profound critique as well. A further implication of her reading seems to be that the specific relationship of body image and body as felt as observed by Lacan might be culturally informed, too. Susan Buck-Morss (1992) offers a possibility to think in this direction.

At one point Lacan characterizes the coherence to which the classical subject aspires as 'the armor of an always alienating identity'. (Lacan in Silverman 1996: 21) It is the result of a cultural logic in which 'wholeness' – a coherent bodily ego – signifies psychic health. Susan Buck-Morss suggests that this cultural imperative has to be understood in the context of sensory alienation typical of modernity. According to her, the significance of Lacan's theory emerges in the historical context of modernity as precisely the experience of the fragile body and the dangers of fragmentation. She presents her critique of Lacan as part of a re-reading of Walter Benjamin's famous essay *The Work of Art in the Age of Mechanical Reproduction*, which appeared in 1936, the year that Lacan first presented his ideas on the mirror stage. According to Benjamin, the very essence of the modern experience is shock. The technologically altered environment of modern city life, the factory, and modern warfare, expose the human sensorium to physical shocks that have their correspondence in psychic shock. It is against this cultural background of modernity as shock that the unitary, well outlined body-as-image as it appears in the mirror appears desirable. The mirror image is a body as seen from the point of view the German writer Ernst Jünger describes as 'second consciousness'. Jünger calls the technological order dominating modern life, a mirror that reflects back an image of the body that alters our awareness of ourselves as embodied beings. 'In the great mirror of technology, the image that returns is displaced, reflected onto a different plane, where one sees oneself as a physical body divorced from sensory vulnerability – a statistical body, the behavior of which can be calculated; a performing body, actions of which can be measured up against the norm; a virtual body, one can endure the shocks of modernity without pain'. (Buck-Morss 1992: 33) In the modern world, war causalities as well as industrial and traffic accidents have become accepted as a feature of existence, and have forced modern man to develop a second consciousness that is indicated in the ever-more sharply developed capacity to see oneself as an object. Jünger writes: 'It almost seems as if the human being possessed a striving to create a space in which pain ... can be regarded as an illusion'. (Jünger in Buck-Morss 1992: 33) The construction of a second consciousness that manifests itself as the result of identification with an image of the body as divorced from the sensory vulnerability of the body as felt from the inside, thus appears as a reaction to the shocks that make up modern life. Benjamin – relying on the Freudian insight that consciousness is a shield protecting the organism against stimuli – comes up with a neurological explanation pointing in the same direction. To protect itself against the constant bombardment of shocks, the ego employs consciousness as a shield, blocking the openness of the synaesthetic system of the body, thereby isolating present consciousness from past memory. As a result, experience becomes impoverished. Sealed off from experience, 'being "cheated out of experience" has become the general state, as the synaesthetic system is marshalled to parry technological stimuli in order to protect both the body from the trauma of accident and the psyche from the trauma of perceptual shock'. (Buck-Morss 1992: 16)

Buck-Morss presents some fragments that form the outline of a fable that lies at the foundation of today's 'reality'. She thus helps to locate the specific constellation of vision, embodiment, and subjectivity that makes up the modern subject within a specific cultural/historical context. Her text suggests that the cultural imperative of assuming the image of the unitary body in the mirror is a symptom of the threat imposed on the subject as a vulnerable body under the pressure of modern life and a technologically altered environment. Furthermore, that this cultural premium informs not only the subject to identify with a particular bodily image, but also the specific relationship of body image and body as felt that makes up the very foundations of the Lacanian model of ego formation. His conceptualization of subject formation resonates the 'disembodied' character typical of the modern understanding of vision, as well as the vigorous privileging of vision over the other senses. It is in the first place through looking that modern individuals are understood to gain insight into themselves and the world, to such an extent that the 'I' of the looker and his or her eye almost seem to conflate. Elements of this fable can still be seen at work in today's understanding of ourselves as embodied subjects and how we experience the relation to the world around us.

Buck-Morss shows the Lacanian model to be the product of a particular historical moment, to be a conceptualization that appeals to a desire at work within the dominant fiction of modernity. At the same time, her historization of the Lacanian model invites one to think beyond Lacan, and to undo the simultaneity of over-simulation and numbness characteristic of the synaesthetic organization of the modern subject, now that the 'grand narratives' of modernity have started to break up and become visible as 'dominant fiction' rather than a natural given. Such rethinking might also grant new actuality to Martin's concept of inner mimicry. Inner mimicry seems to open up the possibility to regard not only the bodily image as constitutive of the embodied self, but also – vice versa – the embodied self as constitutive of the image of a body perceived. This would imply a slightly different reading of proprioception as a combination of *proprius* and *capere*. That is, proprioception meaning to grasp, conceive, or catch what is seen through a process of bodily responsiveness. Inner mimicry, then, would not mean feeling what the other body seen is feeling, but using one's own bodily feelings and kinesthetic responses to make sense of a body seen. Understood in this way, inner mimicry does not present a link to an original universality, but describes a bodily process of culturally specific meaning-making. It would come to mean a way of making things one's own through a process of non-visual mapping of what is seen on a culturally inflected body. Inner mimicry as the process of mapping of a body seen onto the body seeing as a means to make sense of the body seen, might help to overcome the mono-directionality implied in the Lacanian model, and to call attention to the ways in which reactions of bodily responsiveness contribute to the construction of what is perceived as 'just looking'.

Bibliography

Bal, Mieke. *Reading 'Rembrandt': Beyond the Word-Image Opposition*. Cambridge: Cambridge University Press, 1991.

—. *Double Exposures: The Subject of Cultural Analysis*. New York and London: Routledge, 1996.

Buck-Morss, Susan. 'Aesthetics and Anaesthetics: Walter Benjamin's Artwork Essay Reconsidered', in: *October* 62, Fall 1992, 3–40.

Carlson, Marvin. *Theories of the Theatre: A Historical and Critical Survey, from the Greeks to the Present*. Expanded Edition. Ithaca and London: Cornell University Press, 1993.

Case, Sue-Ellen. 'Performing Lesbian in the Space of Technology: Part II', in: *Theatre Journal* 47, 329–343, 1995.

Diamond, Elin. 'Introduction', in: Elin Diamond (ed.). *Performance and Cultural Politics*, 1–12. New York and London: Routledge, 1996.

Foster, Susan Leigh. *Empathy and Physicality*. Unpublished paper presented at the working group Choreography and Corporeality at the FIRT/IFTR XIII World Congress. Theatre and Theatre Research: Exploring the Limits. Canterbury, 6–12 July 1998.

Freedman, Barbara. *Staging the Gaze: Postmodernism, Psychoanalysis, and Shakespearean Comedy*. Ithaca and London: Cornell University Press, 1991.

Fuchs, Elinor. 'Presence and the Revenge of Writing: Rethinking Theatre after Derrida', in: *Performing Arts Journal* 26/27, 1985.

Jay, Martin. 'Vision in Context: Reflections and Refractions', in: Teresa Brennan and Martin Jay (eds). *Vision in Context: Historical and Contemporary Perspectives on Sight*, 1–11. New York and London: Routledge, 1996.

Kleist, Heinrich von. 'On the Puppet Theatre', in: Heinrich von Kleist *An Abyss Deep Enough: Letters of Heinrich von Kleist with a Selection of Essays and Anecdotes*. Edited, translated and introduced by Philip B. Miller, 211–216. New York: E.P. Dutton, 1982.

Lacan, Jacques. 'The Mirror Stage as Formative of the Function of the I as Revealed in Psychoanalytic Experience', in: Jacques Lacan. *Ecrits: A Selection*. Translated by Alan Sheridan, pp. 1–7. London: Tavistock Publications, 1977.

Lehmann, Hans-Thies. 'From Logos to Landscape: Text in Contemporary Dramaturgy', in: *Performance Research*. Vol. 2, no. 1, 55–60, 1997a.

—. 'Time Structures/Time Sculptures: On some Theatrical forms at the End of the Twentieth Century', in: *Theaterschrift* 12, 29–47, 1997b.

Man de, Paul. 'Aesthetic Formalization: Kleist's Über das Marionettentheater', in: Paul de Man. *The Rhetoric of Romanticism*, 263–290. New York: Columbia University Press, 1994.

Martin, John. *Introduction to the Dance*. New York: Dance Horizons Incorporated, 1965.

Melville, Stephen. 'Division of the Gaze, or, Remarks on the Color and Tenor of Contemporary Theory', in: Teresa Brennan and Martin Jay (eds). *Vision in Context: Historical and Contemporary Perspectives on Sight*, 101–116. New York and London: Routledge, 1996.

Silverman, Kaja. *Male Subjectivity at the Margins*. New York and London: Routledge, 1992.

—. *The Threshold of the Visible World*. New York and London: Routledge, 1996.

Notes

[1] *De Zieleweg van de Danser* was first presented at the International Theaterschool Festival 1997 in Amsterdam. Director: Gerardjan Rijnders; choreography: Krisztina de Chatel; performed by: Mimoun Oaïssa and Wen-Cheng Lee.

[2] *De Bacchanten*. Het Nationaal Ballet/Stichting Voorheen ADM. Director: Gerardjan Rijnders, choreography: Ted Bransen. First performance 18 June 1986, Koninklijk Theater Carré, Amsterdam.

[3] *Ballet*. Toneelgroep Amsterdam. Director: Gerardjan Rijnders. First performance: 4 April 1990, Stadsschouwburg, Amsterdam.

Frank Reijnders

The Hide of Marsyas: Some Notes on the Screen of Painting

Now that the screen and its refraction constitute the foundation of everyday events, the art of painting has become the most archaic medium imaginable. At least, this view appears to be held increasingly commonly. At the Documenta X in Kassel, the art of painting was deliberately shut out, and at other international exhibitions, too, it has been condemned to a marginal existence. Paint texture is regarded as archaic because it is said to be too slow and too untransparent to make contact with 'our reality'. New picture carriers such as the cibachrome photograph, the video screen and the computer printout have transformed the art of painting: 'The computer is the revenge of painting on photography', asserts young Dutch artist Micha Klein, referring to the first time painting was certified dead, at the beginning of the 19th century, after photography had allegedly taken its place. Because of its fictitious and manipulable nature, digital photography approximates to painting. Mimesis is still being brought to perfection, 'reality' is pictured increasingly quickly and precisely. It now appears as a 'virtual reality'. All media can be digitalised, except for painting.

It is of course true that, strictly speaking, the art of painting is no longer an established, self-evident phenomenon (painting/linen/brush). Consequently, it is often forced to adopt a defensive position. Or is it the other way round, and has the art of painting – both old and new – secretly conformed itself to the two-dimensional screen? It is in its capacity as screen that painting is totally incomparable. The screen of painting, too, is a surface, but it is not flat, smooth or transparent. There is inevitably thickness, relief and layering. As long as representations are at issue, they are part of a paint-decked surface, which prevents them from coinciding with 'reality'. Therefore, it is questionable whether perfect imitation was ever the aim of this kind of mimesis. Has not our view rather been parried and seduced by the charm of imperfection, the variations in thickness and the different ways in which paint is applied to the surface?

Does contemporary painting manifest itself as a screen? A screen amidst a multitude of other screens? Surrounded by screens, we are in any case compelled to relocate the image, more specifically the image of painting. There certainly is an unbridgeable gap between the picture screen and the paint screen. As the paint screen is not transparent but pretends to be, it provokes ambiguities and contradictions; the ambiguities of a second and a third dimension, and the contradiction between a representation and a paint texture that keeps the representation at a distance. Nobody knows exactly where figuration begins and abstraction ends. Nobody can determine precisely where the borderline lies between perceptibility and conceivability. Because of such ambiguities and contradictions, one has wanted to discard painting. It has been labelled an illusion, a lie, a shade, a poison even (Plato's *Pharmakon*). All these objections against painting, however, can be transformed into strengths, if one simply concedes that painting is an imperfect medium. To its adversaries, this is its greatest weakness, especially in an era when communication and transfer of information are considered paramount. However, it is precisely through the illusion that paint creates that the art of painting preserves its sovereignty. The paint screen is not a metaphor, unlike the window, the mirror, the flat surface and the picture screen. Metaphors belong to the realm of language, and as such they are inevitably related to painting. The paint screen, however, is part and parcel of painting itself. It is not a metaphor, but a metamorphosis. That is why painting, and painting alone, is always able to reconsider its precise nature.

The specific possibilities of the paint screen were already being explored quite early on. In Titian's *The Flaying of Marsyas*, the painting's pigment and the hide of the Phrygian satyr almost coincide. Do we see Marsyas' hide or a hide of paint? Such duplication continues to shock. The painting, which is already impressive merely because of its size (212– 207 cm), was produced by Titian when he was 90, shortly before his death in 1576. It depicts a scene from classical mythology: after Apollo, who played the lyre, beat accomplished flutist Marsyas in a musical contest, he could deal with the loser as he wished, and chose to flay him alive. This Venetian painting bears witness to a different type of mimesis than that developed by the Florentine painters since the early 15th century, when they attained a previously unknown three-dimensionality and authenticity through the technique of linear perspective. Titian's mimesis was, first and foremost, much more cruel. He does not aim at an idealistic construction, but starts from paint: stains, colours and patches of light. The *Pittura di macchia* he developed later in life disorders Florentine premises. The surface of the canvas comes first: after preliminary layers have been applied, it is covered with rough touches, strokes and streaks, so that forms seemingly crumble and the illusion of space becomes undefinable. The ambiguities and contradictions are protected by paint. Palma 'il Giovane', a pupil and assistant of Titian's in the latter years of his life, gave an account of his method of painting: 'The seasoning of the last retouches involved the harmonising of the lighter pitches by applying paint with the fingers, thus gradually bringing them closer to the halftones (…). It is true (if one thinks about it) that he had his reasons for doing so: in trying to imitate the Highest Creator's work, he pointed out, when necessary, that He too used his hands to shape the human body out of the earth.' Titian felt challenged by God, the supreme artist. His device, too, was illustrative in this regard: a bear licking its new-born cub into shape. Titian was the first to hide the secrets of nature in the secrets of paint. This 'Lord of Painters' had a greater impact on the development of the art of painting than anyone else. From the 17th century on, the implications of his 'ultima manera' were further explored by Rubens, Velásquez and Rembrandt. As he approached 90, the 'late Picasso', too, modelled his style on that of 'the late Titian', so that he could be free and imprudent. Lewdness was his theme at that stage: urinating and menstruating women, wild embraces and penetrations. Again, the process involves a literal transformation into paint. Stains, specks and primary signs are his starting-point. One red stain of paint evokes menstrual bleeding; one exclamation mark is enough to capture cunt and asshole at once. For the 'late Picasso', too, theme and method of working coincide. It is as if the painted surface itself stretches out to the erogenous zone.

It seems a small step from Titian's Marsyas painting to *Le grand sanglier noir* (1927) by Jean Fautrier. A black boar that has been cut open appears in an overwhelming close-up, almost obscenely showing off its scarlet guts bordered by stubbly fur. One recognises the same kind of mimetic cruelty in the coinciding of the hide of paint and the boar's hide. Both Titian and Fautrier chose their theme quite deliberately. The painted surface and the painted subject evoke the same sense of touch. The starting-point of painting is again in the paint itself, in its untransparent texture and in the irregularities of its hide. In spite of the similarities, this is not the continuation of a tradition. Titian's métier came to its end long before, and requires painstaking reconstruction. Fautrier's method of layering is different. He does not use coloured glazes for instance. Fautrier considered himself a modern painter, an iconoclast, even though he still celebrated the identifiability of his subject: 'Painting can only be destroyed, has to be destroyed, in order to reinvent it'. Like so many other modern artists from the early 20th century, Fautrier believed in the principle of destruction, though unlike Mondrian and others he was not after purity or new meanings. Fautrier had a distinct preference for the vulgar. His dead body reeks of decay and reminds us of a place which, in modern times, leads a doomed existence: the abattoir. Fautrier's destruction does not result in a restoration of the flat surface, but to its disruption. The unevenness of the surface challenges to a minimal countermove: variations in thickness of paint, varnishing, scraping, carving. His dissolution of the art of painting is even analytical: colour, drawing and matter are detached in order to grasp the 'essence' of the theme. In the 20th century, there is no longer an obvious continuity in the art of painting. It has to be reinvented over and over again, but can only acquire its meaning in relation to tradition. This holds for Mondrian, for Fautrier, for Pollock, for Fontana and for Polke. The power of their art lies in the recognition and problematisation of its proclaimed finiteness.

Scholars are always trying to capture the art of painting within the trajectory of modern art. According to Clement Greenberg, for instance, the importance of Pollock's paintings between 1947 and 1950 lies in their contribution to an ideal envisaged by 'modernistic painting' from the end of the 19th century: restoration of the integrity and purity of the flat surface. This influential American critic experienced the web that was woven of paint threads and paint drops as sublime mirages from which any hierarchic order had evaporated. Pollock, so it was argued, succeeded in refining the painted matter to a purely visual illusion and thus reached a logical conclusion in his art. In the 1960s, when Greenberg's modernistic ideal came under fire and 'the art of painting' came to be regarded as a limited and irrelevant medium – just as it had been at the beginning of the century – Pollock too fell from his pedestal. For the first time ever, 'modernism' and 'avant-gardism' were being theoretically distinguished and played off against each other. Greenberg, who had never made that distinction, was pinned down to his modernism, because he maintained that the art of painting was a central category. He believed that painting had, in its most progressive form, subjected its own procedures to a critical examination and had thus been able to preserve the inviolability of its own tradition ('past standards of excellence'). The avant-garde movements of the beginning of this century (Futurism, Dadaism, Constructivism) had, on the contrary, begun to systematically question all categories, including 'the art of painting' as such. These impulses now had to be carried forward. Likewise, the continuation (neo-avant-garde) in the 1990s may prove in retrospect to be a new impulse. After all, the avant-garde today also calls upon its own continuum. Be that as it may, such idealistic constructions totally ignore the radical nature of Pollock's painting, its 'earthly' and formless qualities, and the piss. Pollock's 'drippings' bear the visible marks of the way in which they were applied, spread out on the floor while he let liquid paint drip all over the canvas in a raging passion. As with any painter, the paint got under Pollock's skin: the painted surface of his huge canvases display the splendour of ornament. In contrast to earlier, more discrete forms, Pollock entangles the viewer in a web that looks quite repulsive from up close: it wrinkles, withers and curdles. In some cases, the paint texture even contains rubbish off the floor: nails, buttons, keys, coins, cigarette butts, matches – as in *Full Fathom Five* (1947). Pollock confronts the horizontality of the picture carrier with the age-old tradition of the erected vertical image from which one can keep an appropriate distance and that corresponds to our own posture. Greenberg's view is therefore one-sided, to say the least. Pollock, assisted by the laws of gravity, was the first to succeed in capturing the painter's gesture as such. He no longer painted brush on canvas. Armed with paint pots and a stick, he sprinkled and poured out the liquid all over the often unprepared linen, thus leaving part of the effort to the material itself. No visual concept can reabsorb these paintings; they are less than an image. The human penchant for transcendent or sublime forms is crossed by a degradation and desublimation of the perceptual field.

In a similar way, the work of Italian artist Lucio Fontana, unlike that of Pollock, was hailed in the 1960s as a worthwhile contribution to the neo-avant-garde. It was regarded as an early impulse to freeing art from the categories it had been confined to, in anticipation of contemporary European conceptual art (in America, his work was ignored). In his 'Manifiesto blanco', written during his stay in Argentina in 1946, Fontana opted for an art 'that is not influenced by our conception of it'. He was considered an artist who literally pierced the integrity of the flat surface, thereby undermining the premises of Greenberg's 'modernism'. When Fontana perforated, carved, cut or tore his canvases, he opened up the infinity of a mental space and succeeded in gaining access to the other side of painting. This assessment, however, ignores the materiality of his 'openings', as if the blockages, the crusts, the crumpling and the crumbling of the edges do not matter. Like Pollock, Fontana's starting-point is the infinity of materiality, but he never got beyond 'formlessness'. The polychrome ceramics from the forties evoke magma, mud, dirt. Or a turd in the case of the cube-shaped mass of blackish material from 1949, with its shiny, iris-like reflective surface, that refuses to rise above itself and become a geometric form. These objects stimulate our sense of the obscene. However, his materiality is not only marked by 'formlessness' and 'obscenity', but also by 'kitschiness'. Cases in point are the brightly-coloured fake gems and the gold and silver sequins that he used to encrust the surface of many a painting in the 1950s. Fontana has never made a secret of the fact that he drew inspiration from baroque art and its formal double, kitsch. The distinction between high and low is no longer an issue in his work. There is no ironic detachment or elegant play with bad taste that one sees in the work of certain Dadaists, Surrealists and Pop artists. Fontana reverses the roles: his work contributes to the proliferation of kitsch within the field of art. He reminds us of the fact that art as a modern phenomenon was launched around 1800 to get rid of baroque excrescence and eccentricity.

When I first saw *La Fine di Dio* (1963–1964), a bizarre series of brightly-coloured oval shapes that had been ripped open and perforated, they made me laugh. These were not paintings, and yet a new kind of painting was being conceived. The title refers to Nietzsche's famous aphorism on 'the death of God'. When Fontana invites the viewer to enter, through the holes he has made, into the insane infinity of space ('the infinite nothingness') that appears after the murder, he does so by illusory, perhaps even archaic, means. The viewer is dragged along by the temptations of image and appearance, by the ornaments of the visible world: shape and colour (green, orange, pink), shadows and light, distance and nearness, movement and rest, space and surface. Paradoxically, these egg-shaped forms are in fact a hymn to the monochrome surface which, far from being destroyed by its 'injuries', is made to shine. Fontana's murder of God is a material gesture. It is impossible to speak of metaphors, symbolism or aesthetic sublimation when its visible marks are reminiscent of an anus or a vagina (especially in the case of the pink examples). The tightly stretched canvas becomes physical as soon as the perforation commences. According to Fontana, the fierceness of this deed 'lasts forever'.

Pollock and Fontana enabled the *art of painting* to take a stand against modern art and its penchant for the transcendental and the sublime. In the course of the 20th century, the art of painting has been certified dead and side-tracked by all radical modern movements; at the same time, the paint itself was – for the first time ever – made into a fetish (though not in a psycho-analytical sense, as no substitution mechanisms are involved). Never before was the hide of paint so thick, so solid, so untransparent. Moreover, the paint increasingly seems to take over the initiative from the painter; more and more often, paintings paint 'themselves'. The painting is not a mere illustration or image, but a process or even the result of a procedure. Quite illustrative in this respect is how German painter Sigmar Polke saw his own work in the 1980s: 'My painting is subversive because it is impossible to talk about its subjects. I apply paint and varnish, both of which leave their own marks on the canvas. The stain starts to move, the image offers us something that was not there before. It is a process on which I have no grasp. The painting decides on its own destiny, it goes its own way'. The work of younger painters such as Frenchman Bernard Frize or Englishman Ian Davenport would also appear not to have been produced by human hands. These artists merely create the conditions for processes to proceed spontaneously: 'I do less, paint does more'. (Davenport)

We may subsume the art of painting within the broader history of the picture screen and its possibilities of representation. This tradition dates back to Alberti's description (in the first theoretical treatise on painting: *De pictura* (1435)) of the painting as an open window through which one looks into a substitute world: a rhetorical means which developed into an indestructible metaphor, because it also holds for photography, film and television. The computer interface is its most recent manifestation. In the course of this history, the art of painting has been overtaken by technique, and a complete reversal of imitation has taken place. The engine of this history was the perpetual desire to connect closer and closer to the real world, by recording it faster and faster, and ever-more accurately ('real time telepresence'). The distance between image and world has been neutralised, and with it the charm of illusion. The world which appears on our picture screens is without illusions. The picture screen has no depth. As soon as we take a look at what is behind the screen, we are disillusioned. We only see digital hardware. In this history, the art of painting has had its day. And not only in this history: the art of painting no longer plays a significant role either in the history of modernism, of the avant-garde, of art criticism, and of the visual media. On the other hand, historical time may never have begun for the art of painting. The thought that the art of painting may be outside of time is more alarming. By this I do not mean that it is 'timeless', in which case it would merely be the dialectical counterpart of 'temporary' and thus remain bound by history. Paint as matter is indifferent, but not inert or passive. It is not interested in *our* infinite manipulations, interpretations, meanings and ostracisms. Its indifference is its power. Consequently it is able to neutralise in advance all attempts to make painting subservient. In this sense, painting resists all efforts to impose upon it a linear and irreversible order that would fixate it in time. The art of painting is never completed. 'Only an empty canvas is ready', proclaims French painter Eugène Leroy, who applies very thick layers of paint in an effort to challenge the current opposition against painting. As he, too, cares for the complex richness of painting, Leroy considers himself a present-day follower of Titian's. Painting may sometimes be labelled a slow medium, but it is nominalist painting. The gravest danger that the paint screen faces is to coincide with itself, which inevitably results in unsubstantial 'material painting'. The paint screen is still too fast for us. In the texture of its paint, its secret remains intact: the secret of the future. The texture need not always be thick and solid; it may be paper-thin. One painting, or even a small detail, can suddenly change the course of history. The paint screen has always been treacherously active with regard to metaphor, which is nothing but a disguised form of idealism. The window has nothing whatsoever to do with the art of painting. What is the 'representational' character of visibility? What is imitation and what imagination when 'nature' is being copied? All painted windows since the Renaissance are equally untransparent as the paint screen. The mirror does not reflect either; it devours. Alberti must have been aware of this, otherwise he would never have identified Narcissus as the inventor of painting: 'Painting is nothing but the embrace of the surface of the pond by means of art'. So what about the purity of the surface that modernism strove for? The surface is not flat at all (level and infinite), but curved. It bends itself around the painter's initial implicating stroke. The surface is always a provocation. Each monochrome is illusory, shadowed by a mental image as a result of which the art of painting never reaches its desired end. There is only a paint screen. One can respect this screen, as most painters do. It can be pierced. It can free itself from the wall and take possession of a space, as is the case in certain baroque spaces and in the black or neon-lit 'ambienti spaziali' which Fontana created in 1949. It may also lead an imaginary existence, as in Duchamp's nominalist painting. The gravest danger that the paint screen faces is to coincide with itself, which inevitably results in unsubstantial 'material painting'. The paint screen is certainly not the essence of the art of painting. It has none.

Translated by ICTS

John Blake, *Untitled (Bone box)* (1994),
cibachrome mounted in light box

John Blake, *S-P-I-N-E* (1993), 25 vertebrae, steel calipers and wiring system

John Blake, *Untitled (Skin Series)* (1969/1996), 11-unit photo construction

John Blake, *Untitled (Well)* (1992), installation

John Blake, *Untitled (Spine)* (1991/1992), dia projection with
3 steel and copper element

Peter Mason

Hard Graft

This article deals with a number of cases of metaphorical ostectomy – literally the surgical removal of all or part of a bone – carried out by the artist John Blake (Providence, Rhode Island, 1945), along with the reinsertion of the bone in a new situation. This iterated process of grafting the bone onto ever new contexts implies a two-way pressure: the pressure exerted by the bone on its context, and the pressure exerted by that context on the intrusive bone.[1]

To Reiterate ...

As Maria Anna Potocka has astutely observed, 'John Blake's "installations" never start out by leaning on the energies or metaphoric contents of a space – in fact, they usually begin in his studio, before the space is even known – but once committed they seem deeply rooted, and they cannot automatically transfer elsewhere'. (Potocka s.d.: 6) Before tracing the trajectory of Blake's bone, then, it may be as well to start with a description of the object as if we were viewing it in the context-free environment of the studio – an obvious fiction, of course, as no studio environment can be regarded as context-free or siteless.

John Blake's *Untitled (Bone Box)* (cibachrome mounted in light box, $168 \times 40 \times 40$ cm), [1] offers the viewer a representation of a bone (not a bone itself; the Magrittean distinction will become important later) in front of an equally vertical fluorescent tube, its verticality enhanced by the verticality of the light source. This verticality can be linked to one of the four elements singled out by the Italian historian Carlo Ginzburg which we use in representing our own bodies: they are erect or vertical; they are bipedal; they are symmetrical; and they are alive. (Ginzburg 1990: 241) Verticality as a basic principle of the morphology of the human body is applied in Blake's work to just one part of that body – a bone. But from this point on the correspondence with Ginzburg's self-representational schema of the body breaks down. To start with, the bone is not bipedal. There is a duplication, but it is not the duplication of two limbs placed side by side in parallel: it is the duplication of a single bone, its reverse image superimposed on it vertically, not juxtaposed beside it. Likewise the question of symmetry: this bone is not symmetrical about a vertical axis, like the human figure, but it is symmetrical about a horizontal axis, at the point where one (image of) bone touches the opposite tip of (image of) bone. Finally, the bone reverses the notion of the living body – bones extracted from a body signal their own death, if not that of the body itself.

But does the bone *stand for* the human body? There are precedents for such a supposition in Blake's earlier work. In *Guard*, originally created in 1985–1986, the walls of a single room housed the black figures of a human-sized 'I' drawn on paper. As the preparatory drawings for *Guard* make clear, this 'I' is isomorphic with the human figure. At the same time, however, the abstract form of the 'I', cannot be mistaken for the human figure. It stands for it, it may be coterminous with it, but it does not partake of humanity on any level except that of the metaphor. And metaphor implies the existence of distinct realms of being. As Paul de Man explains it:

> But 'anthropomorphism' is not just a trope but an identification on the level of substance. It takes one entity for another and thus implies the constitution of specific entities prior to their confusion, the *taking* of something for something else that can be assumed to be *given*. (De Man 1984: 241)

A bone, by contrast, does not *stand for* the human figure; it is a tangible, organic part of the human figure. Rhetorically, it is a synecdoche, the figure in which a part comes to stand for the whole from which it was taken. If the bone is anthropomorphic at all, then, it is so in a looser sense of the word.

Still, we can be a bit more precise about the extent of this looseness. In his study of Gustave Courbet's alleged 'realism', Michael Fried has suggested on the basis of a number of examples that Courbet was attempting to break with the theatricality of David in the direction of a self-representation of the painter. The flow of rivers, the form of caves and rock formations, the very curves (*courbes*) of human figures, can all be read as 'signatures' by the painter himself. Does this make them anthropomorphic? Instead of the painter's body and the representation constituting specific, distinct entities, we seem to be confronted with a 'corporealisation' of the representational field. Within such a system, cases of anthropomorphism are only part of a larger transformational system operating within that field. (Fried 1981: 94–127; 1990: 238ff)

A 'tangible, organic part of the human figure' is not yet precise enough. This part, a bone, is identifiable as a radius, the bone which extends from the elbow to the wrist. As a part of the forearm used in writing as well as in painting, sculpting and so on, it implies a literal, organic relationship between human beings and the artefacts that they create. Just as Courbet's brush strokes may seem to be an extension of his hand and arm into the field of the painting, so John Blake's forearm is extended into the artist's handiwork – bone.

The bone, then, is part of the forearm. It is also a part of the human skeleton. And it is a part of the human body. *Pars pro toto*, synecdoche, it certainly is; but for which totality does it stand?

Suppose it is to stand for the skeleton. As archaeologists know, skeletons tend to be found in a horizontal position, the horizontality of death. But this bone is vertical, the posture of life. Second, bones and the skeleton as a whole are supposed to be invisible.[2] Barring accidental exposure through car accidents, surgery, torture, etc., the right and proper place for a bone is hidden from sight. But John Blake's bone is clearly visible; in fact, its visibility is brought even more to the eye by the fluorescent tube behind it. Instead of resting in the concealment of unilluminated interiority, the bone is plainly on display for all to see.

Suppose it is to stand for the body. Whose body? The bone in John Blake's *Untitled (Bone Box)*, let us hope, is not John Blake's bone. What about its gender: does it stand for a male or a female body; and does it matter?

A cursory reading of the Biblical narrative in Genesis would lead one to suppose that the bone is marked by a masculine sign. As the bone of Adam from which Eve was created only in a secondary moment, the bone would seem to be masculine unless there were clear indications to the contrary. But to raise the question of gender at this point raises the question of a state preceding sexual difference, a state in which the line between masculinity and femininity has not yet been drawn. On this reading, Adam's bone is not masculine; it is neuter, only acquiring a masculine sign within that secondary movement constitutive of sexual difference.

Yet perhaps 'neuter' is already too precise. As Jacques Derrida has shown in relation to Martin Heidegger's concept and usage of terms like *Geschlecht* and *Geschlechtslosigkeit*, neutrality as a refusal to choose between masculinity and femininity remains bounded by the dual structure of 'either/or'. Heidegger, on the contrary, seems to have had in mind a sexuality that was not only pre-differential but also pre-dual, a sexuality that is more originary than the dyad. (Derrida 1987: 395–414)

That this talk about gender is not irrelevant to John Blake's project can be seen from another of his installations, *River* (Aleph, Almere, 1987). Here the Aleph space in the cellar of Almere Town Hall contained not only a partitioning of the space by two walls separated by a cavity only six inches wide – the artist's estimate of the skull's average width – but also two torsos (in fact, a torso constructed from two figures but experienced as one form), divided by a vertical iron beam, one coloured red and one coloured green.[3] In rising from a supine to a vertical position, these two naked bodies, seen from behind and to one side, are indeterminate as to gender. Neuter caryatids, both their anatomy and their pose belies any attempt to bound them in gender terms. Just as we should be on our guard against supposing that the vertical 'I' in *Guard* is a one-dimensional masculine figure, so we should resist attempts to parse *Untitled (Bone Box)* as part of a male figure.[4] And in all these figures, the act of duplication introduces us to something which is always double, always marked by *internal* difference separating its two separate, if symmetrical, components, an internal scission that marks it as the bearer of its own otherness.[5]

Duplication in these cases is iteration, the movement in which self repeats itself as other. The concept of iteration is not the same as that of repetition. While the latter refers to repetition of the same, iteration introduces difference into the same through the singularity of the event. (Derrida 1990: 215–216) Iteration therefore combines repetition with alterity, sameness with difference, at the same time. For how else are we to describe the structure of *Untitled (Bone Box)* than as the superimposition of bone upon bone in which the repetition of the same image is at the same time not the same? The replication of the single bone by vertical juxtaposition produces an object – John Blake's *Untitled (Bone Box)*, which differs from all the other bones that one has ever seen by *bearing such a striking resemblance to itself.*

As remarked earlier, John Blake's *Untitled (Bone Box)* is a representation of a bone, just as his *Untitled (Vein)* is a representation of a vein. But matters are both simpler and more complicated in the case of *S-P-I-N-E* (1993; Galeria BWA, Wroclaw, 1994) [2]. Twenty-five steel callipers, strung from a steel cable network, each grip a single section of the human spine. The vertebrae are arranged in correct sequence, and are genuine human bones.

Matters are simpler: there is no longer any question of the representational status of the spine, for it does not stand for a human spine – it *is* a human spine, the vertebrae are actual human vertebrae. The installation is a *presentation*, not a representation.

But (and this structure of the 'but' is as much a part of Blake's work as it is of the present text) matters are more complicated too. For these vertebrae are suspended each 50 cm from the next one. The resulting skeleton, consisting of human bones, represents a figure on a larger than human scale. Indeed, the exhibit reminds one of exhibits of whale or dinosaur skeletons in museums of natural history. So our apparently simple presentation of human bones – which *S-P-I-N-E* undoubtedly is – is at the same time the representation of something bigger, something of Moby Dick proportions:

> I take SPACE to be the central fact to man born in America, from Folsom cave to now. I spell it large because it comes large here. Large, and without mercy. (Olson 1947: 11)

Within this representational setting, the callipers themselves seem to partake of the nature of bones too, their steel framework a skeletal frame; mirroring the extended human spine, but in a much larger dimension, the callipers from the backbone of some gigantic prehistoric creature, clutching the puny human vertebrae in its claw-like grip. As in *Untitled (Bone Box)*, the bone is replicated on itself: in *Untitled (Bone Box)*, as we saw, by vertical juxtaposition of the same on the same to produce the other to the bone; in *S-P-I-N-E*, through vertical juxtaposition of the same on the different to bring out their resemblance to one another.

   One of the justifications for writing about the representational aspects of works that are also presentational is that they themselves have the quality of textual representation, that is, of script. The 'I' of *Guard* is both the first person singular of grammar and the ninth letter of the alphabet – within certain cultural sets, of course.[6] The 'I's on the four walls of *Guard* also have a relationship of assonance with the earlier installations *Their Eyes II* (Matt's Gallery London, 1980–1981), *Their Eyes IV–VI* (Wielka & Akumulatory 2, Poznan, Galeria Foto-Video, Krakow, 1981), and *600 Eyes for Krzysztofory* (Krakow, 1981).[7] As for the callipers in *S-P-I-N-E*, they have become the crane-like inverted commas or quotation marks which punctuate human speech. This crane-like or plier-like operation of inverted commas has already been noted by Derrida in an interview: 'Somewhere, I think, I have compared quotation marks to cranes'. (1995: 9)[8] To jog the philosopher's memory, it was in his *Éperons* (1978: 44),[9] where he referred to 'This spreading of truth which suspends itself, elevates itself between quotation marks (machination, cry, *thieving grab of a crane* [my italics, PM])'. Why are quotation marks like the thieving movement of the grab of a crane? Because in both cases something is removed from one context and grafted onto another. In the case of *S-P-I-N-E*, the twenty-five elements of a human spine are removed from their human dimension to feature, as a quotation, within a skeletal structure of more than human dimensions. In the following section, we shall trace the ways in which *Untitled (Bone Box)* is removed from one context and grafted onto another.

Dissecting Architectural Space

Blake had already used the radius to shore up the vaulted roof of a wharf-side cellar in the Oudegracht, Utrecht in 1993/1994. On display in the SMart Gallery in Amsterdam in 1994, John Blake's *Untitled (Bone Box)* was located underground too, beneath the surface, in the vicinity of the visceral piping circulating beneath the floor of the building, looking as if it were propping up the building against subsidence. In this case, the -ing of building suggests that there is a process going on in which the building is somehow engaged in the act of build-ing itself, constituting itself as a building, a work in progress. At the same time, it is hard to repress the feeling that it is not a simple work of construction that is going on, but one of de-construction: is this the ruin of something that was once more whole? Or is the ruin-like appearance merely the sensible form assumed by a *Gestalt* in the process of becoming?

This proleptic notion of the ruin as a state of something which is yet to be, as well as, or rather than, as a state of what has been, is borrowed from Louis Marin's perceptive comments on the architectural fragments in some of Poussin's paintings. (1995: 153–160) Marin points out how the use of the term 'ichnography' to refer to an architectural ground plan implies that such a plan can be read as the trace (from the Greek *ichnos*) of the building after it had been completely ravaged by time. At the point where the last vestige of building crumbles, ruin collapses into ground plan, or ichnography. In this structure of presence, time hesitates between flux and reflux, origin and end, between pre- and post-.

In the case of John Blake's *Untitled (Bone Box)*, we may ask the same question: is it a fragment that has been detached from a skeleton, a ruin of what once supported a human frame, a vestigial trace? Or is it a building-block, a first (and, through the process of iteration, second) step towards the reconstitution of a human body? Or even – and this is the direction in which *S-P-I-N-E* points us – towards the constitution of a body that exceeds the human body?

At any rate, that the bone points to something besides, if not beyond, the human is evident, not just from the architectural setting in which it was displayed, but also from the preparatory sketches for *Untitled (Bone Box)*, which already make it clear that the lineaments of the body are like the lineaments from which architects construct buildings. And on the wall opposite them, as it 'happened', – both a part and not a part of the installation – were a preliminary drawing and a 'post factum' photograph of another Blake installation, the one designed for *The Ideal Place* in the 'Haags Centrum voor Aktuele Kunst' (1993–1994). In the upper room of the HCAK, the beams and fluorescent lights on the ceiling had been replicated on the floor, and a thin horizontal stripe drawn along the middle of the walls divided the space into two symmetrical halves. Entry to the space was barred: all the visitor could do was to look into a space which fitted into itself perfectly, a space which bore a striking resemblance to itself, a space which iterated its sameness as difference, a space filled with space.[10] Olson again:

> Space has a stubborn way of sticking to Americans, penetrating all the way in, accompanying them. (1947: 114)

Yet despite the seeming bleakness of this space (Blake himself evokes 'there is nothing elsewhere' from Samuel Beckett's 'Imagination Dead Imagine'), it too may have an anthropomorphic dimension. Philip Peters suggests that the thin horizontal line in the middle of the walls might be a metaphor for the spinal column, and the whole might be a complete human cavity, though manifested horizontally in space in opposition to the, in principle, vertical human form. (1995: 40–42) Even without such an anthropomorphic dimension, however, *The Ideal Place* still relies on the viewer's body. As Blake himself has expressed it: 'In my work the body is an essential ingredient. Sometimes I represent it; just as often I reflect it abstractly, providing the viewer's body with a different job to do'.[11]

This architectural/anthropomorphic lead draws on the similarity between the upright human figure and the building, a conceit going back at least to Vitruvius and pondered by all those who studied his *De Architectura*. The great French classicist painter Nicolas Poussin, for instance, writing to Paul Fréart, Sieur de Chantelou, in March 1642, adds a touch of eroticism to the conceit in assuming that the beautiful girls of Nîmes had delighted him as much as the columns of the Maison Carrée, since 'the latter are merely aged copies of the former'. (1989: 63) We can follow this lead to one of the studies for *Guard*, deriving from a book of drawings by Michelangelo in which architectural and anatomical sketches overlap. This drawing could have been called *S-P-I-N-E*: the spine of the book, which separates two torsos, seen from the rear and one side, consti- tutes the form of the 'I' which was to lead, not only to *Guard*, but to *River* as well. The significance of the convergence of Michelangelo and Blake lies in the analogy between internal and external bodily extension. Michelangelo saw the joints and muscles as the columns and architraves of architecture. Blake inverts the internalisation of architectonic constructions to dissect the anatomy of physical space.[12] In her *Body Criticism*, Barbara Stafford has tried to reveal similar unexpected parallels from within two fields which were considered as distinct, if not irremediably different: artistic and clinical diagnosis. Hence she can juxtapose an architectural etching by Piranesi and an anatomical dissection, since:

> One of the major and I believe still unrecognized contributions of that tireless Venetian etcher, Giovanni Battista Piranesi (1720–1778), was his use of the etching needle as a creative surgical tool to uncover information about an otherwise irretrievable past. [...] He artistically unearthed the mutilated corpse of Italian antiquity. [...] Wielding the etcher's needle like a scalpel, he applied surgical procedures taken, I believe, from medical illustrations, to turn the still-living fabric of architecture inside out. (1991: 58–59)[13]

We have come across the two torsos seen from the rear and to one side in Michelangelo's drawing and in John Blake's *River* installation. In the latter, not only were the two human torsos conceived in architectural terms; Blake saw the Almere Town Hall itself as a torso:

> I have to admit that I went so far in anthropomorphising this building as a whole that I imagined it as the upper half of a torso lying face skyward in an empty field, arms folded in at the elbows, hands clasped together to make a rest for the back of the skull pressed down into the soft earth – all linked together at the apex of the prostrate spine I had pictured to begin with. (1991: 37)

The anatomical/architectural ambiguity is like that of the proleptic ruin – is an architecture being viewed anatomically, or an anatomy architecturally? Take the callipers in *S-P-I-N-E*. In conversation, John Blake described them to me as resembling the tool used by a pipe-fitter to gauge the diameter of a pipe, i.e. an 'architectural' use. There is a certain appropriateness in the allusion to geometrical measurement if we recall that Blake's bone is a radius. Furthermore, the use of callipers by biologists, archaeologists, and especially by physical anthropologists, to measure the dimensions of bones (including their craniometric use as instruments of mismeasure) (Gould 1981) suggests that an anatomical context would be just as relevant as an architectural one. How are we to discriminate? To return to the installation for *The Ideal Place*, the impossibility of describing that space in terms of mirrors and reflections is due to the fact that there is no (secondary) reflection of something prior (primary) to it. As Peters writes: 'There is no illusion, only "tangible" reality; everything is, as it were, "real" '. (1995: 41) So what is 'prime' (a concept dear to both Olson and Blake) and what is representation?

In some respects, the combination of human architecture and anatomy that characterises Blake's constructions is like, say, the 'House of Dior': as a company consisting of designers, salespersons, etc., the House of Dior is a personification of a building; but as a corporation, with its own ramifications, divisions, hierarchical order, etc., it is the reification of people in a 'House'. If a metaphor is a term taken from one semantic field and applied in a different, unrelated field, then Blake's bones are not metaphors, because it is impossible to establish a primary field of reference (architecture? anatomy?) from which the others would be different. No metaphor is possible without the prior demarcation of distinct semantic fields.

We have now run through a whole range of possibilities regarding John Blake's *Untitled (Bone Box)* in terms of presentation or representation; metaphor or synecdoche; anatomy or architecture; masculine or feminine; singular or plural; ruin or building-block; and so on. At a time when discourses and their inevitable disciplinary practices have begun to take an interest in the human body too as an object of study,[14] the resistance of *Untitled (Bone Box)* to encapsulation within any one of these positions is to be welcomed as revealing an awareness of the ambiguities inherent in the bone – it is undecidable.

'All experience open to the future', Derrida has written, 'is prepared or prepares itself to welcome the monstrous *arrivant*, to welcome it, that is, to accord hospitality to that which is absolutely foreign or strange'. (1995: 387) At the same time, this act of hospitality is an attempt at domestication, to make the newcomer a part of the household – though in Derrida's architectural writings, playing on the slippage from *heimlich* to *unheimlich*, what seems most familiar becomes unfamiliar.[15] This double movement of welcoming the monstrous into one's building while respecting its alterity was forcefully expressed in John Blake's installation *Untitled (Bone Box)* in the civil registry office in Utrecht (1995). By now, certain elements may seem familiar, but not in this combination. The bone of *Untitled (Bone Box)* has been vastly enlarged – it is now more than five metres tall – like the effect of enlargement on the human vertebrae suspended in *S-P-I-N-E*. The notion of the architectural frame of a building as a skeleton is still there, as the bone's verticality relates to the vertical columns in the room, and the horizontal splitting of the steel frame in which it is encased continues the horizontal line of the mezzanine. In fact, the relation between the bone and the architectural setting is so organic – and it is reflected in the way that architectonic elements of the space are reflected on the glass surface of *Bone* just as *Bone* itself is reflected in the glass windows facing it – that one wonders whether the work of art was designed for the building or the building for the work of art. But there is something curiously conventional about *this* bone, whether the artist was aware of it or not, for there is a long-standing tradition in the Netherlands of hanging large bones from the walls of public buildings. Two jaw-bones of a whale hung in the Dutch seat of government from at least 1619. This was not the only Dutch public building to be decorated with whale bones. A gigantic whale bone was suspended from the outer wall of the old Amsterdam City Hall; clearly visible in seventeenth-century drawings and paintings, it was certainly in position by 1600, though we do not know how long it had already been hanging there. Pieter Saenredam's 1641 drawing of the Amsterdam Town Hall (now in Teylers Museum Haarlem) reveals a whale-rib hanging from the outside of the building, and it is still visible in his later, more well-known painting of the same building (1657) that is now in the Rijksmuseum Amsterdam. A whale-bone can still be seen hanging from the outside wall of the Campveerschetoren in Veere.[16]

The public display of whale bones antedates their importance as economic products of the whaling industry; like the crocodiles which were suspended from the roofs of a number of churches in the late Middle Ages, they have a magical quality; they are examples of the marvellous, the curious and the extraordinary, which could have an apotropaic function. So the gigantic bone suspended on the wall of a public building in Utrecht (though it is on the inside of the building, it is also visible from the outside) turns out to be a part of Dutch (and more generally European) historical tradition, just as the *River* installation was itself rooted in the Dutch tradition of the manipulation of geography which resulted in the creation of a new polder, Flevoland. As we have seen, the comparison of the human body with the architectural orders goes back to Vitruvius, reinforced in Blake's work through the intermediary of the Michelangelan tradition. The torsos in *River*, caryatids that can be regarded as naturalistic transformations of the Ionic order, go back to the same classical theories of proportion.

There is indeed something immediately classical about the earlier works considered here, whether it is the Beckettian terseness of the installation for *The Ideal Place*, or the Vitruvian classicism of the architectural torsos. Yet they are by no means definable in terms of such cultural or historical conventions. The starkness of a work like *Untitled (Bone Box)* evokes a more elemental response: the response to that liminal area in which a bone both is and is not a bone, in which self both is and is not self, in which resemblance and familiarity – we all have our bones, and what could be a better reminder of the fact than the presence of a gigantic bone in a civil registry office visited by thousands of people a year? – are the very stuff of strangeness. Denied direct experience of our own inner selves, we have to fall back upon the representation and the trace. For the act of recognition – John Blake's *Bone* as one of our bones – is also the provocative shock experienced by turning ourselves inside out.

Large, and Without Mercy

A year later, *Untitled (Bone Box)* reappeared in yet another context: Kunstbunker Tumulka, Munich, this time not on its own but surrounded by other works by the same artist, none of which had been originally conceived to be shown in that particular context. What happens when autonomously created works of art are put on display inside a bunker erected under the Third Reich? Are they taken over by the sheer size and weight of their surroundings? Or, like David against Goliath, can their disadvantage in bulk be outweighed by their canniness?[17]

When John Blake accepted the challenge to exhibit a number of his works, most of them produced over a period of more than a decade, in this bunker, one of his self-avowed aims was to use and simultaneously unbalance the constant pressurising of the body resulting from the claustrophobic, windowless bunker.[18] Given the impossibility of turning a blind eye to this pressure, how did Blake set about redistributing it?

The seven-storey Kunstbunker Tumulka consists of a series of identical 'cells', each of them uncompromisingly rectangular and solid, linked only by the staircase running through the building. So there is already a strongly marked vertical dimension – the staircase supporting the cells like a spine – and a horizontal dimension – the floors and ceilings of the cells themselves. Blake rearranges this spatial economy in two ways through the insertion of a work, *S-P-I-N-E* next to the staircase. Twenty-five authentic human vertebrae, stretched on parallel steel wires, extend in a gradually decreasing scale from the coccyx on the first floor to the cervical bone on the fifth, forming a veritable spinal column to the building. Previous versions of *S-P-I-N-E* were horizontal, as we have seen, the vertebrae extending like the skeleton of some enormous whale. Now rotated through ninety degrees, the work eloquently states what it is – the support of *homo erectus*, a being whose architecture resembles that of an upright building.

The inclusion of the spinal column in parallel to the staircase does not, however, reinforce the verticality of the building. Rather, mimicking the staircase,[19] it calls its monumentality into question, the delicate human bones (they cast the shadows of birds and butterflies) offering a refinement, variation and pose which the staircase lacks.

At the same time, that portion of the spine which is visible on each storey – five vertebrae – is blocked off from the other twenty vertebrae.

The continuity of the column, the fact that each group of five units belongs to the same spine, is invisible to the eye. Instead, situated as it is between the floor and ceiling of a storey, each five-vertebrae section partakes of the same space as the rest of that storey, i.e. its horizontality.

The subversion of the bunker's horizontal and vertical axes is continued on the second storey. One wall is filled by an eleven-panel grid containing seven photographs and four blanks, *Untitled (Skin series)* [3]. The heavy black frame of the grid mimics the structures of the bunker, but the work undermines them at the same time in at least two ways. First, arrangement of the eleven panels within a rectangular grid inevitably means a lack – the lack of the twelfth panel that the symmetry of the grid requires. By 'leaving out' this panel in the lower right-hand corner of the wall, the grid is destabilised. One suspects that it would topple over unless it were firmly attached to the wall. Second, the act of pulling at the skin which is displayed in each of these panels generates a field of opposing forces which is itself in opposition to the inertia of the bunker. Alive, the wall pulsates beneath the busy fingers, while the juxtapositions of photographs create new, imaginary bodies and body parts, a pullulating inventiveness to counter the dumb ponderousness of the building.

Sometimes verticality and horizontality are countered with curves. *Vein*, an installation that was shown at the London Matt's Gallery in 1989 as one of an open series of installations in which the artist presented 'arrangements of an enlarged photographic detail of aspects of the human anatomy […] placed within a construction of industrial materials' (Instone 1989), at that time included a wall on which several irregular lengths of steel tube formed a framework on which sheets of copper were balanced. In the 1996 version, *Untitled (Skin over Vein)*, on the third floor of the bunker, there is no need for the armature of many tubes. Instead, a single copper sheet is balanced over a steel pipe that protrudes from the wall. The copper surface reflects its surroundings, but bends them into curves. In the lower surface of the copper sheet one can see arches, Piranesi-like, extending into an imaginary distance. Stark in their isolation, the tube and sheet take over the space, intruding into it, and allowing the space to intrude into them at the same time; the untreated copper surface reflecting its surroundings but colouring them with its own incipient oxidisation, bending them into curves, bending them to its own will.

In *Untitled (Vein/Hand)*, on the same storey, a photoplate of a hand, palm down, fills the floor, covered by a glass plate, pressing against a copper plate flat to the wall. Not only does this pressure operate as a counterforce to the pressure of the wall of the chamber; as you approach the wall, the prominent veins on the back of the hand ripple beneath the glass plate, introducing a wave-like movement into the space.

On the same storey, the bunker is subverted in yet another way by the installation *Untitled (Bone Box)*. Wedged between floor and ceiling are two box units illuminated by a vertical fluorescent light. One of them is fore-grounded by a photograph of a bone. The rectangular structure of the box units, and the fact that they occupy the entire vertical space of the chamber, suggest an assimilation to or absorption by the bunker. Yet, the image of the bone, symmetrical but not geometrical, floating on the surface of the box unit, detaches itself from its surroundings to become as delicate as the bones of the spine. Moreover, the very fact that the bone boxes mimic the structure of the bunker itself gives them an added resilience: if they seem to be in a metonymic relation to the bunker, their stark verticality echoing the building itself, there is always the risk that they might *take the place of* – both steal the space of and replace – the bunker.

Besides redistributing the pressure of the building, Blake deploys a second deconstructive strategy which involves a reallocation of gender roles. As he noted in an interview, like any vertical urban building, the bunker is undeniably phallic. Yet, built as a shelter for human bodies, it is a feminine vessel. Much of Blake's oeuvre is anterior to any masculine/ feminine division. In line with this, many of the works in the bunker are difficult to pin down in terms of gender. Take the skin in *Untitled (Skin series)*: the body is clearly male, but the folds in the skin and the unexpected curves created by the juxtapositions of the photographs connote femininity. Even the acoustics of the building reinforce this dislocatory effect. For instance, as I experienced in viewing the exhibition with one of its curators, Anne-Marie Bonnet, the high tones of a woman's voice are cut off in the building, reducing it to a 'neuter' tonality without gender.

The storey on which the ambiguous character of the bunker – an aggressively masculine phallus/a tender feminine haven – emerges most clearly is the fifth (at the level of the 'lungs' of the building). The large chamber is filled with the installation *Untitled (Well)* [4], a work conceived earlier but never exhibited before. At approximate chest level, a battery of steel pipes protrudes from three walls of the 'cell', while the fourth wall is painted in a flesh colour to evoke the human body toward which these pipes are directed. Though the installation 'fills' the chamber, the room itself is empty. Coupled with the uncanny sounds emerging from the rest of the building (water pipes, whirring fans), it is easy to imagine that it is the sound of gas filling the chamber, or that the pipes are the barrels of the guns of a large firing squad with yourself in the position of victim. But at the same time, these pipes linking the inside of the bunker with the world outside are a source of life-sustaining air. Though the artist cannot have been familiar with the ambiguities of the word, the installation could have been called *Gift* in German: the duplicity of the gift which poisons, the ambiguity of the pipes (are they for inhaling or exhaling?), is at one with the duplicity of the bunker – a device erected to save the lives of high-ranking Nazis, themselves bent on destroying lives, in 1942.

In the city of the beer putsch, its civic architecture inevitably recalling the days of the Third Reich, which I happened to visit on the public holiday to celebrate the reunification of the two Germanies, how could one be deaf to the historical resonances of a Nazi bunker? At the same time, how is an exhibition to rise above the pathos (shades of Boltanski?) of mere historical recollection or commemoration? Another of Blake's subtle strategies in dealing with this challenge, as deconstructive as his interventions in the spatial, acoustic and sexual dimensions, is to recontextualise both the bunker and the works contained in it within a series of different temporalities.

Surely, one way of transcending the limitations of political history is to go for universals, and in this sense the human body would seem to be such a universal, however historically circumscribed our conceptions of it may be. 'Cell' after 'cell' of the bunker confront the spectator with a reflection on what it is to have a human body, to be built like a building, extending the notion of the anatomy lesson virtually beyond all recognition. At the top of the building whose seven storeys are held together, as we have seen, by the vertebrae of (*S-P-I-N-E*), the large 'cell' on the top floor – the *caput*/capital of the body/building[20] – accommodates the head, seen from inside in *Untitled (Skull)* and from outside in *Projection (Rodin head)*. The latter is an epiphany: floating on, before – who can tell? – the wall is the projected head of a woman by Rodin. Blown up to these proportions, out of all proportion, the heads loses all of its features: sexless, indeterminate, it *is* in an archaic time dimension, anterior to any male/female dichotomy. And anterior to any young/old dichotomy – as immature as an embryo, not yet formed, and as formless as the age-old head of a pharaoh from ancient Egypt,[21] featureless through the erosion of time, the only markings on its face the texture of the wall itself.

Where else in Munich can one see a head like this? In Jonathan Borofsky's *Walking Man* (1995), which dominates the entrance to the Munich Re building in the Leopoldstrasse. Yet while Borofsky's featureless man, looking as if he is in a space suit, strides towards the future, Blake's projection of the Rodin head hovers like a ghost of the past.

There are more ghosts in the Tumulka Bunker. For instance, there are spectres of Blake's earlier work which haunt the interstices of the building, those areas or surfaces on which no identified work by the artist is actually on display, but where the physical surroundings of the building themselves take on a Blakean aspect.[22] For instance, the I-form around which Blake's *Guard* is articulated reappears in some of the walls of the bunker to which works by Blake are attached. This is no coincidence – since some of the walls have been modified by the artist so as not to detract from the viewing of his installations, any I-forms which remain must be regarded as deliberately tolerated, if not deliberate. Another earlier Blake installation, *The Ideal Place*, does not feature in this exhibition, yet the idea of a space divided horizontally into two symmetrical halves runs through both *Untitled (Well)* on the fifth floor of the bunker – a battery of steel pipes all at the same level, – as well as *Untitled (Skull)* on the topmost storey, where twenty-four fluorescent tubes illuminate half of a hemisphere so brightly that neither they and the brilliant side, nor the side which is cast into extreme darkness, are visible. The bisected interior of a skull, blinded by hyperillumination – this show is certainly extreme – operates as an icon of the inability of thought to exceed thought as expressed in Beckett's *Murphy*:

> Murphy's mind pictured itself as a large hollow sphere, hermetically closed to the universe without. This was not an impoverishment, for it excluded nothing that it did not itself contain. Nothing ever had been, was or would be in the universe outside it but was already present as virtual, or actual, or virtual rising into actual, or actual falling into virtual, in the universe inside it. (1938: Ch. 6)

Back on the ground floor, but with this skull in mind, one is confronted by *Untitled (Spine)* [5], the projection of the upper half of the back of a bent human torso, while in front of it (though such spatial precision goes beyond the 'evidence' here) a copper pipe is balanced on a steel bar which presses against the wall at an angle. The intersection of pipe and bar seems to be the point of 'homing in' on – a skull, the dark shadows around the shoulder blades of the bent human figure as blank as the eye sockets of a skull. Here the viewer is caught up in the time which the artist spins around him or her: like the 'reading' of a painting by Poussin, say, (Marin 1995; Mason 1998) it takes time to traverse the field offered to our view, and each journey taken evokes, and modifies, previous journeys in the same space. Once you have been to the top storey of the bunker, the ground floor is no longer what is was. The space of the bunker is transformed within the temporality of a visit, which adds its time scale to a range of different, and homogeneous, temporalities extending from the relatively short term of a 'walk' through the seven stories of the exhibition to an almost immeasurable temporal scale spanning millennia.

It is impossible to forget the politico-historical implications of a bunker erected in Nazi Germany in 1942. But, instead of commemorating that fact in a negative way (I take it for granted that no one will think of commemorating it in a positive way), Blake takes up the challenge of the bunker's formidable physical and historical dimensions and redistributes them on a different time scale – or rather, scales. There is the time scale of the visit – it takes time to cover all seven floors, no matter how hurriedly you do it. Then there is the time scale of the artist's own oeuvre, for some of these installations in 1996 hark back to installations of the 1980s. (As we have seen, for instance, *Untitled (Skin over Vein)* goes back to a series of seven works presented at Matt's Gallery in London in 1989.) There is the time scale of a loan – for *Projection (Rodin head)* the borrowing of Rodin's head of a woman from a century ago. There is the time scale of European history of the 1930s and 1940s, perhaps evoked most powerfully in the upper storeys containing *Untitled (Well)* and *Mehr Luft*. While *Untitled (Well)* is perhaps the work which most directly evokes the former function of the bunker as a bunker, the latter installation (deriving from a series first executed in 1993–1994) is equally uncompromising. In the small 'cell' on the fourth floor, a fan unit rotated on and on, relentlessly, its whining filling the air. In the large 'cell' on the same floor, a series of three boxes mounted on the wall perpetuated the movement of the fan: against an orange box, what looks like a male torso in a Saint Sebastian pose was subjected to a boring into the chest by the fan, itself reiterated next to this orange box in a white one. On another wall, a blue box seemed to represent what is laid bare by this whole movement. The effect on the viewer – cut off from any contact with the air or sounds of the outside world – is a choking for air, a desire for 'Mehr Luft', a desire to escape from this inferno that the artist has perversely called *Mehr Luft*. But in pausing (choking) for breath, the viewer is reiterating the heavy and laboured breathing of those bodies who spent days or nights in the bunker half a century ago. And there is an even more leisurely time scale: the classicism of Blake's work, here as elsewhere, reaches back to the iron symmetry of Greek Archaic sculpture (also evoked in *Guard*) (van Winkel 1991): and in the archaic *Projection (Rodin head)* it extends even further back to the columnar figures of ancient Egyptian monumental sculpture. Yet none of these eras – including the present – is a haven. None of them encompasses the work in question. There is no appeasement in Munich. On the contrary, in the restlessness of the to and fro movement of these installations, they subvert the very solidity of the bunker. Its temporal anchoring severed, the bunker – incredibly – starts to float, at least for the time of an exhibition.

Bibliography

Beckett, Samuel. *Murphy*. London: Routledge, 1938.

Bhabha, Homi. 'Of Mimicry and Man: The Ambivalence of Colonial Discourse'. *October* 28 (1984), 125–133.

Derrida, Jacques. *Psyché: Inventions de l'Autre*. Paris: Galilée, 1987.

—. *Éperons: Les Styles de Nietzsche*. Paris: Flammarion, 1978.

—. *Limited Inc*. Paris: Galilée, 1990.

—. *L'autre cap*. Paris: Minuit, 1991.

—. *Points …. Interviews, 1974–1994*. Elisabeth Weber (Ed.). Stanford: Stanford University Press, 1995.

Egmond, Florike and Mason, Peter. *The Mammoth and the Mouse: Microhistory and Morphology*. Baltimore and London: John Hopkins University Press, 1997.

Feher, Michael, Nadaff, Ramona and Tazi, Nadia (Eds.). *Fragments for a History of the Human Body*. New York: Zone Books, MIT Press, 1989.

Ginzburg, Carlo. *Storia Notturna: Una Decifrazione del Sabba*. Turin: Einaudi, 1989.

Gould, Stephen Jay. *The Mismeasure of Man*. New York: W.W. Norton & Co., 1981.

Greenblatt, Stephen J. (Ed.). *Allegory and Representation*. Baltimore and London: John Hopkins University Press, 1981.

—. *Courbet's Realism*. Chicago and London: University of Chicago Press, 1990.

Instone, Jeff. 'Arm's Length, Fingertip Control: The Installations of John Blake'. *Art Monthly* 129, September 1989.

Man, Paul de. *The Rhetoric of Romanticism*. New York: Columbia University Press, 1984.

Marin, Louis. *Sublime Poussin*. Paris: Seuil, 1995.

Mason, Peter. *Infelicities: Representations of the Exotic*. Baltimore and London: John Hopkins University Press, 1998.

—. 'Lecciones Superficiales: Transparencia y Opacidad en las Américas, Siglo XVI'. *Aisthesis: Revista Chilena de Investigaciones Estéticas*. s.l., 1998.

—. 'La Lección Anatómica: Violencia Colonial y Complicidad Textual'. *Foro Hispánico* 4: Discurso Colonial Hispanoamericano. Sonia Rose de Fuggle (Ed.), 1992.

Olson, Charles. *Call me Ishmael: A Study of Melville*. San Francisco: City Lights, 1947.

Peters, Philip. 'The Ideal Place: Absence, Negation'. *Art & Design*. Profile No. 42. London: The Ideal Place, 1995.

Potocka, Maria Anna. 'Written Down From Memory'. *John Blake in Poland 1980–1994: Wtedy I Teraz–Teraz I Wtedy*. Krakow: Fundacja Wyzwolenia Kultury/Galeria Potocka, s.d.

Poussin, Nicolas. *Lettres et Propos sur l'Art*. Anthony Blunt (Ed.). Paris: Hermann, 1989.

Rykwert, Joseph. *The Dancing Column: On Order in Architecture*. Mass.: MIT Press, 1996.

Sawday, Jonathan. *The Body Emblazoned: Dissection and the Human Body in Renaissance Culture*. London and New York: Routledge, 1995.

Stafford, Barbara Maria. *Body Criticism: Imagining the Unseen in Enlightenment Art and Medicine*. Cambridge, Ma. and London: MIT Press, 1991.

Wigley, Mark. 'The Domestication of the House: Deconstruction after Architecture'. *Deconstruction and the Visual Arts: Art, Media, Architecture*. Peter Brunette and David Wills (Eds.). Cambridge: Cambridge University Press, 1994.
Wills, David. *Prosthesis*. Stanford: Stanford University Press, 1995.
Winkel van, Camiel. *John Blake's Guard 1985–1986*. Apeldoorn: Van Reekum Museum, 1991.

Notes

[1] For a fuller discussion of the process of recontextualisation, see Peter Mason, 1998.

[2] For the taboo on peering into one's own body, see Sawday 1995: chapter one.

[3] The cavity between the two walls also contained two signal lamps, one green and one red.

[4] Jokingly in conversation, John Blake told me that he had sketched an asparagus-like bone like a phallus just for fun; implicitly, then, his Bone should not be read as a phallus.

[5] David Wills connects this with what he calls 'prosthesis' as a movement or spacing of and into difference; see Wills 1995.

[6] Another work which belongs in this series is a drawing for *Guard* entitled 'I + []', in which the 'I' has been vertically split to produce a pair of square brackets, the anthropomorphic figure has become an instrument of punctuation.

[7] The story of this installation and its background is recounted in *600 Eyes for Kryzysztofory–Ich Oczy*, Eric Wierda Artbooks, Amsterdam, 1987.

[8] An interview originally published in French in *Digraphe* 8, 1976.

[9] 'Cet écart de la vérité qui s'enlève d'elle-même, qui se lève entre guillemets (machination, cri, vol de pinces d'une grue)'.

[10] A work dating from 1968 and first installed in the following year, *BOUND*, had consisted of a network of parallel steel cables stretched tight between the opposite side walls of a large, empty room. In turn, it was echoed in *The Vleeshal*, Middelburg, in 1982.

[11] *Untitled (Bone Box)* By John Blake, Dienst Burgerzaken en Gemeentebelastingen, Utrecht, 1995.

[12] I am here following Camiel van Winkel 1991.

[13] This example is discussed at greater length in Peter Mason 1992: 131–155.

[14] The three volumes of *Fragments for a History of the Human Body*, Michael Feher, Ramona Nadaff and Nadia Tazi (Eds.), are one of the clearest examples of the attempt to create a modern canon in this field.

¹⁵ See especially, 203–227.

¹⁶ Other examples in Egmond and Mason 1997: 31.

¹⁷ John Blake–Bunker, in Kunstbunker Tumulka, Munich, was on show from 13 September to 20 October 1996. It was organised by Michael Heufelder and curated by Anne-Marie Bonnet and Susanne Ehrenfried. It was accompanied by a bilingual catalogue with texts in German and English.

¹⁸ See the interview with the artist by Anne-Marie Bonnet and Susanne Ehrenfried, '7 Questions for John Blake', issued as a supplement to the exhibition publication.

¹⁹ On the disturbing slippage produced by mimicry (almost the same, *but not quite*), the classic text is Bhabha 1984: 125–133.

²⁰ On the affinity between head and capital see Rykwert 1996: 34ff. Also relevant is Derrida 1991.

²¹ The installation *Voice-d* (in situ, The Hague, 1987) involved two large, sand-coloured transparencies of the weathered stone profile of an Egyptian pharaoh in a subtle interplay of historical image, urban architecture and autumnal colours.

²² The Tumulka Bunker is not the only site where Blake installations become hard to distinguish from the water pipes and other props of the building. This very complicity between the works and the sites they temporally inhabit is problematised by the works themselves.

Dietmar Kamper

What is That, Which is the Body?

This question is one of a sequence of questions that includes 'what is man?' and 'what is a picture?' The way the question has been phrased goes against the common assumption that we have known what the body is. It reveals a point beyond what has been understood.

'What' questions arise particularly in times of crisis intensifying into catastrophe, after they had already become popular at the start of the era of bourgeois society. They attempt to scrutinise, as well as take risks with, previous knowledge in the manner of secondary naivety. The putative certainties of knowledge have ceased to be sources of information. We know too much and we know it too imprecisely. For example, the question 'what is man?' marks the place of withdrawal. With all the efforts exerted since Kant we have come to radical uncertainty. This is *homo absconditus*. With their science of man, anthropologists have, in the fullness of their analyses, literally resolved 'man'. This outcome now needs to be stated more precisely. A return to the state of knowledge, as if we knew it, almost rules out enlightened contemporaries. The same goes for the picture. The ritualistic and artistic way of dealing with imagination has not been able to arrest the reflux of made pictures. Successful anthropological concepts of history have again been deluged by the current inundation. Today, at the high point of the functioning imaginary where nearly everyone feels compelled to produce something, it is less clear than ever what a picture is. A return to naïve certainty is not a possibility here, but attaining uncertainty, which becomes ever more precise, is. When considering the body and relevant theories pertaining to it, it can be seen today that the concept of always having understood is beginning to fall apart into ever more abstract pieces after the retreat. All this is taking place under the pressure of the third industrial revolution. After the revolution of goods and then of money, there is now the revolution of value which is barely still symbolic. In it the human body is forced to play the ark in a declining world, the last place and refuge of things material in an utterly abstract society. Indeed the drama takes place on the surface but cannot be resolved there. More than this it needs an 'interface' with the subterranean of pictures, a point of pain, a broken edge, a cut in order to be able to get a look-in. This 'point-edge-cut-complex' is still largely unknown. Vilém Flusser has written something on this and left it to us. Here, the complex will be steered in a direction, even towards danger, to completely lose track of what is going on.

Time and again the body has always conformed to the assumption that we knew. It is an archive of phylogeny, a working machine, the body in medicine, the picture in advertisements, the object of desire and the instrument of pleasure, the medium of the media and so on.

According to the findings of historical anthropology, it must be conceded that the body has the status of a 'subject' even when it has no consciousness or will. It has the opportunity of showing itself to be submissive or alluring as far as knowledge, interpretation and power of the mind are concerned – something that can be called neither moral nor rational. In any case what is amazing is the lasting consequence of the epochal *interpretamente*. New interpretations have a hard time of it. It takes a long time to change direction once a certain direction has been taken. The body is extremely inert in the face of disciplining, civilising and colonising. It is far too slow for quick models. This also applies to the solution of compulsive interpretations, particularly its current lack of control through picture abstraction that started off slowly but now can barely be stopped. Everything is happening as if the people involved have made time to learn, as if the body gave those who have it, or think they have it, the chance of explanation. It is given to the descendants of lines who use it as an archive of their symbiosis even when their time is over; to the workers who have to use it as a means of eking out life in a society of contracts until the time of structural unemployment; to the sick whose bodies are seen by the medical establishment as a 'case', treated roughly and maltreated subtly; to the beloved and the lover, even when the desire has gone and desirability has faded; to the 'users' and spectators if they have finally understood that the human body has served its time as the favourite image of the era. Because of these kinds of complex situations, there is no simple evidence and no direct argument to be taken up as far as the body is concerned. What the body really is, is determined by eras in the history of knowledge and discourse that has been made ever clearer since Michel Foucault. We should not, however, assume that this epochal history is as we would like it or that it is subordinate to consciousness and despotism.

The body is more like remnants, rubbish and junk on the conditions of the self-relatedness of the mind. Where powers and monsters meet, the body is the only authority able to portray their mistakes.

It is not only recently, in its third phase of abstraction, that the human mind has believed that it can do without the body. Both with unrestrained suppression, whether it be machine-like exploitation or linguistic contempt, as well as with all manner of wildness, whether it be drugs or pictures, extermination has been going on for centuries. There is an extreme, aggressive and murderous destruction taking place in politics, sex and sport, whilst often the opposite impression is given. The only problem left is the corpses. Yet they will be buried and taken from view, as has happened during this century's countless massacres. After ultimate pictures have been taken of them, human bodies are consigned to rubbish, junk and unusable remains. And that is how they behave. They do this main model of interpretation a favour by obeying it. On the whole, bodies are obviously no longer subversive – or rather, they are no longer obviously subversive. If there is a protest then it is by exceeding the quota – with all the rash aftereffects and unintentional side effects that fill today's world, both unreal and imaginary. Again a widely protracted period of learning begins. People can, if they wish, follow and track the trace that their mistreated bodies have left behind. For they are still responsible for their mistakes as well. In concrete bodies in action, bodies in pain, bodies in effigies, the characteristics, stigmas, monuments to their worthlessness, to their advanced devaluation are pointed to in the picture. The place where these can be perceived is the meeting point of powers and monsters. Above all it is there, where power becomes monstrous and the monsters are in power, that something strange occurs – of all things, those most highly stylised symbols appear. The only prerequisite for becoming aware of picture puzzles like this is the elaborate perception itself. It succeeds through practice that follows learning in history, a truly 'diabolical' competence that revokes allegiance to the symbolic order of power in its double fortification. Suddenly, mostly out of nowhere, the monstrous appears through the official picture and it is spelled out clearly how life, feelings, thinking without a body verges on the criminal. It also shows how pure self-relatedness of the mind is essential for a total, self-eliminating society which can no longer manage the difference between victim and massacre and between inward and outward power.

It is in this respect that the body as a remnant signifies the end of the metaphysical receptacle of thoughts. The body remains the dismembered body. The whole body is not a body, but a picture. In this arena of endless idiosyncrasies it is playing theatre with the unbearable.

Luther's disparaging dictum about the bag of worms containing rotting, decaying flesh stuck almost obsessively to the ideas of the body that had existed since the late Middle Ages. At the same time the long shadow of Greek metaphysics, which determined the entire notion of spatial matters in Europe and then the world, can be found in it. That one feels trapped in a coffin, that flesh *sarx* is a prison of early life, that the skull is too small for the world spirit which only gains its rights of universality in its other home, that the earthly is restricted in time and space whereas the heavenly is timeless and powerful everywhere – all this is in the best Platonic-metaphysical tradition that finally perishes when the tradition is realised. As a dismembered body, the body is the real foundation and the foundation of reality. In other words, there is only the physical that manifests itself in a logic of the 'not quite'. Whoever denies these prerequisites, wanting to leave them behind or omit them while continuing the old theology of meta-physical characterisation as technological-scientific, inevitably enters the realm of the monstrous where things are ghost-like and horrific. Phantoms instead of real things and people keeping all scenarios full of horror. Even people change secretly into the wicked things they always detested the most. The arena where these compulsive performances are played out is a place afflicted by so-called allergies – processes that dismantle and remove the imposed entirety from the body. The body itself is playing theatre with what, for it, is unbearable. Immunity, the bodily reification of a particularly powerful projection of an ancient receptacle of thoughts, is undermined and gradually removed. What is bad is that people cannot live without enemies under the pressure of the historically implanted desire for lost unity and entirety. Because of this they risk death in the aforementioned theatre. Healing strategies with their Latin and Greek, especially in the time of AIDS, are finished. Healing would be the acceptance of mortal life. The cell must also learn about death. If it does not, inevitably it will become cancer-like. The war raging in the arenas of the body is, however, neither 'Armageddon' nor the decisive battle in medicine. It is the decline of a historically effective body-interpretation and the arduous rebuilding of a pile of rubbish in Another Body.

The body is the Other in the world of the Same. It is purely a matter of maturing. That is why a body cannot be cloned, only pictures of bodies. Bodies do not have a frame. Senses are by no means natural, but remain pertinent to the supernatural. Since identifying thinking prevails through-out the entire human relationship with the world, the non-identical only has the chance to portray the other side. The body becomes, as it were, the focus of the Other where only one matters. Whether in doing and suffering, in making and leaving it is always the Same which is alluded to, people turn their own bodies into something quite different, strange, even hostile – something that does not play along. This structural impossibility is an answer to the extended desire for power manifested in the theological–technological Europe–America complex. It is an extreme example of unconscious resistances that extend across borders with the expansion of human authority. A foolish, but short-cut, counter-strategy is already at work. People do not want to understand. People want to clone bodies – bodies of animals and people. People want to come out with a physical sameness – a clone is the same again – and, if necessary, regardless of the consequences. However what is produced is not a body, but a 'living' phantom, a monster, a picture of the body that is 'body-like'. The animal or person cloned have to live their lives in the spotlight as proof, are put on show, photographed to death and exposed to, and violated by, the terroristic regime of the imaginary. What is never achievable, however, is a characterium of an actual body: that of being invisible, unnoticed, simply there, unframed. Human creativity, insofar as it is a creator, cannot shake off the frame within which it creates. It cannot release the creation into the free-for-all of contradictions and contrasts. It could be objected that the incriminated weakness is not just a by-product of clones, but applies to all sorry efforts made by man. That is partly the case. Every technological or political competence, as proved worthwhile in the establishment for half a millennium of a genuinely human world, has always had to suffer from this limitation of pure virtuality. But this is partly not the case too. People have poetic abilities with quite different effects, but linked, without exception, to their personal decline. Only a broken and specifically mortal competence guarantees originality to life created in reality and fiction. There is a big difference between wanting to make the Same – and achieving the monstrous – or to accept the Other as Different.

It is only from the body – in a theory of the inevitably mistaken unconscious – that the universe of the mind can be seen on the outside, although the imaginary essence believes itself to be the entire world with nothing outside it.

Since the separation of belief from 'superstition', and knowledge from the 'incoherent', human senses have undergone a programme of normalisation that did not end until the senses could be used to serve so-called healthy human reason. It was a matter of imprisoning the senses, whose magical reality is incalculable exhaustion, in the narrow environment of bourgeois enterprise in order to cultivate absurd self-interest and take part in the quest for illusionary advantage. Changes for the better were left to the problem-solving mind. Appreciation of higher things was reserved for art, in which one or other sense could make a career, but only under the supervision of those masters of instrumental good sense. At the end of this partially human-killing enterprise, it now emerges that it is the privileged mind itself that led to this narrowness. It produced a calculable illusion, a 'raging interruption' (Paul Virilio), which enclosed the *horror vacui* of the emergent new era in an enormous bubble of thought-up pictures, namely with the essence of the imaginary, and which finally cultivated the unconscious with the claim of universal validity. It emerges that globalness is a local event, although nearly all energy is invested in confusing and covering-up such a truth. The self-regarding mind is a small phantasma extending all the way to infinity. It is the phantasma of the omnipotence of pre-pubescent boys who did not succeed until they had endured necessary failure – something that can be detected right down to the last detail, not from the inside, but rather from the outside. The so-called universal is nothing more than 'becoming one', in any case one in the eyes of fearful children who are afraid of their fear. And that is probably an illusion, even if physically busy and scientifically protected. However, as the senses in the sense of cosmic horizons are blocked up and stuck fast, it will be some time before the lack of a framework allows an unprejudiced view of things, and the imaginary basic characterisation in the foundation of belief and knowledge of sciences moves into the bright light of critical contemporariness. Such leaps forward towards a precise uncertainty have, and will always have, the prerequisite of the human body in its historical contingency.

The fundamental directions of civilisation are known as spiritualisation and incorporeality. This occurs doubly as abstractions of language and pictures. The imaginary, both linguistic and pictorial, is relevant – a surface without boundaries simplifying itself into essence.

Rudolf Kassner's phrase, 'the more sensory, the more intellectual', is not one of the basic assumptions of the theory on civilisation, although it has been highly plausible for some time. Here it is more a case of 'the more sensory, the more inane'. Or vice versa, 'the more nonsensical, the more intellectual'. Mind and body, at least since Descartes, follow the model of a revolving door, tensed with mutual exclusivity. This is the only way that the point can be reached where the intellect is removed from the body. This is the point where everything matters, or rather where everything did matter. For we have gone past this point. As long as the body was maltreated linguistically and indeed with a partially rough, partially subtle oppression, then it could subversively keep up. Asceticism, even at its most extreme, needs the remnants of the bodily, the earthly and the material for its fulfilment. Furthermore up to almost the middle of the twentieth century there was a counter-civilisationary tradition of extreme physicality in carnivals, in excesses and in the grotesque (Michail Bachtin). Subversions like this soon stopped only with the enormous adjustment of civilising methods on picture abstraction. Spiritualisation, as the transformation of everything bodily in the pictorial, acts differently from linguistic oppression. It releases. It celebrates the body by means of a cult of pictorial bodies and body pictures and releases it from the very chains that the old asceticism had forged. It appears to be an immeasurable liberation of measure. The historically damaged human body, may, should, has to realise all its needs for freedom, but not in reality, but in effigies, within a framed compulsive imaginary. This frame is the only condition. Everything else is permitted. Permission is granted definitely to do the definitely unpermitted. We may choose freely in the choice of our compulsions to produce – a repressive desublimation, supported in the middle and on a huge scale, as preformulated by Herbert Marcuse. It happens insidiously and without due notice. People are, themselves, still in the way of perceiving what they are currently doing and enduring. This hindrance is strengthened by the apparent endlessness of the virtual world installed in equipment. The imaginary, thought of absolutely, appears no longer able to stop. It offers a dubious eternity and suggests to people who do not want to, or cannot, die, that they are in the right place. It is literally a ghost ship where there is nothing for bodies to look for and nothing to find. Nothing more material is needed to complete the pictorial abstraction. It creates a world *sui generis*, a world of ghosts and monsters which creates fear from the outset. The surface of the picture itself folds in and forms a comfortable prison, forever immutable and endlessly boring.

It then becomes rock hard. The mind has been harder than matter for some time. Its relation to itself remains a short-cut, forgetting that the eternal is of temporal origin. On the other hand, the body presents a cosmic event. Precisely because of its mortality it reaches up to the starts and down to the earth's core.

The greatest possible significance has to be given to what the body is. For in its vocation as a civilising influence, it has been exposed constantly to the fury of disappearance until its life flame was snuffed out in the matériel battles of the First World War. No more micro-macrocosm; no arranging of bodies according to number, height, weight, perhaps still according to number; the big mystery of height and weight – engendered beneath the surface – is brushed away; beauty, occurring in pleasure and sorrow – is removed by sex and sports pictures; the osmotic skin is toughened and made impermeable by finishing the person as an individual, armed with an identity. All this happened in order to produce a double of the mind, in its image. The mind of abstraction is a self-made man, producing his like everywhere – a monster of irrevocable eternity. This has been the case for a long time, not just recently, not just since modern times or the Middle Ages, but since antiquity. The driving force behind this unending story is probably the fear of death. But towards the end of the second millennium, the increase in it is palpable, coming in useful for forgetting, removing and rejecting. We will have to take a stance. This can be done because it has informally revealed the elaborate perception for some time that people gone towards a world of death by denying their mortality, that is of the mortality of their body. It is a world with dead gods, dead people and dead things. People will die from their illusions about immortality and its 'realistic' effects. No, they will not die, they will change into their creation made out of linguistic and pictorial rubbish. It is a creation which cannot die, but which also cannot live. The question remains. What is there left to organise – through thoughtfulness, through rehearsed awareness, through incessant thinking about bodies – in the face of the invisible superior strength of a closed circle in the orbit of the imaginary? The mind is locked in the prison of freedom. It is imprisoned and has to take its prison with it everywhere and all the time. Yet the body can escape, go where it wants to, if it destroys the mind as a maker of doubles. Whoever can conclude that ignorance is increasing in knowledge, also tolerates the thought that spiritualisation, the main aim of all civilisations, in the end turns out to be a tale of a multi-layered abstraction with many ways of dying. Then people would lose their fear of fear and, in the face of their own mortality, finally grow up.

Translated by Claire Tarring

II. Portfolio

Myriam Van Imschoot

Images Preserved in Liquid:[1]
A Foreword

The following series of pictures of Eric Raeves, in collaboration with photographer Bart Michielsen, are somewhat of a, to say it in theatrical terms, 'première' and a 'primeur'. The series *premières* in so far as this book finally has reached its moment of appearance and presents itself to us in print. The photos are a *primeur* in so far as they, being specifically designed for this book, make Eric Raeves leave his most familiar medium, the medium of dance, to cross over to the medium of photography. And yet, has Eric Raeves really left the medium of dance? Or, to put it another way, has Eric Raeves not *always* been 'leaving' dance even when working in it? So how could he leave dance as a medium for this photo-project, if he had never belonged to it? How can he have left, if he had never settled there in the first place?

Raeves' choreographic work is best known for a continuous blurring of disciplinary boundaries. In 'sculptural dance art' and 'environmental dance installations', Raeves showed a taste for exploring the continuum between the dance image and the sculpture, between the movement and the frozen image, the body and the object, and between different presentation-formats, both in museums and dance spaces. However, it would be deceptive to label Raeves' work as multimedial or interdisciplinary. Rather than transgressing the boundary of a discipline into the realm of the interdiscipline, Raeves seems not to have bothered about those boundaries in the first place. There is no sense of denial or dialectics at work, he does not break rules, is not teasing conventions, there is no self-conscious strategic play at work. The issues related to much interdisciplinary work are for him simply *not an issue*. And if they become an issue it is to people who, however they profess to transcend disciplinary boundaries, still hold on to them to enable the perpetual dynamic of their transgressive aesthetics.

The motor behind Eric Raeves work is not iconoclasm of any sort (in its energy, its gesture, etc.), but imagination. The etymological root of these two words – the *breaking* of an image as opposed to the *making* of an image – is telling in that respect. Imagination reads quite literally as 'image-ination' or 'the making of an image', and that's what Raeves does. He makes images, again and again, with an ongoing concern about how bodies and images relate to each other. What turns a body into an image? How do images turn into carnate 'beings' that speak to us and 'face' us?

This text does not speak *back* to the photographic images in this book. The photos are telling enough to speak for themselves. However, I would like to point to the way the series of photos stand at the intersection of a number of notable recent shifts and emphases in the work of Eric Raeves. More precisely, it is my aim to briefly discuss the shift from a sculpted *object*-oriented languaged to a more *abject* visual language.

The works of Raeves[2] in the mid-nineties were simple and minimal in composition. *Solo Man* (1995) for example, exhibits a naked man on a platform on the spectator's eye-line, who rotates from one pose to another in an extremely slow and controlled way. His face and genitals are turned away, so that the body makes a nameless and plural impression. It is sometimes reminiscent of the idealised bodies of Hellenistic athletes – muscular, broad-shouldered, baldheaded. At other moments the image of the body crumbles into anatomic parts, lumps of meat, strings of muscle or pieces of rump. Remarkable as these images may be in itself, what is truly striking is the way something as basic as a man rotating or taking positions becomes extremely complex for those watching. However curdlingly slow the tempo is, however transparent each pose, however simple each movement: as a spectator you just cannot manage to hold on to what you have seen, to freeze it into a permanent image (or a succession of images). It is not the only time that Raeves points to the fact that a particular presented object can generate in the viewer's eye extremely opposite images. In *Solo Man* it is a clearly articulated and extremely slow moving body with sharp contours that dissolves into an avalanche of images that are slippery, fast and fluid. In the process of looking, the highly sculptured and three-dimensional body breaks adrift into a stream of images from which it is hard to select. Raeves' work is at its best when it challenges, frustrates, hyper-activates and liquidises (makes liquid) the act of looking.

In *1 World*, a collection of 4 nightly lit cages like in a nocturama in the zoo, we see how Raeves questions the sharp and solid boundaries of the body in yet a different way without however leaving the sculptural qualities of the previous work. For example, in *Lichaam op doek 2000-3b* (*Body on Canvas 2000-3b*), the head of a dancer blossoms open into an immense white funnel and in *Insect* a twisting figure fuses into a plinth and a suit of armour. Raeves employs ever more means of manipulating his dancers' bodies: light, projections, body paint, costumes, props, masks, etc. They can hardly be called props, because they are not treated as appendages or additions, but as inalienable extensions of the body itself. The borderline between the physical organicity of the body and an object seem in fact not even relevant. After all, connected in a way that is more symbiotic than oppositional, body and object are simply related quantities in a corpuscular formula with increasingly audacious, imaginative and strange outcomes. As if Raeves wants to stretch out like elastic the fossilised views of the body, so as to include the 'outside', the 'exclusive', the 'non-body' and the 'inanimate' too. In an interview Raeves claims that his model is not reality, but the potential: 'they [the sculptures] sprung from my fantasy and they dare to conceive of the body in ways beyond the depictions we normally see in life. But this other world is not detached from ours. *1 World* is a portrait of our world, but not in the form we know it.' Or to borrow a line from Mr. Spock in *Star Trek*, 'It's life, Jim, but not as we know it'.[3]

In two recent installations presented at the March 1999 Happening in the Cultural Centre of Berchem, Raeves shifts the boundaries of the body not so much by extension but by dissolution. In *Low Table* two twisting figures shut up in a walled-in table cast shadowy reflections on the matt glass tabletop. The bodies here have become ghostly traces on a flat screen. This theme is developed even more strikingly in *Cupboard*, a man-high receptacle. Anyone who wants to see what's inside can look through a hole in the cupboard which contains an ordinary glass (you look through the bottom of the glass which produces a telescopic optical effect). Inside there's a naked female dancer, but the distorting convex base of the glass means all the viewer sees is a syrupy, flesh-coloured liquid, as if in a kaleidoscope. From close-up the skin becomes a meat soup in which spots of skin float round like minestrone.

Taking all these works together, Eric Raeves' main concern is the pragmatism of the image. The leading question behind all these experiments is what an image does (its effect), not so much what it is (the internal visual grammar, morphology).[4] But this is not to say that along the way gradual changes have not been taking place in the image status of the presented. The work slips from nakedness, substance, sculpted three-dimensionality, solidity and definition to another level of treatment: two-dimensionality (projections, photos, surfaces), dilution and delimitation (though it stays within a frame). When Raeves has already liquidised the act of looking, he more and more is making the presented image itself liquid, immaterialised; taking the ground from under its feet.

Eric Raeves thereby comes very close to old theories of intromission in optics.[5] Epicurus, for example, thought that thin layers of atoms from the surface of every object penetrated our eyes in a stream. In his view, to look meant to be saturated. The question of how these injections of 'substances', colours and forms were then transformed into mental images kept not only Epicurus, but also many scholars and alchemists, right down to today's

neurologists, spellbound. Raeves deserves a place in this line. His industri-
ousness resembles that of a pre-modern alchemist, in the way he evokes
in experiments in his choreographic lab the appearance of the body, while
yet abstracting it in the literal sense (ab-strahir): draw off, cream off, break
off – to draw images out of the bodies and inject them into our eyes.

These photos then, I like to imagine, are the jars on the shelf in the
lab of this drawer-off of images. The glass sides (the frame of the photos)
contain a fluid, almost amorphous mass. A leg is incorporated in a trail of
milk or torsos merge into each other and sculptures float in saltpetre;
Images preserved in liquid.

Translated by Gregory Ball

Notes

[1] This foreword was written in 1999 at the time of the presentation of the installations
High Table, Low Table and *Cupboard* during the Happening at the Cultural Centre in
Berchem. I have chosen not to update it with the material of more recent work. Every
last piece creates its own retrospective genealogies and redefines the precedents in
a way that this text has tried to do so at *that* time, *then*.

[2] Eric Raeves started presenting his choreographies in the late eighties with *Amper
Zonder* (1988) and *Mud Man* (1988). A contribution to *Lijn 9* (1989) and *Onbehouwen
Sporen* (1990) – both site specific projects – were prestudies for his first full-evening
piece *Rijkgevulde tema's en donkere kleuren* (1990). *De Perzen/Het Méér* (1992) followed, of which the second part was reworked for *Het Tweeluik* (1992). In the mid-
nineties Eric Raeves takes a new 'start' when he relinquishes the former baroque
aesthetics of his pieces in the minimal solo *Solo Man* (1995). *Solo Man* figures also in
Interesting Bodies, a collection of small pieces or living moving 'sculptures' that were
presented in museums and site-specific locations. After *1 World*, in which the visual
imagery turns bolder again, Eric Raeves makes three dance installations for the happening curated by Marc Vanrunxt in CCBerchem (1999): *High Table, Low Table* and
Cupboard, which got reintegrated in *2 Snelheden* (2000). *Sterk Water* (1999), a solo for
a dancer and video, and *2 Snelheden* (2000), a full-evening piece for three dancers and
video by Stefan Fronck, were presented after this foreword was written.

[3] The motto comes from *Diep in Amerika* (*Deep in America*), Dirk van Bastelaere,
Atlas, Amsterdam/Antwerp, 1994.

[4] The installation works (1999) are no exception to this. In these works Raeves wanted
to approach the body from various angles and thereby radicalise differing viewing
options, such as the worm's eye view (*High Table*), the bird's eye view (*Low Table*) and
the microscopic close-up (*Cupboard*). My thanks to Jeroen Peeters who in a conversation
involuntarily led me to the term 'pragmatism of the image'.

[5] Alberto Manguel makes an interesting comparison between reading and optics
(including the intromission theories) in *Een geschiedenis van het lezen* (*A History of
reading*), Ambo, Baarn, 1999 (the original edition appeared in 1996).

Portfolio by Eric Raeves

Staged Bodies

Photo 1 portfolio

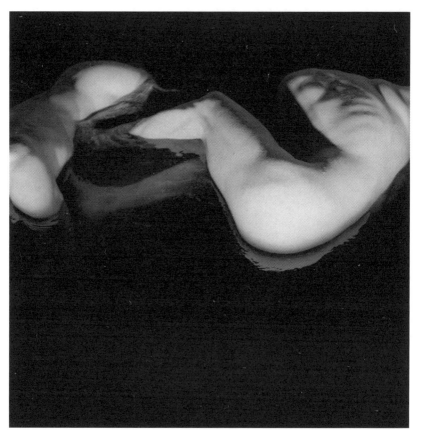

Photo 2 portfolio

Photo 3 portfolio

Photo 4 portfolio

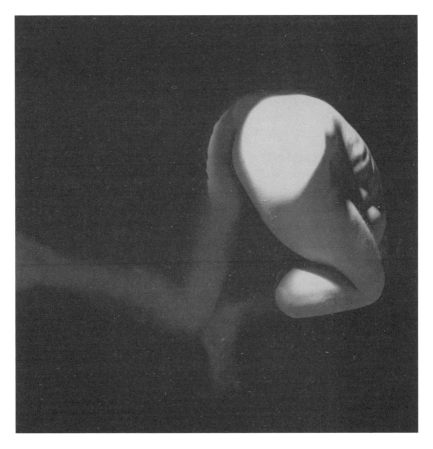

Photo 5 portfolio

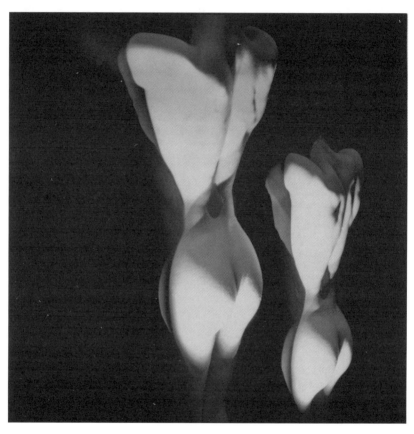

Photo 6 portfolio

III. Interviews

Romeo Castellucci, *Giulio Cesare*, Photo: San Giovanni Silva, agenzia contrasto (Courtesy of Societas Raffaello Sanzio)

Romeo Castellucci

Biography

In 1981, Romeo Castellucci (1960, Cesena near Rimini) established the company Societas Raffaello Sanzio, together with his sister Claudia, a formally trained singer, and the actors Chiara and Paolo Guidi. In 1988, the iconoclastic company moved into an abandoned forge which they renamed 'La Casa del Bello Estremo' (The House of the Beautiful Extreme). Under this name, they also published drama and poetry as well as philosophical writings. In that same year, Claudia Castellucci established a drama school for children: 'Scuola Teatrica della Discesa' (Drama School of the Descent).

The artisan and yet very technological performances by Societas Raffaello Sanzio were a kind of declaration of war against text and language. Their extreme physicality is intended to lay bare the realm of the unconscious, of non-verbal reality. The name of the company was borrowed from the famous Renaissance painter Rafael, because 'in the perfection of his compositions, the body bathes in metaphysics'.

Interview[1]

You state that the body is the character. Do you primarily look for actors with a particular physique? Or, to put it in more general terms, why is the body so essential in your theatre?

It is not so much about a personal choice nor about a certain choice of style. In the theatre one is working with actors and they all have a body. For me, the theatre is the physical form of art par excellence, by definition. Thus, it is an art that communicates through a body that is on a scene. This body is a physical body moving in a temporal dimension. This is about a physical form of art bound by time. The body is the minimum and at the same time the maximum that can be communicated. The search for actors is one of the most interesting phases of my work. The choice grows from a classical dramaturgical necessity and is therefore always linked to the question of the theatre. It would be intolerable to choose people solely for reasons of curiosity, or because of a bizarre or provocative taste. This attitude is not at all mine. It is not my approach to choose anyone unless the choice and the necessity to cast precisely that person arises from a rigourous dramaturgy. In a certain way, it is not me who chooses them. I would not be able to live with that. It is all about an impersonal choice, an obligatory and necessary choice. It is beyond any doubt a formal problem, for I am obsessed with form. For me, it is the sole universal dimension. These actors are a complete form in themselves, which is already perfect. Preceding any methodology even, any examination, any test and verification, they already find themselves in a condition of dignity with respect to the stage. Each body appearing on the stage – I am not only considering the body in its extreme form – is always confronted with a certain degree of amazement. From this it follows that the pathological discourse does not interest me in the least. On the contrary, according to me, each body possesses a form of beauty that attracts me in a certain way, and that takes me along. They are without any doubt forgotten beauties; they are other energies; other, forgotten actions. It is, for instance, very important to me to know exactly how much an actor weighs, for the way in which he weighs on the stage differs in accordance with his physical weight. As a consequence, the way in which an actor weighs on the stage when he is walking on it, is an important element, an element of contemplation, of judging things.

Is this about a material weight, about materiality?
Yes, but apart from the material aspect it is automatically a symbolic weight, too. The curse, the intrinsic nature of the stage is that everything immediately becomes linguistic. An actor who weighs a lot, also has a weighty effect on the linguistic level of the play, as well as on the level of the scene and on the symbolism of the specific language of the scene. To give an example: in the second part of *Giulio Cesare* – for which I have followed a classical dramaturgy of the text – the text imposed a light-footed pace. This is where the choice of bodies that barely seem to touch the stage, barely seem to brush the stage, comes from. In the first part it is about bodies that have a monumental dimension, a dimension verging towards the monument, towards marble, towards something of weight. This dimension was concentrated in the figure of Cicero. So, there is also a discourse of contrast, of reaction between the first part and the second: a contrast based exactly upon weight. The body must absorb and pass on, in a superficial form, although this may seem paradoxical. It is about a kind of superficial evaporation of the new feeling, of the new language. It is always about the creation of a new language. It is a new language that is not simply communicating through a text. It is a physical, superficial evaporation instead.

What does this new language exactly signify? Is it a language outside the linguistic order?
Being on the stage brings forward the state of crisis of our linguistic being time and again. It questions linguistic beings, because the stage confronts the language of our experience with a different language. This is precisely the game of the double in the theatre. One simulates a language. The theatre has a double linguistic nature. The stage is a state of absolute alienation, of unnaturalness, of artificiality.

Is it about body language?
When referring to the language of our experience, I am talking about the language we are using solely as an instrument, a language that happens to consist of empty, circular words. The theatre is an almost parasitical form, doubling the language of our experience of the world. It doubles language in order to create a certain form of doubleness, of transcendence – a way of moving beyond.

This hereafter, is it situated outside the symbolic, linguistic order?
This hereafter is a journey, an adventure, an encounter with the unknown. This state of artificiality, of alienation imposed upon us by the stage should not be taken as a difficulty that must be hidden, that must be anaesthetized. On the contrary, it constitutes an opportunity, a possibility. It is for this reason that I generally cannot stand professional actors – and that is all the more so when they are very good actors – because they respond to this state of alienation enforced upon us by the stage with a typical naturalness. Their naturalness, however, does not possess the force of nature. The central aspect is the nature of the body, of an untrained body, because nature in itself is complete as it is. Nature suffices as such.

Is that nature as a force on its own a primary cause?
It is not something I am looking for, I find myself in the middle of it. It is not a planned dimension. To me, it is a minimal, genital state, in the sense that it could bring something into being. That is what I mean by definitely dismissing naturalness in favour of the force of nature. Nature does not imply spontaneity.

It remains within the framework of artificiality.
Absolutely. One could compare it with a term from agriculture: with grafting – a technique, moreover, that probably came into practice at the time that man gave form to the theatre. It is a part of nature within another part of nature, a cohabitation within new creatures. So they are part of nature,

and not a pretence of nature. These pieces of nature with their destructive ontology create artificial flowers, new plants. A grafted plant is a plant. It is a part of nature but it is unnatural at the same time. Nature in its most simple, rudimentary form of life is uncontrollable. It is about pieces of destructive heaviness and effectiveness, juxtaposed in an unnatural way. In the same way the theatre creates another dimension, another word dimension, another dimension of language and of time. Thus, it frees the way for another language, that cannot be grasped intellectually. This is not sufficient for me, because it is disappointing. It is disappointing because it is comforting. It creates another order of language, another order of things that simply leads me on, that enraptures me.

The form of theatre touches me. I consider the theatre as the form of art to which all other arts are referring to. Painting refers to the theatre, to a small theatre. Music refers to a mental theatre. Theatre is the primary need for artificiality, for the complexity of man. It is also beyond any doubt the form of art most closely linked to death. What strikes me is the fact that the theatre does not claim, does not pretend to tell the truth. I am interested in a theatre that is conscious of its own corruption. One could link this aspect to the discourse on the relation between theatre and rhetoric and also in connection with forms, which we have already discussed. I think it is important to evoke the force of rhetoric. When talking about rhetoric I am of course not referring to the rhetoric that has, rightfully, come to have a negative connotation. I even find it amusing that people are scandalized when simply hearing the word. So I am not referring to present-day rhetoric, which communicates through the language of politicians, through the language of publicity. This form of rhetoric does not have the formal discipline and strictness necessary to be interesting. It is not authentic rhetoric. It is a euphemism. What I am interested in is the old, classical rhetoric. I am mainly thinking of Gorgia, the first theoretician of rhetoric. He made some very interesting, even visionary remarks. To me, rhetoric is not a technique of the past but one of the future. Gorgia stressed the thought that human language does not have the possibility to, is not up to, bear the weight of the truth. This idea is later also taken up by Hölderlin. He formulates the idea that the sacral names are missing. But a long time before him, Gorgia already affirmed the impossibility of truth. In this way, one discovers a completely other function of language: language can no longer tell the truth but its function is to describe itself. Language can no longer describe the truth of things. It can only describe and contemplate itself. Here begins the first mimetic game of language in the history of mankind. The instant that language is no longer taken seriously, that it is no longer believed, the need for fiction is created and the need for linguistic construction, for an artificial body. Gorgia, who forged the term rhetoric, defines rhetoric as 'the way to touch souls'. He inaugurates the aesthetics of emotions. I could also quote Plutarch, who in his turn quotes Gorgia when referring to tragedy: 'He who misleads is more just than he who does not mislead; he who is misled knows more than he who is not misled'. So the one misled is wiser than the one who is not. Language acquires an almost initiating form, as if it were a road to be taken but only through one large construction. The rhetorical discourse is like an artificial flower. That is the aspect that intensely fascinates me in this technique, in this technology of feelings.

Is mimesis the imitation of a pre-existing core?
Yes. It is a doubling that is a greeting to another world. That other world can also instill fear for it is the world of the possible. Theatre is a recreation of something at the same time divine and diabolical.

Is this creation of possibility a choice?
I believe that on a certain level it is a choice but that it is not on another level, in the sense that it is not I myself who is making theatre. I do this in a sort of complete amnesia. But within this amnesia there is a need for technique. It is ambivalent.

Through artificiality the world of possibility can be skimmed over. But only part of that world can be recreated. Is that part a choice or something that imposes itself?
It is a part but the part stands for the whole. *Julius Caesar* does not interest me at all. But there is something special about this: by bringing *Julius Caesar* to the stage I am taking, no, not I, but that which is in the play, makes *Julius Caesar* stop being an object of study and so we can see what comes out of it. It is not a literary problem, but the more time you invest in it, the more the limits widen; they become fluent, intangible. The small object explodes and finally encompasses everything. It is interesting that spectators often ask me if I am preoccupied with the shocking effects of this play. But strangely enough, to me this piece is absolutely not shocking at all. If the spectator experiences it that way, it must be a personal, intimate shock. They are shocked by the confrontation with themselves, by their own intimacy. The theatre therefore starts from *Julius Caesar*, a necessarily ridiculous object or subject, but in the end it stands for everything. The reaction of the audience finally is a predictable effect following the rhetoric mentality, which is one of commotion.

Is this other world a world of archetypes where universal impulses are played out?
Without any doubt it is. Although I would rather talk of fabulous figures rather than of archetypes. In Italian the word fabulous has a strong, powerful significance. The fabulous is at the same time a state of amazement and of fear. The term 'fabulous' refers to a hereafter, to another possible world where things blend. There are fabulous combinations of creatures. There is a sort of circle in which one blends, a circle of initiation, a circuit. In that circle animals talk and people have stopped talking. They exchange forms. Each time a new language is born that is efficient, that is finally adjusted to a body.

Does 'adjusted to a body' mean 'comprehensible to a body'?
Adjusted means without the burden, the weight of tradition. It inaugurates a language, like Adam.

What do you mean exactly by 'without the weight of tradition'? Is the body outside of tradition? And is everything that is outside of tradition necessarily body?
The body I am referring to is a body outside tradition, because tradition allows us to have only one type of body. At the moment tradition forces only one type of body onto us. It has known other forms but now it imposes, with all of its weight, one type upon us, namely the body of publicity. So, tradition, by means of its mechanism, forces us to forget the forms it has passed through in the past. I am preoccupied with these traditional forms, that come from the past but fall outside the realm of tradition.

So, tradition is a synonym of culture?
It necessarily is. Moreover, I am only referring to Western tradition. When I – and not only I but precisely in the amnesia that brings me to it – work with the Anatolian Venus, I am not pursuing tradition but its exact 'contra-tradition'. The course of tradition imposes only one model upon us, namely the most recent one. In a certain way, it is all about turning the movement of tradition, about twisting around the operation of time through tradition. But the question was more complex, if I am not mistaken.

The question was also whether everything falling outside of tradition is necessarily body.
It is, in a certain way. For tradition forces us to filter everything through language, which is very poor. It is a language that pretends to be true. It is a pathetic language, because it thinks it can say, affirm, name things, while it happens to be inevitably separated from things.

So, the body of advertising, the body from the latest stage of tradition is a linguistic body?

Yes, it is a body that wants to communicate. It incorporates all the emptiness, the complete circularity of the language of publicity. It misses the adventure of the other language. Everything is already perfectly acquired, known. There is no possibility left to move someone, to lead him or her to a hereafter.

But is the language of advertising not so powerful that it recycles every chance for another world a priori? Every possibility of a new and different image is permanently taken in, recycled, incorporated by publicity, which makes its creation impossible.

Yes, in the sense that publicity is not a dynamic form. It is a very restricted game, because it cannot escape the communication question. The problem of advertising is that it has to communicate. The theatre does not have this problem. This is the curse of publicity, for publicity is a very powerful form of art, a craft that also invades all other arts. Think of the visual arts, for instance. Advertising is also very much ahead of things. One can learn lots from it, especially from the point of view of precision and from a formal viewpoint and from its icastity, i.e. presenting a figure in a highly concentrated form; a figure of a very commanding appearance; a violent play of forms. To me, publicity is the icastic sister of the theatre. It only has the terrible problem of having to communicate. Apart from the communication problem, publicity also has interests that are never hidden, and that weaken it. Still, publicity is very important today. It has checkmated art, for instance. I have not seen anything as powerful as publicity in a long time.

How do you view the use of technique, of mechanical objects in your work?

Technique and mechanisms are never prostheses. That aspect does not interest me at all. Each mechanism on the stage is invested with a phantasm, a spirit. On the level of dramaturgical meaning technique has the same weight as an actor, a sound or a sentence. Technique is on a level with all other elements. So, it is on a horizontal level and it participates in grasping the complete figure of what one can see at a certain moment.

Things are made alive, are moving on their own. It is something like animating materiality.

Indeed, animating materiality, as in the animistic mentality of children. This is about an absolutely childlike need. This is another key word in my understanding of bodies and of the journey into language. Childhood is a very important state in my view. The use of machines comes from this childlike, animistic mentality. So, when at a certain moment a chair sets itself in motion, – a chair normally being the image of 'staticality' par excellence –, this does not imply one but several things. I do not know what exactly it arouses in the spectator, but it surely suggests something. And by letting a chair move, to give a random example, the suggestion is created that anything may start moving and walk away. As if each object contains a small hidden intelligence, a consciousness, autonomous, hidden to us. But this also holds good for the characters: at that same moment this hidden consciousness of the chair is projected onto them. Cicero, too, might possess this dark power. He is a marginal figure to be sure, and not a good example therefore. Let us take Brutus: we seem to know him through and through. In reality though, there might be a hidden intelligence in this character, a never-explored power. And all of this could be deduced from the obser-vation of a wandering chair ...

After the disenchantment of the world by reason the world is now being re-enchanted again.
Yes, but this time it is an enchantment by reason. This is very paradoxical, but it is not about some sunset or something of the kind. It is an absolutely artificial enchantment, and that is why it is so beautiful and powerful, and also violent. The theatre is the place of violence. The beauty of the theatre is of a violent type. Of course, I do not mean physical violence. It is, as I have said before, a linguistic violence; it is the violence of tearing oneself loose from the habits of language.

Does dramaturgy stand outside meaning, outside the text? Is it about a dramaturgy of the body?
I understand dramaturgy in the etymological sense of the word, namely as the *theurgy* of action. In ancient Greece, *dromena* and *legomena* (acting and speaking) were separated. *Dromena*, acting, – from which the word dramaturgy is deduced –, etymologically means *theurgy*, the practice to bring statues alive, to invest statues with the divine. Dramaturgy is to me the investment of the play and action with a soul; a phantasm. The way in which dramaturgians are thought of today is a total aberration. A dramatur-gian is supposed to be someone who writes a book. This is completely absurd. There is no longer any link with the original word. There are books, to be sure, – but these are only classical texts reaching as far as Shakespeare –, that have within them a deep, hidden dramaturgy. It can be very beautiful to read an absolutely rigid text like a classical text, a classical tragedy for instance, or a play by Shakespeare. You can see how the characters move in

depth; how they are striding over the stage; how they enter and exit; what is the meaning of every gesture; the presupposition of any of the words … A text by Beckett, on the other hand, has a paralysing effect; everything is too self-evident, too clearly put. When talking about choosing the actors, I was referring to this dramaturgy of the depth of texts. Otherwise it would be merely about the illustration of the text, and it should not restrict itself to this.

As far as body language is concerned, are we talking about a body that is directly communicating? Is the body that speaks for itself an Artaudian body?
Artaud is a name you cannot avoid, even if you want to. In reality I am not inspired by Artaud. I think to refer to Artaud in making theatre is out of place, because there is something excessive about him. Looking for ways to bring Artaud to the stage is at once ridiculous and impossible. But he is a kind of prophet of fabulous language, of course. Also, it is very important to distinguish between his different periods: 'Le Théâtre et la Peste' is a text that I do not think is interesting, whereas I very much like 'Le Théâtre de Seraphin'. The latest Artaud, the Artaud of Rodez, definitely interests me most, especially where he works on the translation of Lewis Carroll. The translation of Humpty Dumpty is a cosmic coincidence to me, a planetary event. That was a very meaningful encounter. That is the Artaud that is closest to me. But I cannot name him; I cannot try to repeat him, because that would be an illustration again, or an apostolate, and that is pointless. Artaud, like Carroll, goes through the mirror and meets a new language. That is cruelty: the fact of changing the order of language. And that is why, as someone so poignantly put it, *Alice in Wonderland* really is a horror story.

Does it make sense to separate these two worlds? Breaking through the symbolic wall presupposes the other side; it presupposes the wall.
You need the mirror. It is precisely that condition of contradiction that is beautiful. It is a violent tumble. If this relation of violence, this intimate contradiction of needing the other would no longer exist, it would be as if we found ourselves in that other world. It would not be possible to travel anymore. If someone found himself at the other side, the desire to come to this side would surge up in him.

In your text on the Oresteia *a reference is made to Benjamin. Is there a relation between Walter Benjamin and this discourse on language, too?*
Benjamin is a very strong presence in my reading. That reference within the framework of the *Oresteia* has to do with its subtitle: 'An organic comedy?'.

Benjamin's intuition about tragedy, – which, as all his intuitions, has a stroke of genius in it – has struck me, in particular where he is talking about the complete absence of the cathartic effect. What also strikes me in Benjamin is the absolute importance of childhood experiences, as a world and also as a political metaphor. The significance of the wealth and complexity of inventive childhood experiences.

Benjamin expressly situates himself between the metaphysical and the historical.
Yes. Benjamin is a character that cannot be fully placed in one camp or the other. He was interested in Jewish mysticism as well as in materialism. His intuitions reach up to our time. His way of thinking and the complexity of it are very modern. He worked on just about everything and always from a surprising angle of incidence. But there is no direct link with my own work. They are often discoveries you make later on.

What is your position within the framework of the metaphysical and the historical, of materialism?
I could summarize it by means of a quotation – although I am well aware of the danger of this quotation: Artaud laid claims to a metaphysics of the skin. Or: a metaphysics of the Benjaminian type, which also always revolves around the surface of the material, of a body, of a tangible experience, i.e. of an experience that one can also recount. Maybe I am most of all inclined towards the metaphysical in Bachofen's Matriarchate. Bachofen points out, at first sight, the paradoxical relationship between metaphysics and materialism. He plays exactly on this double aspect. Bachofen's genius is precisely this link with the material. And this link has something intensely feminine about it. For what is at stake here is the disconcertment of giving birth and of the first composition of the cadaver, which in his view is also a female task. He links these utterly physical, bodily practices of blood, flesh and decomposition to the idea of the hereafter. It is exactly in the idea of the flesh that the idea of the hereafter originates. The one presupposes the other. It is wrong to see them as two opposing domains.

So the historical aspect is not taken into consideration?
Unless it reduces itself in its turn to a body, which is what happens in *Giulio Cesare* for instance. This is a historic drama: Shakespeare's version brings a part of history to the stage. It is his only authentic historic play, in fact. But in *Giulio Cesare* history is reduced to a body, to matter. There is no historic authority. Even if Shakespeare represents history, this gesture contains nothing but a circular movement, a reflexive movement.

Time is a circular time leading back to the myths. Within circularity, time is reduced to the myths.

It is almost an acephalous, headless operation. It is a frightening thought that seems to move itself in history, as if an entity, an essence exists that advances through history, and uses it, manipulates it. Shakespeare appears almost like a demon of history, ridiculing everyone who thinks he can make history. *Julius Caesar* is a fine example of this. But there is much of it in his other historic plays as well.

You used the word acephalous, which makes one think of Bataille. Does he form part of your frame of reference?

Bataille has been the subject of my reading as an adolescent. At a given moment he seemed too clear to me: the link between eros and thanatos was something I had understood immediately and that therefore, almost automatically, disappointed me. Heidegger's reflections on the relation between language and death seem much stronger and much more interesting. One finds that only the people who know death have created a language for themselves. It is the funerary character of language that interests me. That brings me back to Bachofen's reflections on civilization or to Benjamin's mourning drama. These are connections in which language is submerged in a bath of violence, as in Artaud. This relation is more interesting to me than the erotic. The genital aspect is what interests me, not the erotic. I think the erotic is incredibly banal. Freud has conceived the link between eroticism and vitalism in connection with death in a more radical way in *Beyond the Pleasure Principle*. To him the principle of destruction is the stronger one; he emphasizes the death wish within the pleasure principle. But then again, these are all themes that interest me, that are touched upon in my work. But there are no literal quotations or references made to all of the names I mentioned just now.

Why does, of all the arts, the theatre come most closely to death?

In this sense it is important, not out of any philological interest, but it is important to know where the theatre comes from. What do these people on a stage mean exactly? In a certain sense, when one looks into the abyss, one could say that it is all about the world of the dead. From its very origins the theatre has been intricately related to the problem of death. To a certain extent each actor is a forefather. And yet, the relation between the theatre and death is not something that can be clearly put into words; it is never completely unveiled. But there is the fact that, throughout our entire dramaturgy – with the exception of present-day dramaturgy, which does not interest me for that matter, death is always brought to the stage. From the early beginnings man has felt the need to represent the dead. Benjamin links this problem to comedy. He asked himself how it is possible that, in classical Antiquity, three tragedies were followed by only one comedy, a satire? How can only one comedy outweigh three tragedies? His answer was that satire had the function to dissolve the lack of catharsis in what probably was a neurotic laughter. The fact that the hero is not rescued at all is dissolved by the comedy. But he does not find justice either. He is being left with his problem, in the unsolvable relation with death, the death of others in most cases, sometimes also his own death. But the problem remains unsolved. Often, the same gods from the tragedies are in comedy situated within a context of inane violence. So, comedy had an almost therapeutic function to solve the lack of a catharsis.

So, we have the impossibility of the catharsis because of the death on stage, of radical destruction. In Benjamin though, the theatre as a whole is being secularized by this destruction of the catharsis; in your own work the theatre is situated much more against a transcendental background.
I am not sure about that. The effect might be one thing or the other. It depends on the response the performance gets from each of the spectators. I could relate my own experience as a spectator. I see myself much more as a spectator watching beforehand than as a director imposing his view of things. To me, as I have just said, both things are true; again, they are one within the other. The voice of Antonius, to give an example, by an actor whose vocal chords have been taken away, is for me a language coming from another world, from the other world probably. It is the language of a dead person speaking to me. But this language is at the same time utterly physical. Exactly because there is a relation with that other world this language creates an absolutely physical experience. So, on the one hand this voice is transcendental, because it takes me away to another world, – that might be the world of the dead, but also the world of fables or of Christian Paradise – but at the same time it is about an experience originating from the flesh, from wounded flesh even. So, in a certain way it is even holier, more glorious, just like the anorexic bodies from the first part of *Giulio Cesare*. They are blinding bodies, superlative bodies, fabulous in their evidence. But at the same time they are transcendental bodies because they are vanishing; they are about to disappear. As with all other things, from the wandering chair to the presence of bodies and words that are pronounced: everything is bound with its own death, with the possibility of no longer being there. The theatre has the most exclusive link with the problem of death, precisely because it is an art that may be interrupted from one moment

to the next. There is no object to be delivered; there is no canvas nor any block of sculpted marble. In many different ways theatre is a form of art that thinks out the relation with death: from the point of view of tradition because a dead person is often brought to the scene, but from an ontological point of view as it is a form of art that is dying permanently; the theatre is saturated with the problem of death.

Is the insertion of the camera into an actor's cancer-damaged throat at the beginning of Giulio Cesare*, entering the inner body as a way to go into the other world?*
Absolutely. As a matter of fact, it looks like a tunnel, a grotto, a trajectory. But it is also nice that an actor not only shows his exterior body, but also his inside. It is an actor turned inside out, and I find that very strong. Moreover, one also sees the origin of the voice this way; it is an absolutely fleshly origin. One sees the contractions of the flesh. According to tradition the voice is spiritual. Throughout tradition the voice is considered to be a vehicle of the mind, because it consists of air. There is a symbolic association of voice with air. But the journey into the actor shows there is also a fleshly dimension, the contraction of muscles; the source of the voice, which is a physical, fleshly source, is revealed. The first part of the play is all about the obsession with the voice, and therefore with the word. It opens with the image of the vocal chords, and closes with an actor talking without vocal chords. The operation on the voice is at the heart of this circular structure. The closing image too, shows a fleshly voice, a voice that can be weighed, a voice that can be brought back to a body, a spiritual voice communicating a text to us, giving the word to us; but not in the least an experience of a body and of the memory of that body. The interesting thing is that this voice without vocal chords originates in the memory of a wound that is under everyone's eyes. The stimulus triggering this choice is in the text itself, in the deep dramaturgy of the play: the text focusses on the funeral oration of Antonius, concentrated on the hurt, the dagger-wounds Julius Caesar's body has sustained. Only a voice that comes noticeably physically from a wound is capable of delivering an oration of this sort. The voice of Antonius is the conquering voice; it is the voice that is above all other voices, dramaturgically speaking. It is the voice that brings down history. It is a defeating voice, and therefore I needed a voice that was stronger. Whereas the voice of Brutus inhaling helium is a regressive voice; a voice becoming a children's voice (this emphasizes the fact that he is a son of Caesar). It is at the same time a voice that is stepping out of history. This is further reinforced by the

little voice of Donald Duck, a clearly non-historic voice, stripped from its claims to monumentality. Thus one arrives at an experience outside history.

Why is Donald Duck situated outside history?
Because his words in no way whatsoever pretend to change anything or anyone at all.

Performances

1981   Diade incontro a Monade
1981   Persia – Mondo 1 a 1
1982   Popolo zuppo
1982   Maiala anziani e malandati
1983   I fuoriclasse della bontà
1983   Oratoria n.1: Rimpatriata Artistica
1984   Kaputt necropolis
1984   Oratoria n.2: Raptus
1984   Oratoria n.3: Interferon
1985   Glory glory, alleluja
1985   Santa Sofia, Teatro Khmer
1985   Mai nati, mai morti
1986   I miserabili
1986   Oratoria n.4: Tohu Wa Bohu
1986   Geronimo
1987   Die Elenden (Kassel – Documenta 8)
1987   Oratoria n.5: Sono consapevole dell'odio che tu nutri per me
1987   La Donna Velata
1988   Alla bellezza tanto antica
1988   Il gran reame dell'adolescenza
1988   La cripta degli adolescenti
1988   L'adolescente sulla torre d'avorio
1988   Oratorio n.5: Sono consapevole dell'odio che tu nutri per me
1988   Dialogo dell'adolescente con se stesso, cioè con la sua icona
1989   La Discesa di Inanna
1990   Gilgamesh
1990   Voce dell'animale
1990   Iside e Osiride
1991   Ahura Mazda
1992   Amleto

1993   Masoch. I trionfi del Teatro come Potenza Passiva. Colpa e
        Sconfitta
1995   Orestea. Una commedia organica?
1997   Giulio Cesare
1998   Genesi
1999   Voyage au bout de la nuit
2000   Il Combattimento

Note

[1] The interview was translated by Erik Spinoy and conducted by Maaike Bleeker, Steven De Belder, Luk Van den Dries, Annemie Van Hoof and Kurt Vanhoutte (June 1998). We would like to thank Annemie Van Hoof for co-editing the interview.

Marc Vanrunxt, *Antropomorf*, Photo: Raymond Mallentjer
(Courtesy of Hyena vzw)

Marc Vanrunxt

Biography

Since the early 1980s, choreographer and dancer Marc Vanrunxt has been a prominent presence in the world of Flemish dance. He is an autodidact and used to dance for An Slootmakers before he started presenting his own work in 1981, often in collaboration with composer Thierry Genicot, visual artist Anne-Mie Van Kerckhoven, and dancer and costume designer Eric Raeves. In his own stubborn and consequential style, he has succeeded in developing an oeuvre of dances. He collaborated on the choreography of Jan Fabre's second theatre production *Het is Theater Zoals te Verwachten en te Voorzien Was* (*This is Theatre As Could be Expected and Foreseen*) from 1982 and also danced for Jan Fabre, Thierry Smits, Truus Bronkhorst and Catherine Massin. In the work of his own company Hyena, Vanrunxt is constantly looking for a balance between poetry and philosophy on the one hand and the art of choreography on the other. The incessant dialogue with the visual arts explains the strikingly sculptural qualities of his work. He likes to perform at daggers drawn and does not shun elements of theatrical camp, which he balances with an abstract, distilled dance vocabulary in a surprising way.

Interview[1]

How would you describe the body within your work?
I have not participated in the discussion of body discourse in the performing arts. In my work the body is a given. It is so manifestly and concretely present in the creation process that it almost becomes intangible as a study object. Nevertheless I am looking for a new language so that I can redefine some self-evident aspects such as corporality, but also, for example, time. This does not involve so much a manageable or exchangeable language but the translation of the research that every performance actually is. During each performance there are certain elements such as location, movement, light, colours, but also the watching eye of the spectator, that can influence the body and our view of it. The discussion of body discourse is embedded in a larger research project into the interaction between these elements. Each performance departs from a theoretical enquiry, which is different

each time and takes changing priorities into consideration. The biggest problem, however, is the vocabulary. How can this research be translated; how do people look at it; how do they understand it? It consists of a search in which one works out the different ways of showing something. This certainly incurs the fear of being too explicit. My medium is the language of mystery, which involves the examination and show of invisible things. For me, this is also a criterion when I go to look at other people's work: the search for the hidden force, the mystery behind things.

The communication to the outside world is not always self-evident. I would much rather present the research as such, but this often appears difficult for the audience. Moreover, a performance requires a certain degree of finishing. Consequently, there is a risk that the audience consider the performance as a terminus; a finished product or final data. We must not forget that a production is strongly subjected to changes and to the different locations in which the production takes place. We do not play at the large theatres, which normally provide a minimum of technical means. You often have to invent everything all over again because the location necessitates this. As a result, the perception becomes totally different and gets to look a bit like a big puzzle. It is an entity but it should be a fluent and variable process instead. Still, you do learn how to present a 'definitive' product although I realize that this is in itself a contradiction.

You have said that you are also looking for the mystery in other people's work. Is this mystery more concretely tangible now in your own performances?
You could translate the mystery as a form of intelligence. It stands for a stratification, not only appealing to all senses but also to rational, emotional and spiritual layers of interpretation. In some performances though, the latter aspects are sometimes missing. This intelligence is especially fading in dance because it is considered to be difficult, and therefore looked upon as uninterpretable. But that does not stop me from looking for different layers. If necessary, I look for something I cannot identify or that cannot be consumed rightaway, but that, by consequence, keeps reverberating.

I do not much associate the first part of Antropomorf *with the word mystery. Personally, I would rather describe it as ethereal. Later on I read that the oeuvre of Bataille has been one of your sources of inspiration for* Mijn solo voor Marie (Vernietigd) (My solo for Marie (Destroyed)) *Bataille's quest for death and the sacral, is that also a quest through which you might find yourself? With reference to* Antropomorf *e.g. I am thinking of the long-drawn-out movements, the reaching for the intangible, the age-old search in the arts to meet with 'a Presence'. The typical reaching-out movement of the arm evokes associations with drawings on Greek vases.*

In the solo for Marie, Bataille indeed was a big source of inspiration. Marie asked three different choreographers to create something on Bataille. Before that, Bataille actually was a great unknown to me. It is true that the longing for something higher, something heavenly is strongly present in my work. That explains the use of cubes and pedestals for example. These are decorative elements as well as a translation of the search for something 'Higher'. It concerns a pursuit of something better, more beautiful or higher but also the destruction of the 'Higher' as happens in *Antropomorf*. It is important to place something against the 'Higher', as a counterweight, as it were. Formerly, the white immaterial part in which you had a kind of immateriality or transparency probably came at the end. Utopia as an ending. Now, reality trickles in at the end – always stylized though – in the form of coloured costumes, tears in the white paper, the black floor that becomes visible. Not only is the contrast focussed, the hinge between the contrasting parts is also shown. Visually speaking, this is a big shock and at the same time also a certain relief. The white parts have a strong influence and the scene lasts a little too long as a means of intensification. In that way the longing for something new finally arises.

Could you tell us something more about the realization of the intervention of choreographer Alexander Baervoets in the middle of Antropomorf *which has breached your choreography in a striking way?*

I had already been nourishing the idea for quite some time to introduce a foreign body in the performance, a virus as it were. I wanted to see what effect it would have on both the dancers as well as the audience. I have also thought about a number of other choreographers such as, for example, Thierry Smits, Jan Fabre and Truus Bronkhorst – all of them people with whom I have worked in the past. We agreed that I would remain responsible for the costumes, the music and the light since I was looking for a kind of continuity in the image. After a couple of weeks Alexander Baervoets joined the creative process. I wanted to avoid the insertion of a seperate choreography by him afterwards. Now, the performance has come into being in a chronological way, which gives a strong sense of imperceptible transition whereas our language of movement is very different. This search for a foreign body in my own work is a quest to let something escape control, to allow a chance element. Still, there are also foreign bodies or exterior factors, as for example a costume designer, that I do not allow in my own work any longer. In fact I consider choreography as one large think tank with a look that comes, so to speak, from one brain. I think it is important that there is a continuity of images without one falling into an illustration or translation of the other. In that way, I want, for example, the audience to find the same sensitivity, present in the body or the costumes or in the light so that the light is more than just the lighting of something. This results in a complex network of different disciplines and media. Of course, I am surrounded by the right people who can translate my ideas into technical terms. I am certainly not aiming at ultimate control, but it is very important that there are some parallels between the different media since they strongly determine your choreography and also the way people are looking at it. The experiment to introduce a foreign body, a strange language of movement also stimulates one to think about phenomena such as identity and signature. Some people do not even notice this intervention. Others notice it, for example, in certain touches between the dancers, as in the shakings of hands, which is rather unusual in my own work.

Does this strict control not exclude mystery?
Certainly not, since my control is not comprehensive either. There always escapes something and that makes it exciting. I find it very difficult to interpret my own work and I do not consider this as a lack. One of the starting ideas for *Antropomorf* was working with the location. I have tried to crumple the space, to reduce it into a little ball. Subsequently the 'writing process' begins. I consider the location and the body as a blank sheet. I usually start in the left upper corner of the location. That is also the place where you start writing on a sheet of paper. The location needs thus to be conquered each time, back and fro, over and over again. It concerns a very intuitive process, it is almost an adventure. A number of elements such as material, colour, timbre and sensitivity are fixed and then we start working concretely. Holding on to the state of mind during a time span of two or three months is the most difficult part. It amounts to finding a balance between permanent attentiveness and intuitive sensing. At the moment clarity and readability prevail in my work whereas in the past I was less occupied with this.

Your work is often described as very graphic, as a web of lines carved in space. You have just spoken about the function of paper in Antropomorf *and you have also compared choreography with writing on a blank sheet.*
Naturally I work within the restrictions of dance. I have learnt to live with the fact that movements are fleeting by definition. Eventually, a choreographer has nothing in his hands. What he makes only remains in the minds of the audience and according to me that is exactly the power of it, too.

Yet, I am also trying to burn movements on the retina of the spectator by means of rhythm or repetitions – a sort of loupe idea, in fact. I want to etch these movements in space. In that way the dancers in *Antropomorf* leave tracks behind in the paper. The walking through confetti in *Fortitudo* represents the formation of tracks in the snow. It almost concerns easily manageable poetry, which is at the same time very clear and powerful. I always try to reach a maximum effect with a minimum of means. They are low-budget translations that have become my credo through the years.

Could you say that the idea of tracks also applies to the body, that every dancer carries traces from his past, his identity and existence? Pina Bausch namely represents the identity of the dancer as a track/memory. On the other hand, other choreographers try to make abstraction of memory.
I would rather place myself somewhere in between. I consider the dancer more like a blank sheet, although I must admit that this is a false thought. Each dancer has his own past that cannot be denied. I believe it is very important to know what the body experiences, what the dancer goes through during the whole process of performing. This is the central idea in for example *The Pickwick Man*, the solo by Jan Fabre for me, in which we worked around themes like humiliation, deterioration and undressing of the body and the loss of a façade. This was represented concretely by means of smudged make-up, sweating bodies, total exhaustion. In that way you reach another essence. On such occasions the working of time and energy is strongly present and also the way in which these different elements influence the body.

A number of theatre makers are exactly trying to rule out this human factor. Edward Gordon Craig for instance, found it very tedious that the body of the dancer was getting sweaty.
I think this factor is too strongly present to disregard it or to rule it out. I accept the physical aspect as something that is simply going on, but it is not a basic assumption in my research. In some of my earlier work such themes were often more basic than they are now, as for instance in a performance like *A. Dieu* (1986) in which the battle of attrition, the strain and the visible perspiring were important topics. I must admit that this subject matter in my case can be brought back to a certain period, and does not interest me to that extent today. The period of thematizing the physical evolution of the body during a performance, the decay and the explicit tormenting of the body, or the ineluctable process of time has clearly reached an end at the end of the eighties. Yet, this process is also implicitly present in *My solo for Marie (Destroyed)*. There is the aspect of destruction, for instance, based upon a phrase by Italo Calvino: 'By lighting a candle, you

are using it up'. Further, there is also the exhaustive falling in *My solo for Marie (Destroyed)*. By dancing this solo Marie is destructing herself, as it were. But the hardest thing apparently is the not letting go of concentration. That would be like committing treason to the entire process.

In my work imagination comes before depiction. That is why the acting, the representation of a character was so hard for me in the solo by Jan Fabre. I feel very uncertain when having to depict something, like e.g. the dandy figure in *The Pickwick Man*. I find it very exciting on the one hand, while on the other hand I feel I am going beyond my depth. Character drawing is not present in my choreography but this does not imply that the identity of the dancers never becomes manifest. This happens anyway. The dancers are performing the same movements. Yet, there is a world of difference within certain margins of common concentration. Exactly because of this latitude the dancers are strongly growing closer. The effect is even reinforced when form takes precedence. By opening up form, in fact, you end up in the same line and you create something like a shared heart, beating for both of you.

The body to me is not a psychological nor an abstract theme. From the moment a person comes on the stage, you get a tale, but not a narrated story, that is. Yet, even in abstract dance this tale remains a story about bodies, about the antropomorphous, about humans. I had an euphoric feeling that way when noticing how a mistake was made during a performance by William Forsythe. All of a sudden this performance became very human.

Your work is often depicted as 'soul dance'. Does this indicate a totalitarian thinking of the body rather than splintering or fragmentation?
I would again want to quote the metaphor of the beating heart. The beating heart cannot exist on its own. The energy streams through the entire body. A hand, foot or arm has its own power, significance and importance. But alone it cannot function. So, I am not departing from a strict splitting up. Three poles – centre, heart and mind – are always interconnected and cannot be unlinked, even if a dancer would be moving e.g. only one arm. I think that the phenomenon of fragmentation is often deemed too important and often interpreted in the wrong way as well. You can move your body in a fragmented way in the sense that the impulses are coming from a certain part of the body, but also with choreographers like William Forsythe or Meg Stuart the body remains existing as a totality.

As an executant you constantly have a certain image of your body. You dispose of some kind of built-in TV, so that you can see your body from the outside the whole time. You are aware of your front, your back, your underside. As a dancer you have so to speak ten video-screens around you, making you conscious of direction, space and of your location vis-à-vis the other dancers and the audience. The choreography is perceived from a larger whole, from the energy of the dancers. In *Antropomorf* you can now and then observe how body parts are brightening, as it were. Hands, feet and arms are showing up because their skin colour is put against the uniformly white scenery. Yet, they keep forming part of the covering unity. Sometimes even a further step is taken, and then the four dancers are forming an octopod monster.

Is this totalitarian thinking spiritually or religiously embedded?
Perhaps I can only function properly within this totalitarian frame of thinking. It certainly has to do with respect for the body, with leaving the value of the body untouched. I do not think there is any philosophy or conviction behind it.

Stepping in and out of a certain demarcated space like in your My Solo for Marie (Destroyed) *e.g. is an element that fairly often returns in your work and that almost creates the idea of a sacral room.*
To me, the theatre is a very important place and I do not want to neutralize or trivialize it. The theatre is much too precious to me, although I feel it must not be worshipped either. For, after all, what is done there, is physical work. I am very well aware of it.

Stepping out of a certain space intends to show that exact space. Empty it has become a different space. I am looking for different confrontations, for different forms of communication. It is here that aspects of my work should be fit in, like the turning away from the audience, or the blackout lasting just about too long to amplify the sound. The audience is watching passively, and yet I am striving for the creation of a kind of overall experience. I want to maximally activate mind and senses. I would like to emphasize the importance of the anonymity of the audience, though: the protection of the dark house. That is the audience situation I prefer.

The battle against the prison of materiality is an element we find in your earlier work. Could you explain this tension between corporality and materiality to us?
This tension is the literal translation of the incapacity of communicating. This aspect as well as my personal obsessions have moved to the background more in my recent work. At present I am rather looking for answers to questions like: What is time, what is a minute, a step, a movement? Emotions have come to be the consequence instead of a starting-point.

The conflict with the costume too, is less important than it used to be. Images are not presupposed that much any more. Much rather they are arising. I am more and more putting my faith in the conflict, in the alchemy of things, while I used to be very busy trying to manipulate things. I try to determine as little as possible beforehand. My point of departure is the body in space, as in the drawings of Laban. I am fascinated by the play between delineation and infinity in spaces. That is probably where my preference for neutral spaces like the black box or the blank sheet comes from. A black box gives you a feeling of infinity and by means of one colour or one movement only you can delineate things. You can create a continuous appearing and disappearing of bodies.

How would you situate the theatre within our multimedia society?
Here, we are coming to the essence of the theatre. To me, a living human being doing something for someone else remains the principle thing. There is something irreplaceable about that. However large and impressive the settings are, you are essentially watching a live happening, which is consequently vulnerable. Faults can never be ruled out.

The fitting in of the theatre with today's multimedia society often involves a ramble. Often the wrong thrills are sought. The techniques of staging and fast forward, which were highly popular in the eighties, are no longer in place in the theatrical medium. In my view, the theatre should not be approached with the criteria of film and video.

Are your video projects to be interpreted as autonomous art projects or rather as the registration of a happening then?
The only way for me to work with video is letting my own universe be adapted by other people, like Anne-Mie Van Kerckhoven, Stefan Franck and Bart Van Dessel, who have already done this in the past. These videos, however, cannot replace a live performance and are certainly never intended to. I find it very exciting to see the views these people develop with respect to my work and how they process them. How they are interpreting my work or filter it through the eye of the camera. They are looking for points of contact between their own medium and my work. You could perhaps compare it to my working together with Jan Fabre. I am letting myself 'be used' by him in a certain way, and it is very interesting to see in which way he uses my body on stage.

What kind of body do you want to show on stage? How about the despicable body or the erotic body?
When choosing the dancers I am departing from the integral body. I think it is very important to work with people who understand me and who are

willing to understand me. It is all about intelligent bodies. Let me explain this: the dancer must think along and we have to be able to take decisions together. I try to find out if they mentally go well together with me, and physically with each other. It is a very intuitive process. And then again, technical perfection is not my top priority. But personality, identity and making a strong appearance are. It does not matter to me then, if the body is old or young or fat within a certain code. I must admit I have not yet worked with extremely obese people so far. A dancer must be conscious of his body and of the appearance he makes, also and especially when he is standing still. Standing still may well be the most important form of movement to me. The co-ordination with yourself, with space and the others is extremely important. I am looking for an obedient and rebellious body, that is terribly alert but that is able to simply let itself be led in faith.

Personally, I am confronted with my own ageing body, which dances differently from ten or even five years ago. This certainly determines my vision as a choreographer and it will certainly even more do so in future. Marie Decorte for instance, is 44 years old and she certainly does not possess the perfect dancing body, whatever that may be for that matter. Without making this ageing body more explicit it is an unintended theme, though. In *My solo for Marie (Destroyed)* you see an elderly dancer, with a pronounced silhouette. She is moreover wearing a tight dress, which accentuates her curves. Instead of showing a declining body I would rather say I am showing an evolving body. In the case of *My solo for Marie (Destroyed)* it is an ageing body but I might as well be showing the evolution in a reversed way. I find the irreversible process of a performance very important, physically as well as materially speaking. Apart from that, the dancer should also feel good in his costume. It should feel like a second skin.

As for the erotic body, I am much more looking for a certain sensuality and a consiousness of the dancer. Eroticism and sexuality are not really at the centre of my work. In the same way I am not longer consciously interested in the dangerous body. These aspects are present indeed, but they are no longer observed as extraordinary elements. To me, they rather form part of a normal body.

Performances

1981	Eerste dansvoorstelling (composite programme (50'): Kleinigheden. Van iemand over iemand. Over mensen. Stella who. Again/weeral)
1982	Tweede dansvoorstelling: Lente 82 (composite programme (45'): Dans voor vrouw in water. Verkeerd standpunt. Herinnering)

1983	Beweging drie (composite programme (45'): Solo voor 1000 manen, No puedo mas, You must understand that we lived in an atmosphere of euphoria youth and enthusiasm that can hardly be imagined today)
1983	Vier korte dansen (same programme as Beweging drie, complemented with a fourth dance: Absolute Körperkontrolle)
1984	Poging tot Beweging (70')
1984	De vier uitersten (6') (video)
1985	Hyena (65')
1986	Aï (80')
1986	A. Dieu (36')
1986	Hyena (20') (video)
1986	Bewegend gezelschap maakt gebaren 'zonder melodrama' (28') (video)
1987	Ballet Battage (20')
1987	1/5 (18')
1987	Urania (25')
1987	Sleeping Boys (60')
1988	Ballet in wit (70')
1989	Sst, de natuur is dood (15')
1989	Victoria (11')
1989	Landmark gedeeld door Vanrunxt
1989	Sleeping Belgium (composite programme with Ballet in Wit (3rd part), Victoria and 1/5)
1989	Victoria (5') (video)
1990	Moderne Compositie (70')
1990	Aquarius (90')
1990	Ballet in Wit (25') (adaption for television)
1991	Sur Scène (50')
1991	Avenue de l'Hippodrome (6') (contribution to the RTBF dance film 'J'aurais aimé vous voir danser, Madame Akarova', by Michel Jakar and Thierry Genicot)
1991	Fragment of the 7 veils (6') (video)
1992	Triomf of Dood (22')
1992	O lichaam bleek en schoon van zondigheid
1992	Dalida Act (20') (Performance-act as homage to Gerhard Bohner. Later incorporated into Kult-Star)
1993	Kult-Star (50')
1994	The Power of Love (33')
1994	Antilichaam (65')

1995	Dies Irae
1996	Ex-Voto ('22) (glimpse into a study in which the themes of Antilichaam and Dies Irae are further elaborated, before entering a new phase in Fortitudo)
1996	Antwerpse Angst (11')
1997	Fortitudo (60')
1997	Klassiek effect (20')
1997	Mijn solo voor Marie (Vernietigd) (30')
1997	Persona (7') (video)
1997	Ogni Pensiero Vola (35')
1998	The PickWick Man (directed by Jan Fabre, in the series De 4 Temperamenten)
1998	Antropomorf
1998	Walking on thin ice
1998	Private collection (part of the Triptych)
1999	Antimaterie
1999	Performer
2000	Performance
2001	Some Problems of Space Perception

Note

[1] The interview was translated by Hannelore Devlieger and conducted by Maaike Bleeker, Steven De Belder, Luk Van den Dries, and Annemie Vanhoof (March 1998).

Eric Raeves, *Interesting Bodies*, Photo: Bart Michielsen

Eric Raeves

Biography

Eric Raeves (Beerse, 1958) is a Belgian choreographer, dancer and costume designer. He is an autodidact. Raeves has worked regularly with choreographer Marc Vanrunxt, both as a dancer and a designer, and he also danced for Jan Fabre. He has been developing an oeuvre of his own since 1988.

Eric Raeves's art is based on the moving body. His productions could be labelled 'choreographies' were it not for their sculptural quality and compelling visual power, as a result of which they may be regarded as a form of plastic art. He creates environments in which the human body is a self-evident element; not in order to express a story or emotion, but as a pure, almost abstract, moving image. His two most recent major productions are *Interesting Bodies*, an exhibition of slowly moving sculptural bodies that are shown in daylight in museums, and *1 Wereld* (*1 World*), a theatrical composition of four living installations that transform the stage into a nocturama of mysterious human apparitions.

Interview[1]

Do you regard your work as visual art or as dance performances?
As dance performances, though I realise that their strength lies in the visual qualities. The way in which I approach movement has changed over the years: movement now arises from the physical shape and the visual qualities of the dancer's body. The need to express myself more specifically arose from a feeling that I had got bogged down in my previous work. I had seriously started to wonder whether it was still interesting to be involved with dance in a Flemish context. I had also begun to doubt whether I was still strong enough? That is why I was interested to explore the extremes within myself, my own personal fascinations. These turned out to be the dancer's body: its physical shape and how it can be used.

The formal starting point grew organically from, among other things, my own experiences as an artist's model. It is fascinating to try and look at yourself, the shape of your own body, its contours and volumes from the point of view of someone who is watching you. This experience opened up a range of possibilities for showing interesting things, from a position where you are observing yourself from above, for example. On the basis of this very formal starting-point, I wanted to create performances that the spectator would watch in a similar way. Movement thus originated from choosing and combining poses that possess an unidentified power. At first, this seemed to be too simple, but then I discovered that all elements of dance were present in the visual aspect: the choice of movement, timing, rhythm, intention … in the transition from one pose to another. I then discovered certain forces, such as the tension between the abstract and the real: the body is not so much shown in its identifiability – sex and face are often hidden. At the same time, it concerns the naked body, which is very real and human.

Are you also looking for the boundaries between the abstract and the concrete in the body through the extreme of abstraction, where 'minor flaws' become productive again?
What you refer to as the imperfect, I regard as the authentic or the personal. Often this is the starting-point onto which specific movements can be grafted. Peculiarities of someone's body are often the source of abstraction, and they can be very inspiring. They always make you question your own set of values and standards, and other elements on which you are compelled to base your actions. This makes the body interesting in a new way.

In the case of some of the performers in Interesting Bodies*, you had to look out for very specific types of bodies: older people, bodybuilders … Does that mean that the content lies within the body?*
The content that is offered by the form does not only result from the bodies, but also from their movement and the context in which they are placed. At first, I wanted to create a context in which a 'more perfect' body was confronted with an older body, but this soon threatened to become too emphatic. The search for 'interesting bodies' is the search for the body's possibilities, a search for an intensification of its power through movement and context. It is not about the perfect body, but about the interesting body. Each body possesses a certain beauty, and represents an occasion to create something interesting, whereby the body itself points the way. I never intended to look out for the most perfect of bodies. There is of course a certain margin, because the balance between the different bodies is important. A corpulent body amidst a group of less corpulent figures creates a surplus of content.

At the centre is the search for an expression of the power of the body through movement, an attempt to make the body more interesting, to add something to it. By creating a context for the body, I invite the spectator to look at it in a different way each time. *Solo Man* was the most simple example. In *The collection* from *Interesting Bodies*, the naked bodies were simply put in the light of day. In *1 World* I created a different context – a different world – for each installation. One recognises the same poses and movements, but at the same time, I create different points of view by using different 'tricks', by reverting to theatre, by adding light or colour, by incorporating video, by arranging the audience in a different way.

Interesting Bodies conveyed the almost pure physicality of naked bodies in the daylight, but within that context, you were looking for the more amazing aspects of the body, for unexpected movements and images. In 1 World, *you use a lot more theatrical aids to create the same feeling. Straightforwardness, banality and sweat are of no interest to you?*
Astonishment is indeed what it is all about. It sometimes seems possible to describe in just a few words: a search for the intangibility of beauty, for the indefinable reasons why something is beautiful, and for the desire to possess it. If my work was intended for myself only, I could simply place a number of heads before me and look at them. I want to gain insight into the reasons why something captures an audience, I want to discover wherein lies its power and I want to show it.

How important is the choice between male and female dancers? You seem to have a preference for men?
The choice is not really essential, though intuitively I often start from the male body. On the other hand, what do masculine and feminine mean? A number of people I look upon as very feminine, clearly go against the cliché of femininity. This tension might have to do with a certain animal-like quality. But I do not think my work really has anything to say about the relationship between men and women. Its visual quality is the starting-point: shapes, volumes, contours. Intuitively, it is easier for me to start from the male body, but I do try and look for what fascinates me in the bodies of either sex. I am looking for bodies in which both poles are present: the super-masculine as well as the super-feminine. The perfect body would then be the most androgynous, but then again this would be too one-sided and too restrictive. That is why I try to broaden the spectrum, from the outside to the androgynous centre, where both poles merge and cancel each other out.

In the case of Thierry Smits, one can tell his sexual inclination from his images and movements; in Anne Teresa De Keersmaeker's case, it is obvious that a female choreographer has been at work. In your case, this is less clear. Sexual contrasts seem to cancel each other out.
That is precisely what I like about it. My sexual inclination probably filters through; I certainly do not try to hide it. But I do not think about this aspect

explicitly when I am working on a performance. People apparently need to have things defined. If they are not, the production becomes less tangible, less understandable to them.

Does the search for the 'intangible beauty' exclude ugliness?
Everything is beautiful and ugly at the same time. It just depends from which angle you are looking at it, and in which context it has been placed. Just as good and evil must necessarily exist side by side. A body which is said to be ugly in classical terms – a fat or deformed body – can become beautiful if one looks at it in a certain way, for instance by taking one's time. All that is required is the appropriate perspective.

Even when you combine corporeal images in unexpected ways by shifting perspectives, you always seem to refer to classical Greek sculpture, where balance and proportions are paramount. Do you agree?
For me, that is not a deliberate goal, though one can hardly escape from the ideal image that society imposes. It is a matter of fact that if you work with dancers, whom you need for their technical qualities, you will be confronted with well-trained and therefore well-defined bodies. This is because the formal aspect *within* the body itself is also important: their contours and volumes approximate to the classical ideal. Often, these proportions are only highlighted when the body moves; certainly in the case of some dancers, you would not suspect an ideal body at first glance.

Should the quest for beauty and the pretty side of things be interpreted as a statement on ugliness and banality?
I do not want to teach people how to enjoy, but simply allow them to enjoy things, including ugliness, because it too is beautiful. Ugliness is not present in my work as a shock, a disenchantment or interruption. I invite the audience to a contemplative way of looking. There is no rupture. Nor do I believe that an intentional rupture automatically stands for ugliness. I regard it more as a contrast, with which people deal in a more rational way. In this respect, I would not really feel comfortable, as it implies too much of a message. There is a message involved now, but not at a theoretical level.

One criticism of your work is that your corporeal images are too idealising, as a result of which they have an unintentional affinity with an aesthetics such as that of Leni Riefenstahl's.
I do believe there are certain similarities between Leni Riefenstahl's aesthetics and mine. Whether the starting-points are the same, I cannot say.

I think that she looks at the body and searches for beauty in the same way as I do. Her athletes are not ideal people and nor are my dancers. You are observing shapes and proportions, not a whole person. And, much like she probably did, I do indeed determine the set of contours and proportions that you get to see. If, however, she purposely set this as her goal, I differ from her. I doubt, though, whether this is the case. In her later work, she made underwater pictures of fish with the same kind of aesthetics in mind. I personally am not looking for ideals, but for specific strengths in every single body; strengths that initially are formal, but that get a search process in me going. Why do we humans appreciate these strengths so much? What is their purpose? What do they do to us? What is their true significance … ?

How important is the element of 'time' when looking at these bodies and their context?
It is very important to give people plenty of time to look at something, and to give something enough time to be what it should be. As far as I am concerned, the performances may last a lot longer, but this would be unbearable for both the audience and the dancers. Slowness is central, but I presume that the opposite may also be true. Speed is more problematic, though, as it is less tangible. I am still trying to discover how the same effect can be created by fast images. But perhaps its power lies in the fact that you can grasp it no more than beauty.

Speed can easily result in a rupture or a shock, and will then interfere with the pursuit of beauty. How do you see this fit into your future work?
Even at speed one can maintain stamina, avoiding ruptures. In the same way, an image can be fixed, and then it would coincide with slowness; the result would be a homogeneous image, not a sudden cut from a to b. Slowness does, however, offer you a better opportunity to get a hold of things. But I would like to achieve the same through speed. At the moment, it is still about uncontrollability and fleetingness, but it does not have to stay this way. I want to look for a way to work with speed and yet make a lasting impression. This would mean a dimensional shift away from what I am doing now, as I would have to treat the space and the dancer's body in a different way. This complicates matters within the concepts that I have applied so far, but I regard it as a challenge to try and find the right solutions for it. One possibility is to let the body of the dancer go for just a moment, and to maintain speed and aggressiveness longer by means of video and space, by switching from one medium to the other.

*The images you create resemble puzzles made out of body parts: some are
hidden, others are singled out. The result is rather 'unnatural', a new composition consisting of loose fragments. Is this a reconstruction out of the
fragmentation of the corporeal image?*
The fragmentation can be understood in different ways. Even if the pivotal
element in a certain movement is the shoulder blade, the entire body is still
involved. The entire body – even the parts that you do not see – dances
along. From the dancer's point of view, awareness of the entire body is very
important. A certain fragment only works because of the entire body's
stance. The dancer's shoulder blades in *Insect* can only create that particular image because the head is not visible. As a choreographer, you can look
at the body as a landscape, and concentrate on certain elements. I would not
call it a puzzle. It is not even important for the spectator to be aware of the
fragmentation. Fragmentation makes it possible to show new things. The
spectator is well aware of this and probably realises that another, new, reality thus emerges which we would otherwise ignore.

Which parts of the body do you hide?
In fact, I would like to show everything and look for extremes, but as a choreographer, I am perhaps not up to that yet. I want to show the intangibility of
beauty, but at the moment I do so in a pleasing manner, as a result of which
beauty is glorified somewhat, and the audience feels happy. It could also be
done in a manner that the ground seems to give way beneath your feet. But in
that case I would have nothing to go by, and I want to be in control.

In *Interesting Bodies*, the face and the sex were hidden. These are
important parameters of an individual's identity, and as such may lead to
identification. They were hidden in order to divert attention. Through neutrality, the body is given an opportunity to speak for itself. The face determines too much. One is so used to looking at it that the rest of the body
becomes interchangeable. Take away that point of reference, and other –
less definable – layers emerge. This way of focusing on other signals fits in
with the search for less explicable forces, which are part of the dancer's
body and are also at work within the spectator.

*Do you eliminate the subjective in this way in order to bring the objective
qualities of the body to the surface? Or does the particularity of that single
body still come first, even without a face?*
Solos or movements are always conceived with a specific dancer and the
qualities of his body in mind. Consequently, the particularity of that body
still takes precedence. Apart from that, you can kill two birds with one
stone: the dancer's body is turned into an object which is reflected on the

watching subject. For anyone accepting the challenge, this may represent a reflecting or a confronting interaction. You can look at those bodies in many different ways: fleetingly, purely formally, attentively, introspectively – who am I, why, how, what and where – or simply pleasurably.

Do the dancers object to not being allowed to show their faces?
During the performance, it is not really a problem that they are used as objects; the acknowledgement at the end, through the audience's applause, is what matters. But it is hard to let them stand up and look the audience straight in the face, because this breaks the spell of the performance. Everything the performance stands for is then thrown overboard. I do not like to bring people down to earth. At the end of *Interesting Bodies*, the dancers covered themselves in bathrobes. This kind of rupture, which brings everyday reality into the piece, was necessary because otherwise the audience would stand there for too long. At the end of *1 World*, the lights are not switched on in order to prevent the audience from examining the installation of *Insect* and discovering the theatre trick, after which they would leave with only that image in mind. This would undermine the performance too much. It would be marvellous if the whole thing could simply go on until everyone had had enough and left of their own accord. But this would be impossible for the dancers.

It nevertheless involves two sorts of reality: on the one hand there is finiteness and the banality of having to stop, the bathrobes; on the other hand, your performances are about the reality of the body. Is one of the two more important or more real?
In *1 World*, I want to show another world. If I show the disillusionment of reality, I am again occupied with other elements of contents. The elements I want to convey in *1 World* already demand enough time and attention – any reality beyond that is too much for me.

What is your assessment of the view that there lies a danger in too much abstraction: it could paradoxically lead to a denial of the reality of the body, a voyeuristic image without materiality?
A body is and always remains matter, both in its beauty and its ugliness. Letting the audience in as a voyeur, observing beautiful and ugly bodies, is inherent in the work of a dancer, an actor, a performer, a sculptor and the like … Showing different aspects, points of view and layers testifies to the creative power of man to be able to look at himself. Both in the creation of images and in the execution of movement, the artist-performer strives for total control over this body. He only shows what he wants to show. To begin with, the artist has to decide whether what he is showing is honest or not. A large degree of

abstraction therefore does not deny the reality of the body. It gives us a brief opportunity to reflect on the particular focus that is offered through abstraction. What is shown, is not a goal as such. It is an instrument to confront oneself. Therefore, I do not think abstraction passes over concrete matter.

You seem to want to keep the audience at a distance from your images. Each time the audience of 'Interesting Bodies' came too close, it was resolutely pushed back by stewards. How does this relate to the intrusiveness of the microscopic view of the body?
I deliberately opt for distance. My performances are still conceived as 'dance'. When I am working on a piece, I decide what the spectator should see. If I let the spectator come too close, I am no longer in control of what he is going to see. Now that I am working with video, I can let the camera determine the angle of observation.

Each of your performances has an obvious mark of reference. But in 'The collection' in Interesting Bodies, *the perspective of the audience standing around was very broad. Is it not interesting for a spectator to have different possible perspectives?*
I direct the spectator's view very consciously, because I want to make sure that my message comes across. I do find it interesting if a spectator tries to find the right perspective by himself. But I insist on manipulating the angle of view, because I am concerned with showing a side of the image that is not obvious. This is not a beach. You can look at bodies in a different way. And this fascination I want to convey. Even when I try to imagine what an audience might feel, I still depart from myself. When I observe an image, I immediately look for the ideal vantage point.

Perspective is important in order to see the right proportions. Distance is important in order to connect correctly with what is shown. If one is too far away, one can lose contact; if one is too close, there is a danger of disillusionment. Each object has an ideal size. Take a stamp, for example: its purpose, its recognisability, its spatial position, its beauty or lack of beauty.

As the spectator is partly free to choose his own perspective and the amount of time he wants to devote to observing, he is under the impression that the distance is bridged. You are drawn in, presumably partly by repetition, although the starting-point was formal and abstract rather than emotional. You become part of a sort of ritual. The distance is neutralised, you become one.
Such things are never intentional. They simply come about in the course of the creative process. If I become aware of them, I decide whether or not to use them. For the dancers too, it is a sort of ritual, and that makes it fun to

do: it neutralises practical problems and nuisances, such as the body paint in *Insect*. It also helps if I can show them how the audience sees them.

Why do you avoid a traditional theatre setting, in which the perspective of the spectator is to a large extent also fixed?
The idea of an exhibition is central to my two most recent performances, because I want to give the audience a certain degree of freedom. You can leave as soon as you get bored, which is easier to do in this kind of setting than in a theatre with rows of people. The spectator is under the impression that he is able to choose. I also think that, in this arrangement, it is easier for an audience to accept that the concept of time used is different than is usually applied in theatre. Technically, it leaves more room to show different things in one location, in a single space.

There is a commonly held view that things can only exist if they are put into words, while one can, of course, also think in images. How does your work relate to language, image and reality?
I was always convinced that we could think only in language, until someone pointed out to me that children can also think in images. This came as an incredible shock to me. Body and mind cannot be separated. The body is real. Interestingly, man is confronted with all kinds of forces on which he has no grip. The unnameable fascinates me. Creating all these performances has made me realise that the desire to grasp the intangible, the desire for the unattainable drives my work as well as my existence.

Do you ideally want to create a sort of referencelessness, so that the image stands entirely on its own?
It is too easy and too obvious to lapse into a frame of reference. I do indeed feel the desire to create things that stand on their own. I try to attain a higher level, a concern which is of course related to the search for the intangible, instead of the recognisable. The spectator is invited to look at things creatively, or perhaps on an even higher level, to be affected without having to look for associations. To transcend human consciousness: one body colliding with another, on-looking, body; two bodies communicating in a direct, undefined language. It may sound very New Age-like or futuristic, but as an image it is beautiful.

In Insect, *the body becomes a very literal quote. It is an almost linguistic reference to images, resulting in something resembling a language. Is this due to the clarity of the insect-image?*
I sometimes feel the references in *Insect* are a bit too explicit. What do you do with language? Words are used to communicate, to put things in

perspective. That perspective, however, does not become clear in this solo. I do not look at it as a linguistic approach. There is of course a theme: the comparison between man and animal. Man has a hard skeleton inside, with muscles on the outside. Insects have an exoskeleton, with organs on the inside. Another starting point was the idea of draping many costumes over each other and to peel them off one by one in order to get closer and closer to the essence, to man. Perhaps this is no longer recognisable, and in fact it does not really matter, because these are not profound ideas as such. But starting from them, I get to work with the body both visually and kinetically. Also, this solo depends a little too much on technical aids. It is fascinating, but less moving than *Solo Man*, for example. But, like a painter, I can sometimes find it pleasing to use many colours.

If Insect *rests on too much technique, is it perhaps your intention to transform the body into something else? Certainly this impression is also created* in Body on canvas *and* Duet.
I am looking for things that can influence the body while staying part of it. First and foremost, this means playing with the material of the body as well as other materials. Through this play, I want to give pleasure to myself and others. At the same time, I want to enter into further confrontations that evoke emotions, that raise questions or suggest answers, that provide insight into myself, my mind and the world. Most importantly of all, I want to search for the forces and energies that drive us.

Is it not the case that the entire performance of 1 World *rest more emphatically on technique than any of your previous work, not only because of the construction of* Insect, *but also because of the importance of lighting?*
Sure, but it still is a variation on the theme of the body in motion, its visual power, the fascination for the combination of all those indefinable forces. In spite of these aids, *1 World* does not differ substantially from *Interesting Bodies*. It has only been wrapped up differently. Often an artist is interested in just one thing: in my case this is the fascination for the human body, the search for control over all these different forces, the quest for grasping what cannot be grasped. This reminds me of Auguste Rodin: I can imagine that, whenever he had finished a sculpture, he felt as if he had grasped 'it', whatever that 'it' may have been. The delight at being able to grasp something, the astonishment and fascination with creating, is of central importance; to be affected by it, to feel as if I myself can bring about and shape beauty and strength, or rather, to know how to go about looking for them.

Performances

1988	Amper Zonder
1988	Mudman
1988	Lijn 9
1990	Onbehouwen Sporen
1990	Rijkgevulde thema's en donkere kleuren
1992	De perzen/Het 'Méér'
1992	Hippos
1995	Solo Man
1996	Interesting Bodies
1997	1 Wereld (Insect – Solo Man – Duet – Lichaam op Doek (Body on Canvas))
1999	Kast – Tafel – Hoge Tafel
2000	Sterk Water
2000	Twee Snelheden
2001	Zelfportret

Note

[1] The interview was translated by ICTS and conducted by Steven De Belder, Luk Van den Dries, Annemie Vanhoof, and Kurt Vanhoutte (March 1998).

Thierry Smits, *Corps(e)*, Photo: Luiz Alvarez

Thierry Smits

Biography

As a child, Thierry Smits (1963) took classical dancing classes at the Municipal Academy of Beringen, a Flemish mining town. After a short stay in Paris, where he performed in revues, he returned to Belgium and took training in classical and modern dance. He was instructed by Udi Malka, Andreï Gligovski and Peter Goss among others, and also spent some time in the renowned Mudra of Maurice Béjart. At the age of 26, after having danced for several years for the company Plan K, he started working on his first choreography, *La grâce du tombeur* (*The grace of falling*). Since then, Smits has worked in several fields; besides the choreographic work that he has done for his own account and for other companies, he now also creates cabaret and co-ordinates dance sequences in popular shows on Belgian television. Apart from his stage work, this artist is politically active in Brussels, where he was among other things closely involved in the establishment of a militant AIDS movement called 'Act Up'. Smits is one of the Belgian choreographers whose creations are produced alternately in the Dutch and the French-speaking parts of the country.

Interview[1]

Could you perhaps give us an outline of how your work has evolved? What different points of interest do you examine?
I am mainly interested in the more formal aspect of the work. I then attempt to transfer the investigation and place it against a thematic background. Which is an exploration of how the forms created in the first formal phase of the work acquire meaning in a thematic context. My work therefore consists of constantly focusing on a formal examination, and placing the solutions that emerge from it in a more theatrical context.

I am also interested in exploring popular forms and providing them with a new meaning, showing them in a new light. When I use the term 'popular forms' I mean drawing from things such as the sort of cabaret one finds in champagne bars, or bits of folklore or tradition. I have already worked on these a number of times.

A combination of the two brings us to a third point of interest: not being afraid to be eclectic.

Does the term eclecticism refer especially to the choice of forms?
To the choice of forms as well as to the language of dance, neither of which, as far as I am concerned, are linked to any scale of values. From the point of view of culture, I find an extreme form of contemporary dance to be of no more or less value than something that already exists or comes from another tradition. And it is in this that my form of democracy lies. These days there is a strong tendency in the theory of dance to link democracy only with the contemporary idiom of dance. For example, Laurence Louppe, who is a French dance philosopher, states that a democratic body is one that carries out its own investigation and totally rejects any form of authority. She therefore places this body only in contemporary dance, but no matter what anybody else says, I believe that the contemporary body is an integral part of history. Why then should it be rejected?

This eclecticism expresses itself in the use of a wide range of aesthetic settings. In CyberChrist *for example, one sees the influence of both Vesalius and Madonna's iconography.*
This is perfectly true. However, it is very often seen in a negative light. Apparently I am not pure enough, I am not a purist.

Is this criticism based on a need for absolute dance, on the notion of pure movement?
The strange thing is that choreographers who are normally associated with pure dance, often go far beyond particular boundaries. Because pure dance is in fact dance that prohibits the use of music. The strongest adherents of this are Merce Cunningham and Trisha Brown. There is very little evidence of this type of pure dance in Europe. All works involving dance in Europe are actually a profound mixture of pure, formal dance, such as Lucinda Childs and Judson Church and of highly expressionistic forms of dance. Europe is really the melting pot of it all.

How would you then define your own work?
Also as a mixture of influences. But in my case there is an even stronger element of a conscious lack of coherence in the building up of my oeuvre. For me it is something that is almost non-existent, because I constantly move from something formal to something theatrical and vice versa. So you have a certain style of dance but not a coherent oeuvre.

How would you describe your style of dance?
It is the result of the way in which I work in the studio. I often give very short phrases of movement, which I then teach to the dancers. In these

short phrases there is very little rhythm or nuance between poetic and non-poetic. It is merely one *brut* stone (raw material) that leads to another *brut* stone. And this often gives it a certain angularity. It is only when there is a certain phrase that lasts for one or two minutes that I instruct the dancers to try out the fragments in different rhythms, and have them explore the best way to perform the material at hand by finding a rhythm that feels comfortable. This way of working is very different to that of many modern choreographers, who ask the dancers to improvise and then use these improvisations in the final cut. I only use improvisation once the building blocks are in place.

I would like to broach the subject of authority in your work once more. Is there a link between this and the way in which the body is used in your performances, where the body is presented as the material of the language of dance. In Corps(e) *for example, one often gets the impression that bodies are being used and manipulated, and that they enjoy being manipulated, which is also a form of exhibitionism. Is the fascination of manipulating bodies a theme in your work? Not the free body, which takes us back to the democratic body, but the used, the consumed body?*
The manipulation of bodies is part of the work of every choreographer, but yes, it is present, even though in a weak form. There is a certain theatricality in seeing the submission of one person to another. It is this that makes Jan Fabre's *De Macht der Theaterlijke Dwaasheden* (*The Power of Theatrical Madness*) so fascinating. The interesting thing about manipulation is the illustration of the balance of power. It is the balance of power on stage that is interpellated most by the audience, in all sorts of ways. Their response may be abject, but can also take on the form of a process of identification. The manipulations do have an effect on the audience. Some women react negatively and accuse me of misogyny. I am prepared for this and have at hand a number of examples illustrating that there is as much manipulation by strong female personalities as there is by men. This is just to illustrate that such manipulation demands a personal interpretation and that it is interpellatory and for this reason so interesting.

Do you use these scenes simply for their theatrical power and because manipulation scenes have the greatest theatrical impact, or are they inherent in the dance?
Manipulations are highly stylised in both classical dance and contact improvisation. It is a form you even encounter in traditional dance as well as in acrobatic rock and roll, and is therefore a form that has existed throughout the history of dance. It is inherent in dance itself, which brings

us back to form, which can be striking in itself, but can be even more so when it is linked to a theme or a dramaturgical context.

But in your case, the main issue is not sublimation but de-sublimation, a sexualising of the manipulation.
This is especially true of the work I did around Mapplethorpe. Because of the way it is staged it loses its crudity, its rawness.

In other words an aesthetic screen is placed in between. Is it important for it to lose its crudity?
Yes, I think that it is important for something that has been sublimated to retain a certain poetic quality. Poetry is an important aspect of the performance. Rimbaud is also poetry, just like Lautréamont.

Poetry in rawness, you do not believe in this, do you?
As far as I am concerned, there is no poetry in rawness. An example of this is Ron Athey's production, but of course this is my own personal opinion. Other people might regard it as being poetical. However, what you see on stage is no different to what you see in any discotheque. I find it too unambiguous.

What strikes me about your images and bodies, is that you seem to be searching for the darker side, the side that lies behind what is usually regarded as normal.
This is true. It has to do with trying to find the boundaries of tolerance. I very much enjoy trying to extend these boundaries. This is what I find so interesting about the performing arts. I have no idea of how well I succeed, but it is something I consider important.

To all appearances it is the aesthetic and aestheticising layer that makes it easier for the audience to keep its distance. Where does the extension of boundaries fit in?
It is possible to extend the boundaries of tolerance for example, by using three different aesthetic forms side by side on the same night, and asking the audience whether it can identify with them. The main issue is not only a certain use of the body, but different aesthetic forms ...

And what about moral tolerance?
That too. One can refer to moral tolerance when it concerns the use of the body. The aesthetic aspect is something very different and has to do with taste.

There are a number of recurring themes in your work that could be linked to the extension of the boundaries of tolerance. The icon of the devil for

example, which is a preoccupation that is linked to a certain moral…
This might have something to do with discarding years of Catholic influence, with discarding the fact that someone knows what is good and what is bad. It is a reaction to a society that continues to preach normality. The fact that I bring sexuality to the stage, even in my more formal work, is an important act. I find that too few performing artists make use of the opportunity. Certainly with regard to dance, in which sensuality and sexuality on stage should be perfectly self-evident, particularly in view of the fact that the work involves the use of the body.

Does this mean that you automatically link the icon of the devil and sexuality?
Of course I do. Sexuality is still seen as something diabolical. More than ever before.

As far as this is concerned, the final image of CyberChrist *speaks volumes. The developments between various icons which up to that point have followed a winding course, suddenly result in the resurrection of an antichrist who also has strong sexual connotations…*
It is strange how everyone comes back to this. Someone even talked about the second part, and that diabolic number only lasted for one minute! It was a sort of exclamation mark that I used because I found that there were enough aesthetic works that did not pose any questions at all. I find productions that are no more than charming utterly boring because they evoke an aesthetic emptiness, however heavenly they may seem. I found it an apt moment to call a halt to all the beauty.

How do you link this diabolical exclamation mark to Vesalius, Madonna, Christ and other icons in CyberChrist?
The dramaturgy of the piece was a 'Way of the Cross', leading to the Antichrist. The main issue was emphasising Christian iconography, in which there is evidence of diabolical iconography; it is a part of it and it would be a pity to forget that. I enjoyed breaking off the aesthetic first part and its images that refer back to Holbein, with a wink.

What do you think of the concept of the mannequin as an image of the body? In the sense of the perfect body?
I enjoy working with beautiful people, and it is true that this often plays an all-important role when I cast. It is an aesthetic choice. Most of the people I work with have had a highly classical training. A classical training forms your body in a particular way. In addition to this a classical training

requires certain skills, which means that you have a certain type of body, a certain muscular build. What could be interesting – and I have not yet worked on this, but William Forsythe for example, has – is to make something abject of a body that is sublime. Jan Fabre has also done this. But I have not yet used that as a basis, and up to now I have preferred to go on a highly aesthetic trip.

In the movement material and the positioning on stage, do you always make sure that the body is shown to advantage, that it presents an aesthetic image.
Yes I do. Beauty is actually also design, it comes very close to graphic art, and one actually makes drawings.

So the boundary of tolerance in the representation of a body image remains within an erotic pattern. Is it explicitly non-pornographic?
That basically depends on how it is viewed. An example that comes to mind is Bruce Labruce[2] who made *Het Hoerenjong* (*The Bastard*), which contained a great number of erections. He was accused of being involved in pornography, which he denied on the grounds of there being no ejaculation. There are certain people who regard Jeff Koons' photographs as pornographic. I do not. I find them extremely humorous. Certain people see it as being crude enough or going too far, while others do not.

However, I do think it is important to have a second-degree version. I see the first-degree as coarse, whilst the second-degree produces a smile. When dealing with sexuality I use a second-degree interpretation.

But could the explicit nude interpretation not evoke a first-degree interpretation?
So a naked body is first-degree?

When dealing with sexuality a naked body is more direct…
Jérôme Bel only has naked bodies on the stage and it is not the least bit erotic. It is the way in which you use a naked body that determines whether the interpretation is sexual or not. Of course it is true that when I use nudity I often do it sensually, and not in a manner that is trite. That too has its own place, but I rarely do that.

Elsewhere you refer to Deleuze in your work. Could you explain in what way he has provided a breeding ground for your work?
In the sense that whatever the subject, he always starts off with a *contrepied*, with the opposite to what you would expect. The *contrepied* is an interesting factor when you are involved with artistic work, thinking the opposite to what you should think.

So it is mainly Deleuze's attitude towards things that inspires you. Another important factor could be his eclecticism, which he formerly referred to as nomadism.

It would be true to say that I do not settle down into a certain form of comfort. This rejection of comfort largely determines my method of working, both in the production process as well as the final performance. Too much comfort is lethal.

Does this nomadism go so far as gleaning elements from other cultures? At the moment you are positioned very much within Western, historical, pictorial conventions...

I must admit that I dislike multiculturalism. The search for what is multicultural often has the opposite effect on me. It is a concept without content. It is a fad that smacks of neo-colonialism. Our culture is already multicultural. The influence of jazz dance is Afro-American and there is so much Eastern influence in cabaret dancing... When I did a production on the Holy Grail, my inspiration came from books on the culture of the Celts. That was an absolute revelation; it is largely influenced by Indian art. One should not explicitly go in search of multiculturalism, it is already a part of our culture.

What is the difference between working in productions by your own company and television assignments for example?

Working for television is different. It brings in a lot of money, very quickly, and the criteria of television are not high. You are required to work at a standard level. It may sound strange, but when I do television work, I am very, very professional. I want it to look 'finished'. This is what television demands; I have to be precise, just like Madonna's dancers, that sort of precision. The pressure of time is important, it has to be perfect, and this reinforces your professionalism. It also has to be efficient, and this appeals to me. I look for a certain efficiency in my own work too.

Does television work stimulate your own work in any way?

No, not at all. The main reason I do it is not to lose the dancers I work with, because even if you have a structural subsidy, it does not mean that you are always able to pay your dancers a salary. So I have always sought extra work outside our own productions. It also helps me to develop a certain handiness. For example, how does a group of thirty people function on stage? It is very instructive.

Have you ever felt the need to use the medium of television to stage something that would appeal to you?

So far I have never used it. I find it difficult to imagine and often see it used in productions to fill in time. Filling in time is something I do not understand, whereas filling in space is something I can understand. And I always have a tendency to rebel against what I see around me.

However, I am a fanatic admirer of the silver screen, the cinema. If there is one art form in which I am able to lose myself, it is cinema. In fact I find it far livelier than the performing arts. The editing leaves you with such intensity. You can achieve a highly condensed intensity that is far more difficult to realise on stage.

Does this influence the very short sequences in your work?
Yes, of course it does. But I think that this effectiveness only works up to a certain point. I think that you can achieve intensity by using time in a different way.

Bob Wilson time?
Yes, for example. But personally I have a great problem with very long pieces.

Do you identify speed with 'televisual' culture?
Yes I do. In fact I believe that this is true of a great many productions.

Do you see a connection between your own work and close-ups? The tendency to place bodies close to the audience?
In most of my work I have always aimed for a great intimacy. But there comes a time, also for career reasons, when you have to move on to the big stage. On large stages you often lose intimacy and you have to try to gain this in spatial composition, in an intelligent composition of space. I think that I have been successful in this. Also, I did not want to stay put in the studio-work sector. My ambition is also to have a larger acting area, which is an enjoyable instrument too.

Performances

1989   La grâce du tombeur
1991   Eros Délétère
1993   Sang de chêne
1993   Cyriel
1993   Vesalii Icones
1994   Diabolo
1994   L'âme au diable

1994	Surprise
1995	CyberChrist
1995	Soirée Dansante
1996	Baklava
1996	Op Reis
1997	Traffic
1998	Sentier du bois
1998	Corps(e)
1998	Nat
1999	Red Rubber Balls
2000	Achter de spiegel
2001	Richard of York Gave Battle in Vain

Notes

[1] The interview was translated by Gregory Ball and conducted by Maaike Bleeker, Steven De Belder, Luk Van den Dries, Annemie Vanhoof, and Kurt Vanhoutte (May 1998).

[2] Bruce Labruce is a gay director who is working and living in Los Angeles. After a number of semi-pornographic movie shorts (super-8), he made 3 full-length movies: *Super 8½* (a movie about the pornographic cinema scene); *No Skin of My Ass* (an ironic commentary on the gay milieu's sexual fascination with skin heads); and *Hustler White* (a movie set in the male prostitution milieu of Los Angeles – with the performer Ron Athey).

Jérôme Bel, *Shirtologie*, 3rd Victoria Festival 1996–1997
Photo: To Sang Foto Studio (Amsterdam)

Jérôme Bel

Biography

Jérôme Bel (Paris, 1964) was trained as a dancer at the Centre National de Danse Contemporaine d'Angers. He has danced for Angelin Preljocaj, Joëlle Bouvier and Régis Obadia, Daniel Larrieu and Catarina Sagna, and assisted Philippe Decouflé at the ceremonies of the Winter Olympics of Albertville. He has been creating his own work since 1994, balancing on the borderline between dance and theatre, and with a special interest in the possibilities and limitations of representation, originality and copyright.

Interview[1]

By slowing down movement and purifying theatrical gestures, are you hoping to get a specifically physical response to your work from the audience?

Yes. I try to get the audience into a particular frame of mind – I prefer them to be calm and peaceful. But the strange thing is that to get them like this you have to irritate them a lot. They are either calm, or irritated and bothered. Critics say that it is fascinating and irritating at the same time. The audience is drawn to what is happening on stage, but it bothers them all the same. People do not clap very much but I do not think it is because the production has been bad. After a while people come and tell us they thought it was good. I do not think I annoy them, it is just it takes longer for them to react.

So it is not like you are lulling them into something. You want to irritate them into it?

That is right. I always want to perform in theatres because I like people to be seated comfortably. I know my performances are going to be difficult and I do not want them to be bothered by something like uncomfortable seats. The environment should be warm and quiet with soft chairs. I know it is important so that things go well.

Is it not also because theatres are able to provide a focal point, drawing people's attention to what demands that attention?

It is extremely important. Lots of people think that I can perform in places other than a theatre, but until now I have always refused to do so. I want there to be a focal point and the theatre is a great place for that.

In your productions reality invades the stage, but it is a reality which is taken out of context, a reality taken apart and put together again in a different way but with no new story to it. It is more physical and temporal. Usually in theatre, if external elements are brought in they are re-contextualised very explicitly. What is your aim in baring all, and not only in your per-formers baring all?

I absolutely refuse to use theatrical illusions. I am only interested in reality, in touching upon what is real. I try to give shape to things in a way that is familiar to everyone, without them having to be actors or dancers. Then there are very simple things which are dealt with in a straightforward way. Of course there are people who say that a child could do it. I want to do very simple things so that the audience identifies with them as much as possible. For example, *Jérôme Bel* features an older person to give the audience someone with whom to identify other than dancers who on the whole are between twenty and thirty-five years old. Maybe it is pretentious, but I want to show different ways of living, close to life and ridiculously simple. I only realised myself afterwards that it is wonderful imagining what goes on in everybody's lives. I just cannot get beyond this infatuation with very simple material. It is true to say that I am not creating a new story.

What is the main difference from traditional methods in theatre, where the aim is for the audience to identify with characters? Maybe they are not true to life, but the act of identifying with them is a reality. Is it about not creat-ing a story, not giving things an agreeable shape?

I don't ever want the audience to forget that they are at the theatre. I want them to be aware that they are watching a performance and that it is not reality. If there is fiction anywhere, it is on that level and not on stage. It is not strong emotion that makes people believe in the reality of the stage. It is only a representation of things. They should always be wondering what they are doing there, what it all means. It comes from Aristotle and Brecht. The little I have studied about theatre makes me rely on Brecht's alienation effect and Aristotle's mimesis, identification and catharsis – two theories and a combination of them. For theory of theatre, I use these two.

Does Shirtologie *want to make theatre out of ordinary things that we do not even notice anymore?*

It is really focussing on things that we do not see. If very little is shown, it is because very little can be seen. That is what I found interesting with the T-shirts in mixing the body and language. I am a dancer, but it was like writing a script for theatre with T-shirts. The script is where actors and materials meet. What is going on between these young people of between

16 and 20, the T-shirts and me? What did we talk about? That was the most interesting thing about it – having to reduce the words because of the T-shirts, reducing language to a language we all understood. The production was mostly about desire. The first half is about the erotic investment each member of the audience makes in the actor – it is always the same story in theatre, with them thinking 'I am sure you are looking at me'. The second half shows the desire between couples in the slow dances. We had to find common ground between what they think about and what I do. And it came down to a love affair.

Jérôme Bel seems like a game with dolls, with the body reduced to a manipulated object. It is pretty unusual to see a naked body on stage doing practically nothing. The body was like an object, which then looked like a normal body which then went on to make human, anthropomorphic actions.
The thought of dolls never crossed my mind. The idea here was to look at the body as the instrument of the dancer, with a visible distinction between the subject and the object. I see the distinction most clearly at the neck where the separation can be seen physically. The actors look at their bodies. The subject is in the head and active, and the object is what he is manipulating, his own body. I admit that there is something doll-like in that, but the idea from the start was to look at the instrument of the dancer. The violinist has his violin and the violin is made by the instrument-maker, whereas the dancer's instrument is his own body. The other factor in this was Roland Barthes' thoughts on the 'degré zéro de la littérature' (the zero degree of literature) – whether writing can be free of connotation. Is it possible for the dancer's body to be the 'degré zéro' of dance, free of signification? This led to the doll-like impression which many people find hard to accept, thinking that you cannot treat a body like that. I am criticised a lot for the way I use the body because they believe it is something sacred. I do not see it like that at all. The body is sacred, but it is also made up of molecules and muscle and is all of these things put together.

Does the body get in the way of communicating meaning? The body could be 'degré zéro', a blank canvas for reconstructing meaning, but at the same time it is a large mass, a medium able to distort meaning. This makes the body both a foundation on which meaning is constructed and an instrument of sabotage. Meaning can be constructed according to a certain idea, but at the end of the day the body can mask the way the messages are read.
This friction between meaning and its essence, construct and nature is part of what it's all about. This is most evident with the girl wearing the T-shirt

with Madonna on it. She looks a bit like Madonna and has Madonna on her T-shirt. It is the phenomenon of the gap between meaning and 'who I am'. Also, when the woman in *Jérôme Bel* writes 'Christian Dior' on her body, adding a brand is going against the archetypal idea of a woman.

It is also something which prevents the most intimate contact with the skin and which also invokes all clothing which are temporary constructs and representations of the clothed body. My belief is that everything contains a meaning because I have come to realise that the neutrality written about by Barthes does not exist. There is only meaning, and social and symbolic constructs, even with a naked body. For example, it was really hard deciding what to do with their hair! It shocked me every time because I could not work out what to do with their hair so as not to convey an impression of something. A hairstyle can represent the 1980s, or a certain age or a certain taste. Everything we did created impressions of our culture. There were some things in the production that were not understood. For example a number of people told me it is universal. I think it is a dreadful comment to make – I hate this reaction. Because the performers were naked and we were doing very simple things, part of the audience thinks it is universal. That is absolutely not true. It is only culture, to which I add certain elements to encourage certain ideas. What annoys me most is that they do not realise that it is their own culture and their own vision of the world. I only want this production to be put on in Europe, and even then I have big problems in different countries. Some are shocked, others are not at all. Some people understand some bits, some people do not. Even in Europe there are a lot of cultural differences. That is what I have been trying to show, that there is no one kind.

Nom donné par l'auteur *is like an experiment enlarging the meaning of objects, taking them out of their usual context and attempting to give them a new meaning. And in* Jérôme Bel*, the body's meaning is reduced, naked and exposed as it is. Does this mean that the body has too much meaning and objects not enough?*
It is giving bodies and objects another meaning as objects, giving an alternative to how they are normally perceived. It is very pretentious of me, but you could say that that is how it is. For example I did not use eroticism or violence with the naked bodies in *Jérôme Bel*. But these seem to be the first impressions people have today when confronted with naked bodies. Whether this has always been the case I cannot say. But it is true to say that a poetical body is created, a slightly weakened body, an imagined body, a strange body too. This means that the body is not this sacred thing which

is just sex and power. It is the same with objects. You can reduce the meaning of objects to say that there is more to them than that. There is a poetical vision in this kind of ordinariness.

So in both cases it is a question of enlarging their meaning?
I do not know if it is enlarging it. I would say it is giving them another meaning, presenting a different view of them from what is normally understood. It is evident with the performance with objects because they never stop taking on new meanings.

Your work is very minimalist and has an aesthetic quality of its own. Do you always aim for an aesthetic quality in your work?
I am often asked that, but I do not want aesthetic quality. Choice does not come into it. I take things that are usually already there, which obviously have an aesthetic quality of a kind. This was a problem for a while because I found it difficult to accept. When I was putting together my first productions I did not see the minimalism in them, but little by little, talking with colleagues, I started to see it. But that is not all. I love things that are shambolic, wild and outrageous, but at the moment I cannot achieve it. Now that I admit that is how things are, it really is an aesthetic quality of my own. At the moment, more and more, I just want to show barren themes. This minimalism makes the audience more active, it is up to them to make the performance work. They are the other protagonists in it. I am always thinking about where the audience are, what they are thinking. There are plenty of people who do not like what I do and I understand that they do not want to.

Has there been an evolution from Nom donné par l'auteur *to* Shirtologie*? In* Jérôme Bel *there was a search for something universal or pure, only to discover later that it is a never-ending search.* Shirtologie *is like a game of mecano but with T-shirts, constructing identities with things around us that demand to be used.*
It's retrospective and speculative at the same time. *Nom donné par l'auteur* has an extremely cerebral and mechanical aspect to it, and almost nothing to do with bodies. *Jérôme Bel* takes things further with the cerebral combination of very strong dramatic effects and constructs, with bodies. It was an interesting concept to put the organic – a word I do not like very much – with the cerebral and it is what gave the work its power. Then *Shirtologie* is a kind of acceptance of signs of alienation. First I wanted to see if we could achieve Barthes' neutrality, and I then wanted to go for it with *Shirtologie*. I can see that fashions like Nike or Michael Jackson pass and I can accept that. I try to take hold of them and see what they signify whilst

accepting them, without despising or rejecting them. No, living with this
world is about culture. How can we be aware of these things and manage to
get by with them? I think that is the step that needs to be taken between
Jérôme Bel and *Shirtologie*.

But is there nonetheless not a sort of idealism in Shirtologie *when all the
young people at the end are wearing different monochrome T-shirts and
one person is naked. The last T-shirt has 'United Colors' on it. Is there a
sort of morality there when it is been about playing with people's identities
but at the end everyone is their own person and there is no need for external and commercial things like T-shirts.*
Yes, but we still cannot forget that the last T-shirt has 'United Colors … of
Benetton' on it. That is exactly what I mean – the idealism of there just
being colours, a multitude of things, blue, infinity, hope and then it ends.
That would be great, but I do not believe in it, I am not an idealist. But
everyone else dreams of it. I can see that I am disappointing a lot of people
at the end. It is annoying that there is just blue; it is a small sign but they are
happy because I give them hope. But the final T-shirt brings them up short.
'United Colors of Benetton' is a slogan that is commercial and idealistic.
And then I ask them to decide for themselves; that is basically what I ask
them. I am not modern in that sense, I do not believe in liberation or whatever, unfortunately perhaps. But in any case that is what I feel.

*Are you presenting a critique on the reification of body and mind, or are
you searching optimistically for a symbiosis of the two, abandoning the
idea of the mind being above the body?*
There is always critique involved, but the problem arises from the subject of
the performance. The production is about studying this problem, carrying
out a critique and finding solutions to it. In *Shirtologie* we tried to see how
we could get by with poetry, humour and awareness. Usually at the end
there should be a solution which is acceptable or not for everyone. If there
had not been a conclusion for us I would not have put on the production.

*But it is a solution that does not ignore or obliterate the problem – it
remains part of it. One possible solution to the problem of reification could
be to have the mind as the alternative totality.*
'Obliterate' suggests violence to me and it is one thing I try never to use. I
might be giving you a roundabout answer, but it is a question of acclima-
tising and adapting to things and certainly not destroying them. It is more
about getting by, eating away at things rather than destroying them. That
is one of the points made by Roland Barthes. Destroying codes is no use

because everyone knows they are there. I do not want to start a revolution, but rather try to get by, materialising, alienating or resisting. It is subversion without explosives or destruction.

And do you consider yourself as non-violent towards theatre or dance?
Absolutely. When I am putting on a production, I think it is of such simplicity and gentleness that everyone can accept it. Afterwards I can see that its properties are extremely violent, that temporality is violent. I have made mistakes there. I do not want to use violence on stage for the sake of it, but in the end I use it in another way. Is that violent? We cannot be rid of it. Should we respect the pious desire not to use violence because we hide it from ourselves? It is strange but when something difficult happens I tend to suppress it. But I have been treated as a rebel when it comes to dance and other choreographers. I was very taken aback. I like what my colleagues do. I would like to do things like them if I could.

In the past you have worked with Catarina Sagna and Philippe Decouflé, whose contemporary dance is more 'traditional' than yours. Have you broken with this 'tradition'? And what have been the most important and positive elements you have gained from your apprenticeship?
I decided to do things differently, but I use a lot of things I learned from Philippe Decouflé and Catarina Sagna. I like their work. When I think about it, I made choices – how to organise myself, how to think, how to rehearse. That is all I think about. I cannot see how anyone could do otherwise. I could not give meaning to T-shirts until after T-shirts, I could not give meaning to *Jérôme Bel* until after the bodies of the dancers. The material I take on, I organise, re-position, move about, reconstruct. But I do not think at all, like many others, that I have erased my past. There are of course some people that I rejected, but others have influenced me enormously. I do not believe in the idea of creating something out of nothing – there is no such thing as originality. I believe it is a question just of working with culture, that is what fascinates me and that is why when someone tells me it is universal I get so annoyed. It is simply not true. Some people are obviously shocked by *Jérôme Bel* and some who can accept it only because there have been plenty of productions before it. They tell me it is very 1970s and reject it. Then there are others who think it is something completely new, totally avant-garde. In my opinion, it is neither one thing nor the other, it is adapting things, more and more *Le dernier spectacle* will discuss that a lot, about culture, about the culture of performance, how we fear them. *Jérôme Bel* taught me that there is no such thing as natural. All we saw was down to what we knew about bodies.

*The bodies you show seem to lack energy because there is so little move-
ment. But they communicate a lot of meaning. Is there a conflict between
energy and generating meaning?*
I would be a monster if I said yes. I think not.

Maybe energetic bodies produce too much meaning?
Yes, perhaps. I do very little to make the audience come up with a meaning.
I want to produce something that has meaning, so I use a code of my
choice. In *Shirtologie* it is simple. First of all I show the code: the first
shirtology is the most basic code of numbers which even a four-year old
would understand: one, two, three …. Then I tell them how the code should
be read. I put a structure in their head, then re-use the code and the structure and break them to end up with certain effects and in order to intervene.
I admit it is as simple and basic as that. I impose a rhythm and I know that
little by little people are going to know that nothing is gratuitous, that they
have to learn patience but also that they will always have an answer.

At the same time you force the audience to look for a meaning.
Maybe that is where the violence is. There is no violence on stage but I
want them to come up to the stage. For example, I say that I put on indirect
performances. Usually there is a distinction between the stage and the area
containing the seating. There are some theatrical techniques to enable you
to project. I learned how to look beyond the area of the stage, to go towards
the audience, into them even. I want to do the opposite – I want it all to be
on stage so members of the audience have to throw themselves at it. I am
very proud of myself when that happens. There is not a lot of movement
on stage, but movement comes from the audience going towards the stage,
physically, but especially mentally, because it is the only way. There is also
this idea of weakness, like the desire not to have violence, not wanting to
shout, not wanting to push ideas at people, but rather to let them work
things out.

*Do you realise that this kind of weakness might provoke a kind of violence
on the part of the audience?*
It does provoke violence because many in the audience ask to move, shout-
ing sometimes, 'come on, move!' Nowadays people cannot bear doing very
little, not going fast, not putting on a show. I do not really want to draw
negative conclusions about society, but it is very irritating. I can see that
people come in order for someone to take charge. We go to the theatre and
cinema instead of reading a book. They are really saying, 'Well, tell me what
I have to do. Give me meaning'. I give a meaning, but only the building

blocks to it, like a metaphor. I was recently in Salzburg for the preview of my new work and there was a discussion afterwards with the audience to find out what they thought of it. There was a group of young people – it does not matter who they were – and one distinctly told me, 'I did not like your show because if I go to the theatre I want to be told what to think'. I said, 'Fine, I understand perfectly, but I would never do that'. That is fascism to me, there is no question of me telling you what to think. I make suggestions, I show what the problem is from all angles, but with infinite perplexity. I am confused myself, I am not sure of what I am putting forward. And it is like cement that has to be made, whether it is a wall like that or a very solid wall. I think that is what bothers people.

Why do you use professional dancers, whereas in Shirtologie *they were all young people with no formal training?*
I am a dancer too, so I know more or less what the language of dance is. But it is obvious that playing with choreographic and theatrical codes supposes a subversion of these codes, a destruction of them even, although I do not think we achieve it. If they are dancers I try to break these codes. In *Jérôme Bel* half were professional, half amateurs. Then I had no hesitation in working with amateurs from Ghent because what I make use of is theirs, the fact that they do not have these codes. They come on stage without the codes of theatre or dance and it is amazing. That is why I gave them such a long time at the beginning because if I said, 'Do not do anything', they did not. If I tell an actor 'Do not do anything', he is on stage and wants to justify his position on it, so looks back on his training for something which means 'do nothing' and then will not do nothing. But the youngsters from Ghent managed to do nothing and it was great because so many things did happen! There were some who started to cry; emotions came out which were real and it gave me an amazing opportunity! I was fascinated by it and by them. They put up no resistance, they had no preconceived ideas about theatre and were as they naturally were. It was the most beautiful thing I have seen.

Was it also important from the point of view of their physicality?
A professional dancer walks on stage very differently from a youngster from Ghent, because there is a code. My dancers have worked with choreographers who have those codes and I do not want to break them just like that so I give them different ones. It is not a question of rejecting other people's codes, they just enter into mine. I do not think I save them or teach them freedom at all. But for an audience used to seeing certain ways and codes of how the body is portrayed, it is a big change. When they are

amateurs and young people and they do not move for six minutes, other things are going on. It is always a question of working with what people expect and know, because I am part of the audience too.

Is the distortion of the body in Jérôme Bel *a kind of fetishism, even if it is not performance art or the bodies of models? Maybe it is a strange kind of fetishism because the bodies are so normal.*
I had not thought of fetishism at all. But I think there is a fetishist element for the audience, whereas for us it is not the case at all because the actor and I are coming from the perspective of dance. As a dancer our body no longer has this sacred side to it. We work with it and manipulate it. It has given us pleasure and really unbearable pain. So it is something we are very familiar with, there is nothing fetishist at all about it. Our starting point was a body as an object we know well and which is very ordinary. But even so I had problems getting a cast together. There were dancers I had worked with who completely refused to be naked or to do what I wanted them to.

So it is about vulnerability then, the opposite of fetishism?
Completely. Bodies are weak and incapable. They lack ability, they do not move fast, do nothing out of the ordinary, they stay constant most of the time. We never slow down and we never speed up. So, people always think we are doing things very slowly. We might wait, we stop, but it is what I call the real speed of things. It is never quicker, never slower.

Is this vulnerability a kind of masochism because the indirect effect you want to achieve is just as violent?
There is an expression in French which is 'prêter le flanc'. It means that I will not defend myself. Whether that is masochism or not, I will have to think about it. I do not think it is, it is just a question of accepting it.

The distortions of bodies in Jérôme Bel *and all the changes of T-shirts in* Shirtologie *are always temporary, they are never definitive changes. Does it after all go back to the idea of a foundation with constructs on it?*
It is funny but I have never thought about it! I come across something and I decide to put on a performance for an hour. I tell myself that I could go on, but do not. I play with this code a lot as they nearly all last an hour because I get to a point where I say to myself, 'Be careful, I could go on'. In *Nom donné par l'auteur*, it goes dark in the middle. That is what is required. It is saying 'Stop', because I could go on making infinite combinations. So it goes dark, like chapter 11, the hero in Bangkok, chapter 12, the hero's wife in Brussels in the middle of .... It has to stop, it is temporal like that. They take off their T-shirts until there are none left, because that

is the material side to things. It is true that in *Jérôme Bel* they were writing and they rub it out. It is really based on constructing effects, and the new production is more of the same.

Performances

1994   Nom donné par l'auteur
1995   Jérôme Bel
1997   Shirtologie
1998   Le dernier spectacle
2000   Xavier Le Roy
2000   The Show Must Go On

Note

[1] The interview was translated by Claire Tarring and conducted by Steven De Belder (July 1998). We would like to thank Sabine Hillen for co-editing the interview.

Wim Vandekeybus, *Her Body Doesn't Fit Her Soul*,
Photo: Wim Vandekeybus (Courtesy of Ultima vez)

Wim Vandekeybus

Biography

Wim Vandekeybus (Herenthout, Belgium, 1963) first came into contact with theatre at a workshop. He subsequently took a number of dance courses (classical dance, modern dance, tango) and also devoted himself to film and photography. After a successful audition with Jan Fabre, he went on tour with the latter's *De Macht der Theaterlijke Dwaasheden* (*The Power of Theatrical Madness*), in which he performed one of the two naked Emperors. After his tour, he decided to start working on a production of his own, retreating for several months with a group of inexperienced dancers who called themselves Ultima Vez (Spanish for 'the last time').

Vandekeybus was never interested in movement for the sake of movement. His dance vocabulary finds its inspiration outside the realm of dancing, in a non-artistic, everyday world. Important ingredients in his dance and theatre productions are the hidden areas of reality, the underlying (internal or external) motives and objectives of actions.

Interview[1]

Your work is often described as instinctive and impulsive. How do you feel about such descriptions?
I work very intuitively. Perhaps the result is not all that important to me. Apart from that, I never received any formal training and I have therefore never learned a specific dance technique. That is probably why I find it hard to distinguish between the technique and what comes about instinctively. I have recently been asked how I separate dance and theatre. I answered this question by means of a metaphor. A movement is like a plant. As time goes by, the roots of a plant are no longer separable from the earth it has blended with. This metaphor stands for a kind of contagion that also occurs in my dance performances. The starting-point does not stand on its own; as time goes by, it can no longer be distinguished from the final result.

When I started out as a choreographer, I had to look for existing movements out of sheer necessity, without being able to steer them. Instincts and reflexes, which are now used increasingly rarely, played an important part in this respect. Everything is much safer now, less physical, and minimal contact – as with television – has become possible. Only in emergencies does one feel a kind of survival instinct, a protective function. In the same way, movement can be minimised dangerously. This leads to artificial divisions, so that people will tend to specialise obsessively in one particular technique (take sporting persons, for example). I personally find it interesting to work with people who do not so much excel in technique but possess a certain intuitive capacity to adapt themselves to different circumstances. In that respect, I began to work with movements that are part of human nature. These can of course be stimulated. You could, for instance, imagine that the stage is balancing on a needle. Movements could then be created to serve this image, and the result would be an illusion.

In *One for sorrow (7 for a Secret never to be told)* we have tried to dance pain by dancing everything backwards. 'Sorrow' means to move towards where you cannot see. In Japan, studies have been conducted of the so-called 'body buffer zone', a kind of emanation or aura which has been photographed and which turned out to be egg-shaped. It is much wider at the front than at the back. So walking forward is safer. Then the idea occurred to us to dance everything backwards. Walking back-wards was like an eternal trap that never shuts, so that it creates a kind of suspense.

So the things that belong almost to the genetic material of human history, these kinds of age-old instincts, are in fact your basic material?
They are certainly some of the basic materials. 'L'état' is also important, 'the state of doing something', an almost emotional kind of concentration. How do dancing bodies mingle, and which contact is there? One such state is that in *What the Body Does Not Remember*, as the title suggest. During the working process of this performance, I introduced a lot of pictures that I had seen and stories I had read. The story of the drowning person, for example, I found very interesting. Inadvertently, a person who is drowning is extremely dangerous. His fear and panic can be lethal. When your life is at stake, social courtesy – as that which prescribes that you cannot touch a passer-by in the street unless there is a specific context – is quickly thrown overboard. Necessity compels you to do things in order to save yourself. Such extreme situations are unknown to the present generation, which has not experienced the war.

Is this combination of vitality and fear of death, this primal power, connected in any way with the Dionysian? Would you characterise your work as Dionysian dance?
Perhaps, I am of course inspired by certain things, but up to now I have created very few performances that refer explicitly to anything. I think I refer less than Jan Fabre, for instance. When I was on stage working for him,

I always felt like a commentary on another reference. His inspiration sources are shown very clearly, through slide projections in the background for example. In my own work, such references are far less explicit. Especially now, at a time when I am occupied with the invisible, with texts on hallucinations, fear of death and superstition. Superstition essentially represents man's need to explain things. Out of fear and ignorance, people think they recognise signs and they ascribe qualities to things that remain indifferent, such as animals or the forces of nature.

A human being becomes interesting when he is aware of his own weaknesses. In this sense, it is important that there is such a thing as death, so that man is confronted with his own mortality. The more extreme one lives, the more extreme the vitality in one's dance, the closer one comes to death. This is also apparent from research into human emotions. If you take the positive and the negative to their extremes, it is as if the two meet and merge in a different landscape.

How are subconscious elements in your dancers brought to the surface? Do you have certain techniques to achieve this?
It is not necessary for everyone to possess the same imaginative powers as the director. The method of working is also important. The starting point is always an idea. Movement is not there from the very beginning. First we think and talk about what the performance should or could be, and from this concept the dancers should then be able to distil something tangible fairly quickly. I, for instance, came up with the idea of gravity as a form of security. I was inspired by a story I found fascinating as a child. The biggest fear of astronauts who have to leave their capsule to carry out repairs, for instance, is to drift out into space. There is no friction, so you can drift out forever. The chances of coming near to a planet or of bumping into one so that you stop are very remote. Gravity provides protection against the fear of continuing infinitely. Virilio asserts that life is a 'humble fall'. People are constantly dropping down onto the world; when you take a step, you fall from one foot onto the other. And then there is the accident involving a parachutist which I witnessed when I was sixteen. Studies have been made of what is the best way to fall. When your body is relaxed, you can actually fall without feeling any pain. Out of this amalgam of stories and information, the idea arose of taking that moment of fragility when neither foot is touching the ground as the starting-point. That is how we discovered that it is much easier to manipulate a body when it is suspended in the air. It becomes much easier to rotate the shoulders, for instance. With this material in hand, you get to work, and I can assure you that the first days of exploring the possibilities of movement are always very exciting.

It is of course important to work with people who are well aware of what they are doing, who trust themselves and each other. Only then you can arrive at the extremes of movement. The instinct to protect others and to catch them when they fall is essential. During the dance itself you stop thinking. That is what I mean by 'état'. It becomes pure passion. You have no choice.

Is there a connection between freeing oneself from gravity and freeing oneself from other restraints? And do you consider thinking to be such a restraint?
Initially, it was important to me to have danced my own performances. The direct, emotional contact with an audience is by far the most important aspect. Aesthetic and intellectual considerations come after that. But the forgetting and letting go of restraints can also occur on the audience's side. Watching a performance can be a liberating experience.

It seems that people require more certainty nowadays. As a director or as a choreographer, I always have to be able to explain what I am doing. An audience wants to know what a performance is about. I often let different things happen at the same time and use very few unisons. When there are three duets on stage at the same time, the audience has to make a choice. I like that. The chaotic character of such a performance appeals to me. Choreographing is too often seen as creating a solo, which can then be copied by six other people. This is easier to watch, but to me it is also less interesting.

You often use horizontal and vertical images as well as reversals of perspective?
As a photographer, I used to take a lot of pictures from a bird's-eye view. I asked people to lie on the floor and to leap at each other or to make another movement.

When reversing perspectives, I tend not so much to look for technical solutions. Imagination is more important to me. In *7 for a Secret never to be told*, we had giant feathers falling down to the stage and penetrating it by means of nails. From that sprang the idea to do exactly the opposite with people: the dancers lifting each other up by the throat and being suspended from their skulls, as it were. It is like dying temporarily and returning to life the moment your feet touch the ground again. Cutting is very important. Just like in a movie, you have to switch from one energy to another without a fade in or a fade out. Each movement must have a clear beginning and end. Otherwise, you diminish the sense of rhythm and lose the percussive element.

What does the invisible body mean to you?
What happens in your head, the intangible, the fantasy world, fear. These are very hard to portray on stage, hence the idea of using film. Images can show things that otherwise are invisible. *Bereft of a Blissful Union*, for instance, contains the image of a girl whose eyes move independently: an editing trick. The invisible may also stand for a certain atmosphere, as in *Her Body Doesn't Fit Her Soul*, in which the actors were suspended by ropes. This image stood for a sort of eternal fall, as if they had been hanging there for ages. Invisibility is not always related to emotions and dreams either. When you use text, you have to look for what is in between the lines.

As for the invisible side of the body, the 'état' is important. How do you do things? Apart from that, the element of play and the treacherousness that comes with it are essential. You can be inspired by actual events, such as childhood experiences that you carry with you. During the first days of rehearsal, you look for such authentic feelings inside your body. Later on, you can start pretending; you no longer need to actually feel things. In the initial phase, one feels 'amongst each other', as it were. And by working with each other's bodies so intensely, it becomes possible later on to summon emotions and feelings on the spot, without actually feeling them. In that respect the rehearsals are the most important stage of the entire process. The performance itself is important because it involves an audience. I consider this to be the strength of my work: the growing awareness that you did not stop at the first obstacle creates a new energy. That is why it is necessary for a performance to have lived before it is put up on stage. Dancers need to explore their own limits. I, for instance, need to be told where to stop: this defines the boundaries within which I can work. And in a duet, many frustrations can arise that influence the dancers' bodies, while the audience remains unaware, even though there will always be a perceptible tension.

I treat all of my dancers differently. I prefer to respect the individual than to let team spirit prevail. Each body has its own limits, which – as a choreographer – you must learn to discover. I do not think I use psychological tricks to explore the limits of my dancers. I am however aware it is quite possible to blow up an entire company in a single week. It is therefore important to handle tensions in an honest way and not to play off different characters against each other. Certain choreographers need this in order to work efficiently. But I am convinced that a constructive and positive atmosphere can achieve a lot more. During the production of *Bereft of a Blissful Union*, many people lost sight of what exactly they were doing because the performance was so chaotic. Some lacked an overall picture, because they could not see the pieces of film that were being used. In *7 for a Secret never to be told*, we used a different approach. When we first discussed the performance, everyone had to select the elements they felt were closest to them and most distant from them. Then we talked about what that meant to everyone. This approach created an incredible sense of order.

As for *Immer das Selbe gelogen*, a production about Carlo Verano, a 89-year old man with a worn-out body but a healthy mind, the basic idea behind it was that it is less important to be able to do something than it is to want to do it or to desire it. If you concede that you are no longer able to do something, you will not do it. Take my knee injury, for instance. I feel I have to get back on stage. The same principle holds for medicine. In the past, one almost automatically opted for surgery. Now, the muscles around the injury are exercised. You need to adapt your body.

Is it important to you to attract new people?
New people can provide fresh impulses to the people you have been working with for a longer period of time. For example, for the Pasolini project – *The Day of Heaven and Hell* – 18 newcomers have been recruited. They are neither dancers nor actors, which can be very inspiring. Dancers do not read much and they tend to have similar backgrounds. But sometimes it is more important that people have lived a life than that they are formally trained dancers.

Especially with texts by Pasolini, it is extremely important to be able to talk about how the written material should be interpreted and adapted. His writing contains elements of attraction as well as of repulsion. As he did not think in terms of good and evil, Pasolini was clearly ahead of his time. In his work, the body is a walking contradiction, always looking for its own destruction. He died that way too. Not that he did not take care of his body; sport, for example, was very important to him.

I see very little destruction in your work. Perhaps in this instance destruction should be interpreted as a form of montage. You, for example, set out in search of the body's limits, but the body will inevitably re-establish itself in its own power.
Even when the body survives a catastrophe or a shock, the catastrophe will remain a part of it. The shocks are probably stronger now than they used to be in the past, because they have been interiorised. In *What the Body Does Not Remember*, shock and danger were depicted by the throwing stones; these elements may live on in certain tics or impulses.

When I watch your performances, I always get the impression that you put the body and its possible destruction in a romantic context. The body is taken seriously, it is not ridiculed or 'uglified'.

It is indeed true that my dancers emanate a certain beauty. It is more difficult to achieve that effect with an abject body, although it too will possess a kind of beauty of its own. This is however possible with film. Dancers are often chosen because they look better on stage. The stage creates an illusion. When you meet that same person at the bar after the show, you may be in for a surprise.

There is an extreme division in contemporary society between the anti-body and the artificial body. On the one hand, many people train almost fanatically to attain the ideals of beauty; on the other hand, it is often very hard to get kids to exercise, especially so it seems in southern countries. Dancers, by contrast, exercise to build up muscle strength, not to look a certain way. Many dancers have destructive lifestyles; they drink and smoke, but they seem to be able to cope with destruction.

Conversely, it is not easy to work with people who are physically less capable. And yet, I have worked with blind dancers. Blindness, too, is a form of destruction, but it is not ugly. It is an inward flaw. For the same reason, I will never magnify a disability on stage. On the contrary, it is ignored in order to show what else is there.

Is there a connection between your working with blind dancers and your interest in the invisible?

It is often said that the blind can access the invisible more easily. My choice to work with blind people in *Her Body Doesn't Fit Her Soul* stemmed from the fact that this performance was about the senses. How does one experience things? And can you create limits in how you experience? The process of working with blind people was perhaps more important than the final result. How do you arrive at a kind of visual language? How do you explain images to them? As they do not think in images, the image is of an entirely different order to them. Although both blind dancers were once able to see, the texts we used had been written by people who were born blind. It is striking how the blind are often able to form more accurate and more varied images than people who are accustomed to visual images. In that respect, it is true that the blind are concerned more with the invisible, more specifically with experiencing non-visual things. A blind dancer has a kind of aura or peculiarity other dancers often lack. It is striking how the audience is hardly able to notice that there are blind people on the stage. This only becomes apparent at the end, when the dancers are expected to take a bow: then the blind dancers need to be accompanied. In this manner, the spectator comes to realise how much one tends to rely on images.

Do you feel men and women are equally strong when it comes to lifting other dancers. Is there an essential difference between masculinity and femininity, or are the two interchangeable?
In certain scenes, the male and female dancers are interchangeable. Duets, however, are very different depending on whether they are being danced by two men or a man and a woman. The theme of the duet is also important. When it is not about passion, it matters less to me.

There is an obvious difference, though, in creating scenes with only men or only women. Men are more likely to talk to each other. The one dancer may be able to help the other. Women, on the other hand, tend to need their own territory. The female body, though, is stronger. In *Bereft of a Blissful Union*, one female dancer carries three male dancers, as if a monster attaches itself firmly to this female body. The effect that these merging bodies create is quite alienating.

Speed is also very important. You are not supposed to be able to see how a movement is made or to be able to analyse how someone prepares for a leap. It is no longer interesting when things become too analytical. Movements have to seduce; they have to retain some mystery. In this sense, speed protects movement.

Is ritual movement, whereby the body connects to a broader social fabric, of any importance to you?
A ritual is a sort of 'état'. It is an incarnation rather than a technique. It is a manner of movement that belongs to the order of 'gestures'. These are specific movements that suit a person; in other words, body language. You have to invent the ritual yourself. It can be very interesting to study rituals from Bali, but since we do not come from Bali, they do not apply to us.

It is always necessary to retain a degree of freedom within a ritual. Besides, tripping on stage is dangerous. Like superstition, the ritual belongs to the inner self. You should be able to feel the soul in the dance or the dancer. A body without a soul is an object. A dancer should not be afraid to use his body to adopt different souls in the course of a performance. The audience forms an image of each scene. It is important that a dancer is first able to create this image and then to destroy it in the next scene. A dancer has to be able to vary, to transform and to change shape as it were.

Performances

1987   What the Body Does Not Remember
1989   Les porteuses de mauvaises nouvelles
1990   The Weight of a Hand
1990   Roseland (video)
1991   Immer das Selbe gelogen
1992   La Mentira (video)
1993   Her Body Doesn't Fit Her Soul
1993   Elba en Federico (film)
1994   Mountains Made of Barking
1994   Saïd and Mary (film)
1995   Alle Größen decken sich zu
1996   Bereft of a Blissful Union
1996   Exhaustion from Dreamt Love
1997   Lichaampje, lichaampje aan de wand …
1997   7 for a Secret never to be told
1998   The Day of Heaven and Hell
1999   In Spite of Wishing and Wanting
2000   In as much as Life is Borrowed
2001   Scratching the Inner Fields

Note

[1] The interview was translated by ICTS and conducted by Maaike Bleeker, Koen Tachelet, Luk Van den Dries, and Annemie Vanhoof (May 1998).

Meg Stuart, *Appetite*, Photo: Chris Van der Burght
(Courtesy of Damaged Goods)

Meg Stuart

Biography

Meg Stuart is an American dancer and choreographer whose work is strongly connected to the present-day plastic arts. She studied dance at New York University and was a member of the Randy Warshaw Dance Company, where she was also assistant to the choreographer.

Since 1994 she established her company Damaged Goods in Brussels, where she is artist in residence at Kaaitheater. Her evening-length pieces *Disfigure Study* (1991), *No longer Readymade* (1993) and *No one is watching* (1995) were presented in Berlin and toured internationally. In 1994 Meg Stuart made *Swallow my yellow smile*, a commission for the Deutsche Oper Berlin in collaboration with visual artist Via Lewandowsky. Since 1996 Meg Stuart created a series of projects with different visual artists: *Insert Skin # 1 – They live in Our Breath* (with Lawrence Malstaf, 1996), *Remote* (scenography: Bruce Mau) for the White Oak Dance Project (1997), *Splayed Mind Out* (with Gary Hill, 1997) and *Appetite* (with Ann Hamilton, 1998). She comments her work as follows: 'My choreographic work revolves around the ideas and images of distortion, privateness, memories and exposure. I usually associate these elements with simple human tasks: a hug, a chase, walking, running, falling'.

Together with Christine De Smedt and David Hernandez, Meg Stuart organises *Crash Landing*, an ongoing improvisation initiative, with a new edition in Moscow fall 1999. *Highway 101* will be Meg Stuart's next project and will go on until the end of year 2000.

Interview[1]

The first production you introduced in Belgium, in 1991, was titled Disfigure Study. *Disfigurement seems to be an important motive in your work, but what does it really mean to you?*
I have always been interested in deconstructing the body, in breaking it down into body parts. Since I was about fifteen, I have been creating physical studies/sketches of the body. The exploration of each body part independently became a way of exploring what dance could mean to me. I was not simply interested in how many ways a single body could move,

but what it could express emotionally. In this working process I developed distortion as a body language, which allowed me more possibilities of expression than the vocabulary of release technique, which I had studied and was familiar with. I incorporated basic movement studies such as sitting, lying, running, and falling. I focused primarily on the inability or failure to complete these simple movements and the dramatic possibilities of these actions. These investigations – while becoming increasingly complex and multi-layered – continue to be the fundamental basis of my choreographic work.

Appetite *does mark a change in comparison to your former plays, doesn't it? Where does this lightness come from?*
It was a choice that evolved out of the collaboration with Ann Hamilton. We discussed the impossibility of shedding one's weight or burden. We were curious to find out what it is that makes a person feel weighted … their history, family, memories, fears. From this questioning we started to work on the opposite idea of weightlessness. The lightness was absorbed in the process and became an atmosphere for the whole piece. Everything that did not fall into this world was excluded. Searching for lightness became a physical task.

Does this choice for lightness have anything to do with a kind of renewed embodiment after the dismembering, a reconstruction of your work on the independence of separate parts?
I do not know if I reconstructed the body, but in *Appetite* the body is more integrated, more interdependent. The independent body parts may be out of control individually, but together they find a new logic and freedom. Ann and I wanted to create a work that extends out of the experience of being a physical body. Through the skin and the sense of touch the body is an interior and exterior, a container and a contained.

This logic of the body is based on the energy that spontaneously arouses as the body starts moving in space, or is it more like a conceptual logic? I mean, you often seem to work from a conceptual point of departure. How do these two things, the abstract, the planned and the spontaneous, interrelate in the idea of the logic of the body?
A crucial issue in my work is the idea of physical task. A choreographic idea works for me if I can hook on to a physical task that has different layers of meaning. There is a section in *Appetite* that could simply be described as dance, but it is more the result of the task that the dancers have to bounce on the floor with various parts of their body. You could say that

they are trying to mark the clay floor with their bodies. Maybe they want to defy gravity. Or viewed in another perspective, they might be rubbing out a kind of visible experience or touch, as if they are erasing a memory. But every move – and this is the most important to me – is in this effort to bounce. There is always this task, this intention, this 'have to' and then the body moves. When you fly off a cliff you do not think about how you are going to fall down, you just do. Somehow there is this self-consciousness that is removed from the performer in the ideal case and once you are connected to that, it can suddenly start to work. You can see this in almost every part of my work. Sometimes one task is more visible than others, but this intention towards a task is what I focus on. It can be abstract – 'I want to be invisible, I want to enter in someone else's skin, I want to fly' – but it is always there.

My main approach to dance is making samples of physical experience and then splicing them together, joining abstract movements, gestures or involuntary movements together in complex series. One process I use to develop this material is an exercise I call 'change'. The dancers are asked to move without thinking and as soon as they are in a physical or emotional state, I say 'change' and they have to do something else, completely unrelated to the previous state. Afterwards we make a series of the different sequences, mixing them with signs, other gestures, and movements.

You seem to be testing the limits of the body. Are you exploring how independent each body part can be? Where would you locate the edge?
The limits are a drama in themselves. There are certain physical forces – gravity, the decay of the body, ageing, exhaustion – that are present in every choreographic work. Rather than conceal them I have chosen to exploit these issues. At the moment I am fascinated by the power of the body to regenerate. You break your arm, yet it can grow again. If I would work in visual arts, my work would consist in breaking things and then repairing them with objects that do not really fit. I say this because I think it is a metaphor for what fascinates me. It is not the breaking in itself, but the recovery. Why is something broken, how does it repair itself, how did it move forward?

Does the working with organic material, like the clay you used in Appetite, *effect the movement?*
I think it does. The relationship to the floor is unique in dance. It is rare that a dancing surface transforms during a performance. The clay dries and cracks throughout the show, acting as a skin that responds to and interacts with the movements of the dancers.

What is also particular about the clay is the fact that it cannot be applied to the floor by a machine. The only way to cover the floor with clay is by getting down on one's knees and spread the clay out on the floor with your hands. If you water down the substance, it is not solid enough anymore, so it really only works when you spread it by hand. Before each performance 15 strangers share the task of applying the clay together. It is incredible to witness.

Are the blankets you put on the seats of the audience a kind of translation of the feeling of clay?
Ann and I talked about making a gesture to the audience. The blanket being a domestic object evokes connotations of comfort and intimacy. The blankets are displaced on the chairs of the audience. It is a present as well as a burden, similar to the gestures that are exchanged between the dancers in *Appetite*.

Earlier you talked about the physical limits of the body. But does the notion of the subliminal self, of a spiritual borderland, relate to your work? Is there something like an unconscious tic of the body?
I am fascinated by involuntary movements and what I call 'physical states' or 'emotional states' in the body. For me it is related to the question what exactly can be described as dance. I focus on those moments when my heart is beating too fast or when I am short of breath or other direct physical reactions that point to the idea of the body moving without being dictated or controlled. During the improvisation project *Crash Landing @ Vienna* we worked with disabled dancers. There was a woman performing who had no arms and no legs. She described how, although being born this way, she still had memories or experiences of her legs and her toes. She would move her shoulder and say: 'Now, I am moving my hand'. One could imagine there is a past life involved. And when you look at it this way, I might be dancing the story of other people. Sometimes, when you are improvising you get into a trance-like state, a very deep state where the dancer is beyond self-consciousness. At that moment, movements emerge that are hard to define and of which you do not know where they come from. Maybe these movements started out as images or projections of the world the dancers just captured when they were walking through the day, images they absorbed in daily life and that resurface, like radio feedback. This has nothing to do with therapy. It is more like a catalogue of movements, a potentiality of moving, a way of reprocessing or translating the images we experience.

What intrigues me is finding the key that can trigger this flood of movements. Once I read an article about the possibility of stimulating a specific emotional state by learning to control your breath. For example if I breathe in a very short breathing pattern, I can become truly upset. Of course this can all be understood as being a part of the acting technique by which you just learn to appropriate a physical rhythm. When you look at the history of dance, you see that it is mainly about disciplining and controlling the body, trying to align it with an idea of symmetry. Since then I have been drawn to this idea and I have been exploring and testing it again and again in collaboration with my dancers. The search for a physical language and its limits is a thread in my work. Matt Mullican did a performance where he was hypnotised on stage. I was very impressed by what he did and at the same time it was very strange. He was completely unaware of his actions. He went on for about an hour or so, sometimes it was quite uninteresting, sometimes quite terrifying. But always his expressions were very recognisable and shareable, there was always a connection to the reality of the spectator.

How important is it for you to work with dance-trained people?
The first time we worked with non-dancers was in the performance *Splayed Mind Out*. We invited people to meet the dancers and to work on the idea of 'meetings': small interactions we then integrated in the piece. But for *Appetite* I worked with a highly trained group of dancers. This was a very specific choice, because I wanted a unified group, so that they could all do one gesture completely together if needed. I need dancers who can throw away their training and do not look like dancers. But when it comes to improvisation and learning and remembering material from a video, then you really need dancers with training. It is easy to find great improvisers or great movers who are very spontaneous, but it is hard to find people who can remember and repeat spontaneous movements acurately.

It is important for me to question my working process with every new project. Right now I am at the end of *Insert Skin*, a long series of collaborations with visual artists. And now I need some time to explore and develop new ways of working.

Performances

1991   Disfigure Study
1993   No Longer Readymade
1994   Swallow my Yellow Smile

1994	This is the show and the show is many things
	(dance-installation project)
1995	No one is watching
1996	Insert Skin # 1 – They Live in our Breath
1997	Remote
1997	Splayed Mind Out
1998	Appetite
2000	Highway 101
2001	Alibi

Notes

[1] The interview was conducted by Steven De Belder, Luk Van den Dries, and Kurt Vanhoutte (September 1998).

Index

new from the mit press

CTRL [SPACE]
Rhetorics of Surveillance from Bentham to Big Brother
edited by Thomas Y. Levin, Ursula Frohne, and Peter Weibel
The unknown history of surveillance in relation to changing systems of representation and visual arts practice.
450 pp., 950 illus., 350 color
$39.95 paper

Melancholia and Moralism
Essays on AIDS and Queer Politics
Douglas Crimp
"Crimp's essays document the struggle of the AIDS decades with an intelligence, courage, and poignancy that is rare during these times. This is queer scholarship at its best: urgent, brilliant, and unrelenting." — Judith Butler, University of California Berkeley
304 pp., 38 illus. $29.95

Seeing Double
Shared Identities in Physics, Philosophy, and Literature
Peter Pesic
"Drawing on philosophy, literature, and physics in accessible prose, Peter Pesic illuminates the meaning of unique personhood. A challenging and civilizing tour-de-force." — Gerald Holton, Harvard University
192 pp., 11 illus. $24.95

now in paperback
History of Shit
Dominique Laporte
translated by Nadia Benabid and Rodolphe el-Khoury
"Few manage to link so many ideas, as Laporte has done so effortlessly."
— Architecture
192 pp., 59 illus. $12.95 paper

now in paperback
Dreamworld and Catastrophe
The Passing of Mass Utopia in East and West
Susan Buck-Morss
"A brilliant and thought-provoking work."
— David Wild, The Architects' Journal
432 pp., 178 illus., 13 color $24.95 paper

From Newspeak to Cyberspeak
A History of Soviet Cybernetics
Slava Gerovitch
"An exceptionally lively and interesting book. This is by far the best informed and most insightful account of cybernetics in the Soviet Union."
— David Holloway, Stanford University
357 pp., 30 illus. $35

zone books

Publics and Counterpublics
Michael Warner
Investigates one of the central fictions of modern politics and culture—the idea of a public—and the pervasive conflict over its meaning.
Distributed for Zone Books
318 pp. $30

now in paperback
Two Sisters and Their Mother
The Anthropology of Incest
Françoise Héritier
translated by Jeanine Herman
"This is a fascinating book, full of detail and example." — Henrietta L. Moore, Times Literary Supplement
Distributed for Zone Books
341 pp. $18 paper

now in paperback
The Expressiveness of the Body and the Divergence of Greek and Chinese Medicine
Shigehisa Kuriyama
"This is comparative history of the highest order: a captivating reflection of different ideals of bodily life and on the place of language in communication."
— Francesa Bray, American Historical Review
Distributed for Zone Books
340 pp., 26 illus. $18 paper

http://mitpress.mit.edu

To order call **800-405-1619**.
Prices subject to change without notice.

Add dimension to your sociological research

sociological abstracts

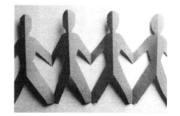

Comprehensive, cost-effective, timely

Abstracts of articles, books, and conference papers from nearly 2,500 journals published in 35 countries; citations of relevant dissertations as well as books and other media.

Available in print or electronically through the Internet Database Service from Cambridge Scientific Abstracts (*www.csa.com*).

Contact *sales@csa.com* for trial Internet access or a sample issue.

sociological abstracts

Published by CSA

Cambridge Scientific Abstracts

| 7200 Wisconsin Avenue | Tel: +1 301-961-6700 | E-Mail: sales@csa.com |
| Bethesda, Maryland 20814 USA | Fax: +1 301-961-6720 | Web: www.csa.com |

Death's Showcase

The Power of Image
in Contemporary Democracy
Ariella Azoulay
translated by Ruvik Danieli
"[A] most valuable, comprehensive statement about the changing relations between art, culture, and power in contemporary democracy."
— Yaron Ezrahi, Hebrew University of Jerusalem
296 pp., 45 illus. $34.95

net_condition

art and global media
edited by Peter Weibel
and Timothy Druckrey
Richly illustrated writings on networked global media and their effect on contemporary society.
450 pp., 475 color illus. $39.95 paper

Crepuscular Dawn

Paul Virilio
translated by Sylvère Lotringer
The "genetic bomb" marks a turn in the history of humanity. Artificial selection is leading the way to a new eugenism. This is the dawn of a new racism, no longer endo-human, but trans-human and exo-human. The "biological accident" of science is a war waged against the human race.
Distributed for Semiotext(e)
164 pp. $12.95 paper

Hatred of Capitalism

A Semiotext(e) Reader
edited by Chris Kraus
and Sylvere Lotringer
Jean Baudrillard meets Cookie Mueller in this gathering of French theory and new American fiction published in the Foreign Agents and Native Agents series over the last fifteen years.
Distributed for Semiotext(e)
320 pp. $16.95 paper

now in paperback

Technoromanticism

Digital Narrative, Holism,
and the Romance of the Real
Richard Coyne
"This book provides the most comprehensive philosophical and cultural context for understanding information technologies that I have ever seen."
— N. Katherine Hayles, University of California, Los Angeles
A Leonardo Book
408 pp. $19.95 paper

the mit press

Clean New World

Culture, Politics,
and Graphic Design
Maud Lavin
"This book should make design a key component of all histories of twentieth-century culture . . . I know of no other book like it." — Anne Higonnet, Wellesley College
208 pp., 81 illus. $27.95

Architectures of Time

Toward a Theory of the Event
in Modernist Culture
Sanford Kwinter
An exploration of twentieth-century conceptions of time and their relation to artistic form.
232 pp., 31 illus. $29.95

Metamorphosis and Identity

Caroline Walker Bynum
Explores the Western obsession with the nature of change and personal identity, focusing on the Middle Ages.
Distributed for Zone Books
288 pp., 15 illus. $28

Pure Immanence

Essays on A Life
Giles Deleuze
translation by Anne Boyman
introduction by John Rajchman
Essays by Gilles Deleuze on the search for a new and superior form of empiricism that rethinks the relation of thought to life.
Distributed for Zone Books
100 pp. $24

A Society without Fathers or Husbands

The Na of China
Cai Hua, translated by Asti Hustvedt
A fascinating account of an agrarian society in China which functions without fathers, husbands, or the institution of marriage.
Distributed for Zone Books
512 pp. $33

To order call 800-356-0343
(US & Canada) or 617-625-8569.
Prices subject to change without notice.

http://mitpress.mit.edu

The Cultural Practice of Latinamericanism, I and II

dispositio/n 49
dispositio/n 50

**Guest Editors:
Alberto Moreiras
and Marcus Embry.**
Contributions from Richard,
Williams, Moreiras, Levinson,
Legras, Poblete, Avelar,
Kaminsky, Castillo, Beasley-
Murray, González, Vincent &
Muñoz, Bora, Embry, Kirk,
Healey, Hershberg, Beverley,
Fernández Retamar.

These two issues only:
$15 to individuals;
$40 to libraries;
$7.50 to students.

dispositio/n
Department of Romance Languages and Literatures
4108 MLB / 812 E. Washington St.
University of Michigan
Ann Arbor, Michigan 48109-1275 U.S.A.
TEL (734) 764-5363
FAX (734) 764-8163
kojo@umich.edu
http://www.lsa.umich.edu/rll/journals.html